WE'RE NOT
LEAVING

▲ **Members of several companies** of the New York City Fire Department arriving on scene at the World Trade Center collapse. *Photo by Steve Spak.*

WE'RE NOT LEAVING

9/11 Responders Tell Their Stories of Courage, Sacrifice, and Renewal

Benjamin J. Luft, M.D.

Director of the Long Island Medical
Monitoring and Treatment Program

State University of New York
at Stony Brook

GREENPOINT PRESS
NEW YORK, NY

Published in conjunction with the:
Long Island Medical Monitoring and Treatment Program
Benjamin J. Luft, M.D., Director
State University of New York
Stony Brook, New York
http://www.911respondersremember.org

Designed by Robert L. Lascaro
www.lascarodesign.com
Typeset in Times New Roman and Din
Cover display type: Masterplan

Printed in the United States
Printer: Lightning Source

ISBN 978-0-9832370-2-0

Greenpoint Press
A division of New York Writers Resources
P.O. Box 3203
Grand Central Terminal
New York, NY 10163

www.greenpointpress.org
www.newyorkwritersworkshop.com
www.ducts.org

▶ **On the cover:** Police officer William, who relates his experiences as a 9/11 responder
in Chapter 20, rests briefly on a barricade before resuming work on the Pile.
Front cover photo by John Botte; background photo of WTC steel structure by Alex Fuchs

*For my parents, Robert and Sonia, Holocaust survivors
whose own harrowing stories of survival and renewal taught me
about the thin line between the rescuer and the rescued.*

*For all responders:
May the Lord bless you and guard you—
May the Lord make His face shine upon you and
be gracious unto you—
May the Lord lift up His face onto you and give you peace.
And to this, we all say: Amen.*

"Without heroes, we are all plain people,
and don't know how far we can go."

—Bernard Malamud (1914–1986)

▲ **Responders carry the recovered body** of a police officer or a fireman in a Stokes basket draped with an American flag. *Photo by Steve Spak.*

CONTENTS

PREFACE

THIS BOOK EMERGED FROM THE CONFLUENCE of two journeys that each began on September 11, 2001. One was the journey my colleagues and I embarked upon that morning when, as Chairman of Medicine at Stony Brook Medical School on Long Island, I gathered together a medical team that stood ready to treat what we expected to be droves of wounded from the disaster. The other was the tortured journey the responders to the disaster undertook when they rushed to the scene of the calamity without consideration for their own safety and well-being, and did everything humanly possible to rescue and give aid to the victims.

Initially, our journey seemed to end before it even began. We waited and waited for patients to arrive, yearning to be able to care for those innocents caught by chance in the horrific maelstrom perpetrated by the terrorists. No patients arrived that day. People either escaped the buildings, or they were killed. The hospitals in the city were able to handle the comparatively few wounded. They didn't need our help out on the Island.

The responders had to face that tragic reality as well. Too soon, they had to shift the focus of their efforts from rescue to recovery. When it became clear they would not find survivors, they began the excruciating, painstaking task of sifting through the colossal mountain of debris, which came to be called "the Pile," for body parts and any kind of personal effects that might bring some comfort or closure to the families of the victims, or at least some sense of connection to their lost loved ones.

The process of recovery and reclamation of the site at Ground Zero was protracted and grueling. Initially it had been optimistically scheduled that the cleanup would be completed in a year, but due to the truly herculean efforts of the responders who worked around the clock, often to the point of exhaustion, the daunting task was completed in nine months. Throughout their work on the Pile, the responders inhaled the caustic fumes of burning debris and the stench of decomposing bodies. They were exposed to rapidly recurring episodes of significant trauma from the gruesome loss of colleagues, friends, and fellow citizens, witnessing death, destruction, and repeated episodes of threats to life and limb by the extreme and unstable environment.

Several days after the attack, I went down to the World Trade Center site. I witnessed the smoldering destruction and the all-pervasive dust, inhaled the caustic odor that permeated the air, and was humbled by the extraordinary response. As a trained clinician and scientist, I observed a situation containing all the ingredients needed for the development of significant mental and physical disease as well as social disruption to those who responded. Returning to work the following day, I decided to change our course. We established a voluntary clinic for responders from our community, both professional and nonprofessional, to help meet their medical and psychological needs.

To our surprise, our effort was not universally embraced initially. Politics, avarice, and fear set roadblocks in our path that at certain points seemed insurmountable. However, we persevered. We enlisted the support of labor leaders and local voluntary fire departments. Today our clinics are found across Long Island. We serve more than 6,000 responders from across the greater New York metropolitan area as well as from states as far away as Hawaii. We developed a unique, collaborative model that has broken down the traditional separation of medical, psychiatric, and social services and instead delivers care in an integrated manner. Thus we joined with the responders on this leg of their journey, involving the quest for recuperation and healing.

Our integrated approach to delivering health care to the responders provided us with especially penetrating insight into the complexity of the experience of 9/11. This led us to establish a seminar course for medical students entitled "9/11: The Anatomy of a Health Care Disaster," in order to understand the multidimensional nature of the event. In the seminar, we examined its physical, psychological, medical, sociological, religious, and economic impact, and how those factors drove the response. The final session consisted of group interviews of two responders. The impact of the interviews was profound beyond our expectations. Highly intelligent, extremely rational, scientifically trained medical students (and their professors) were left with their mouths agape, not knowing how to respond except with tears and thanks.

Out of this experience, our oral history project was born. We purchased a high-definition video camera, some lights, and a photographic backdrop, and set up a studio in my office where we recorded the responders' stories. We also established a website, www.911respondersremember.org, to describe the program and offer sample interviews for public viewing. The stories are powerful. The responders speak of their actions, motivation, courage, foibles, and resiliency, their altruism, patriotism, and sense of community. Their language is simple, frank, and descriptive. As much is learned from their pauses, loss of words, and emotional outpourings as from the words themselves. Although they speak of sorrow and pain, to me they are a source of celebration of the human spirit's ability to transcend unimaginable hardships, and still maintain its humanity.

Often in the interviews, the responders allude to the ambiguity of roles that arises between the rescuer and the rescued. The one rescued provides the rescuer with meaning, which often sustains and empowers the rescuer to live through the rescue effort. A similar experience happened to all of us who were touched by this process of bearing witness. At first we were touched by the events, feeling a great sense of empathy and camaraderie, However, it wasn't too long before the stories of the responders caused the interviewers and participants to question their own understanding and values. The stories impacted us directly and informed us about ourselves as citizens and human beings. Our collaborative care model took on a new dimension, with the patients offering their own form of treatment to the care providers. This became the motivation for the writing of this book. We feel that those who read these stories will become part of the process of bearing witness to the events of 9/11, and ultimately aid all of us in the healing that is needed as a result of that infamous attack.

ACKNOWLEDGMENTS

THIS BOOK REPRESENTS A TRULY COLLABORATIVE effort of both the interviewers and the interviewees. I would like to thank the responders for their forthrightness and generosity of spirit. Recollecting these stories under any circumstance is difficult, but especially so when one was intimately involved and witnessed the loss of colleagues and friends. It only became apparent to me while working with the 9/11 responders of the potent role of the patient in healing the physician. Because of this reciprocal relationship, it is therefore natural to me for the proceeds of this book to be predominantly used to support this project and to establish a scholarship fund for the children of the responders adversely affected by 9/11.

The actual writing of this book, from the first interview to the last edit, occurred over an eighteen-month period of time. The schedule was intense, and resulted in this book as well as a documentary film and a number of different curricula that will be used in schools and libraries. It required teamwork and partnerships. I was very fortunate to have an extraordinary team lead by Julie Broihier. Julie was a partner both intellectually and administratively. Her high-mindedness, organizational skills, and keen intellect were indispensible. Special thanks also to Kathryn Melodie Guerrera, the administrator of our World Trade Center Program. She helps create the environment for the highest level of compassion and care, and keeps things humming.

The selection of interviews presented in this book was derived from more than 125 that we had initially compiled. Putting together a team of interviewers, videographers, transcriptionists, and editors, both literary and video, in order to review and edit, within a short period of time, is a feat in and of itself. Without the Internet and sites such as Craigslist, it would be difficult to find some of the best personnel throughout the United States to work on this project. It was amazing to see that everyone who became involved in the program became totally committed and added both substantive as well as intangible and intellectual value to the project, often offering insights and advice, much of it finding its way into the short commentaries within the book itself. In addition to myself, Julie Broihier, and Melodie Guerrera, our interviewers were: Allison Brons, Stephanie Brown, Andrew Flescher, Deborah Hawkins, Janet Lavelle, and Eliza Marcus. Our videographers were Nandita Ajitanand, Christine Collins, Stephen Edwards, Deborah Hawkins, Dan Maccarone, and Andrew Wright. Natasha Mattola and Denise Rolhfs transcribed these interviews, and editing was done by Jeffery Green, Jaime Leick, Liliana Nayden, Travis Rave, and Jane Yahill. A special thanks to Sonia Fore for organizing the interviews. Several photographers donated their photos to our project: John Bombace, John Botte, Roy and Lois Gross, Philip Mattera, Gulnara Samoilova, and Steve Spak.

We were very fortunate to have Joelle Delbourgo as our literary agent. Together with her Associate, Jacqueline Flynn, they have enthusiastically supported our project, offering advice and encouragement. Their organizational skills were especially appreciated given the extremely short timeline involved in this book. We also thank our publisher, Charles Salzberg of Greenpoint Press, for his innovative perspective, Bob Lascaro for the book's design, and Joy Aquilino for her copyediting and proofreading.

We are also grateful to Janet Gabriel, who provided the initial funds to help get this program started, and for the very generous gift from Henry and Marsha Laufer, who acted quickly to fund the project at a critical moment and allowed this book to become a reality. I would also like to thank my wife, Martha, for the countless hours she spent reading through the manuscript and offering her critical and insightful perspectives.

▲ **A Lincoln, Nebraska, firefighter** and her search and rescue
dog rest after searching for human remains on the Pile.
Photo by Roy and Lois Gross.

INTRODUCTION

THE UPCOMING TENTH ANNIVERSARY will mark an important juncture in our remembrance of September 11th. There will be many articles, books, shows, and documentaries that will examine the day in a distant and intellectualized manner. The testimony in this book is different in that it speaks both from and to the soul. Through their deeply personal and unique perspectives, the stories of 9/11 responders, in their own voices, help us understand the human impact of the World Trade Center disaster and encourage us all to heal.

Few of us really know what transpired after the Towers collapsed. Our recollection of the morning of September 11, 2001, is almost a cliché. The sky was an impossibly clear blue. It was late summer, and the air was warm and dry and pleasant. The new school year had only recently begun. People in Manhattan moved about more freely. There were fewer security checkpoints, and on the subways we weren't constantly reminded: *If You See Something, Say Something.*

Nowadays it is rare to think back to the disaster in detail, to recall meticulously the horror that was felt on that day and in the following months. Nor do people delve into the bare fear, the vulnerability, the confusion, and the chaos so widely felt at the time. More often than not, September 11th has become political, and, too often, primarily a talking point. On its anniversaries, we tend to recall just that one day, as if the horrendous shared experience was limited to a single point in time a decade ago.

A deep understanding of the singular impact of this disaster requires us to examine more than the statistical facts and the foreign and domestic policy consequences. It is important to remember that 9/11 is far more than the catalyst for two wars and onerous security restrictions. In addition to the horrendous loss of almost 3,000 lives and the resulting devastation to family, friends, and society, it is an event that a group of *individuals* experienced in a very personal way, bearing long-lasting consequences. Many of the heroes of September 11th, the men and women who responded to the call, are still recovering from the disaster. They suffer from post-traumatic stress disorder (PTSD), nightmares, sleep apnea, anxiety, asthma, persistent cough, and in many cases, anger and disillusionment about how they were treated by a society that dragged its feet in responding to their needs when they became ill as a result of responding to the disaster.

9/11 also had a profound effect on our national psyche, challenging us to re-examine and re-affirm our values. Our discourse should focus on the courageous actions of the people who responded to the disaster, in uncompromising detail, in order to see how patriotism, brotherhood, altruism, and a deep commitment to the community allowed them to prevail. We must consciously avoid sentimentality and partisanship and refrain from ascribing feelings and motives to the responders who acted so heroically. Instead, we should hear them speak in their own words and embrace the values they embody and that all Americans revere.

What motivated people from all walks of life to respond? What price did they pay for their altruistic generosity, and what sustained them through the collapse and the recovery efforts? Ultimately, what allowed them to achieve some type of renewal? In the face of extraordinary devastation and human carnage, responders reacted with courage and conviction, putting themselves in harm's way with the hope of saving the lives of their colleagues and fellow citizens. When the futility of their efforts to find survivors became apparent, they searched for bodies and ultimately for body fragments, with the hope of bringing peace and resolution to the families of the victims of this atrocity, and to our society at large. The impossibility of bringing closure to so many was extremely troubling to the responders, and in many ways appeared to deprive them of the meaning associated with their response.

The stories in this book are extraordinary journeys told with great humility of the restoration of hope and meaning through a strong sense of community and country, duty and responsibility, brotherhood and tolerance, oftentimes with new spirituality and religion. While some think with nostalgia of the "Greatest Generation" of Americans from the past century, one need look no further than these September 11th responders to find a current Great Generation, right here in our midst.

The conditions under which these interviews were conducted are uncommon and uniquely well-suited to eliciting frank and deeply personal material. The setting was the World Trade Medical Monitoring and Treatment Center Clinic in Islandia, New York, where the responders had been receiving health care for years. The interviewers were Clinic staff members who have done their best to help the responders come to terms with the disaster and the effects of their suffering. The interviews are therefore very intimate, often excruciatingly detailed and unfiltered.

This book is presented as a first-person narrative, containing five parts and an epilogue. The responders' voices require no interpretation, and the force of their words would only be diminished if an attempt were made to retell their experiences. Their order of presentation, although chronological, is overlapping; therefore, they do not need to be read in succession. Each account is preceded by an introduction written by the editors. These introductions provide an overview of the narrative and insights into the individuals telling their stories, as well as into the conflicts experienced by them. In addition, approximately thirty photographs of the World Trade Center responders, as well as those of the disaster environment, are presented.

Part One, "Caught in the Collapse," contains seven chapters that group together responders who arrived at the scene prior to the collapse of the Towers and who miraculously survived. They present some striking common trends. Initially, there was an inability to comprehend what their eyes were actually seeing, and an assumption that they were witnessing an accident. Only when the second plane crashed did reality sink in, and, well-honed by their professional training, they all switched immediately into action mode, with only one goal in mind: to save as many of their colleagues buried under the debris as was possible, with total disregard for their own safety. All struggle to this day to find the appropriate language to describe the horrors they were witnessing. Many of them retain the memory of the eerie "clicking" sound of the firemen's emergency locators underfoot, buried with their owners. The courage that is displayed by the speakers is breathtaking. Yet, to a person, they maintain that they were not heroes.

Part Two, "Looking for Survivors," follows with six stories of responders who arrived at the scene shortly after the collapse of the Towers to search for survivors, which, initially, they frantically did. A couple of days later the realization set in that there were no survivors, and the responders turned to look for bodies. They all intuitively understood that families wanted to have a body to put into a coffin and to bury, and they wanted to provide families with that sense of closure. When no bodies were found, they lowered their expectations, and searched for body parts or personal belongings—anything that would identify people who perished in the collapse.

They shared an intense sense of responsibility, some working twenty-four to thirty-six hours at a stretch, almost nonstop, at immense danger to themselves. They share similar expressions to describe the scene on the "Pit" during the first days: "organized chaos" is the most common. They stress that most responders were strangers to each other, yet soon became a family. When describing the most striking memories of these early days, the responders recall most forcefully the smell—the smell of decaying bodies, "the smell of death."

Part Three, "Recovery, Recovery, Recovery," as narrated by eight responders, focuses on the tedious, painstaking recovery efforts. The interviews display the broad spectrum of professions and specialties needed to dismantle the remains of the Towers. These responders describe the painful, emotional drain of doing their work with no hope left to sustain them, the feeling that the rescue effort had turned, over time, mechanical. They all refer to the "Bucket Brigade": the passing of buckets containing debris lovingly collected from hand to hand, the contents to be ultimately searched for human remains. In the process, they felt that they had turned into parts of a machine, or into ghosts. They commonly express a feeling of numbness, and experiencing a loss of self. Yet they all were determined to appear strong, and did not permit themselves to express emotions. Crying was often done in secret hiding places.

Part Four, "The Responders Need Help," reveals the support—medical, physical, mental, and emotional—that was provided to the responders on the Pile through six narratives. This segment of our story comes from the perspectives of a massage therapist, a podiatrist, three policemen serving in different police branches, and a private contractor. They shared the experience of working for a long duration of time at the disaster site. They convey the wonderful spirit of volunteerism that developed following the disaster. They tell of national organizations that chipped in to provide needed services and supplies, primarily socks and boots. They marvel at the teams of firemen and those from other agencies arriving from all over the country to volunteer. However, they also share their bitter disappointment and anger at being misled by the authorities about the toxicity of the materials they were handling, and the quality of the air they were breathing. Over time, many of them have suffered serious medical problems resulting from the long exposure to these toxins. Despite these problems, they share a firm conviction of having done the right thing, and concur that, if a similar situation were to present itself in the future, they would do it all over again.

Part Five, "Renewal," consists of testimonies from five professionals who brought their organizations' support to aid the responders. They include a psychiatrist, a police veteran who created a peer-help organization, a union leader, a clergyman who ministered to responders' families at home, and a priest from St. Paul's Chapel, which stood adjacent to Ground Zero, miraculously survived, and became a haven to the workers on the site.

This group recounts in detail the common needs of the workers at Ground Zero that became apparent over time, and how they and their organizations provided for these needs over many months. They reveal their own fascinating observations, emotions, and contributions, and candidly also divulge the heavy toll they too paid through their experiences. After all, they were responders as well.

The epilogue is the testimony of a widow of a 9/11 responder who died several years later, following a protracted battle with cancer. The story of her struggles, her pride in her husband's heroic work at the disaster site, and the way she instills this pride in her orphaned children, is an inspiration to us all.

Because of its widespread and lasting effects, September 11th is embedded in the experience of many Americans. It is estimated that 25 percent of the residents of this country have been directly or indirectly affected by the disaster, and as a community we are only beginning to come to terms with it. We hope and trust that this book will aid in this process. The oral history interviews presented here provide a means of transformation for the responders. No longer are they the victims of history, they are the authors of it. Out of this disaster a special type of community is born: its members share symptoms, a common history, and, we fervently hope, a certain salvation.

The rest of us have much to learn from the responders about the many aspects of human behavior when called to serve in response to a disaster. We see them as the generous and altruistic heroes that they are: men and women who faced violence and horror for the sake of the greater good, men and women who risked their own lives for others, who do not see themselves as heroes, but rather humbly tell stories of the bravery and courage of *others*. We learn that the substance of who we are as Americans is not defined solely by our government and institutions; it is ultimately defined by the character and actions of our people. It is something to be proud of.

PART ONE

CAUGHT IN THE COLLAPSE

None of us knows for certain what we would do in an emergency if our lives were on the line. Would courage prevail? Would survival instincts overpower our desires to help? Would we succumb to death? On September 11, 2001, while thousands fled, hundreds rushed toward the burning Towers. Upon seeing the panic-stricken and injured, these well-trained emergency responders went into action, pushed aside their own fears, and focused on evacuating and treating the survivors. The stories that follow are the accounts of these initial responders. They all faced death. They all escaped, but barely. Their stories are not about escaping, but about courage, devotion, guilt for having survived, and fear, once realization set in.

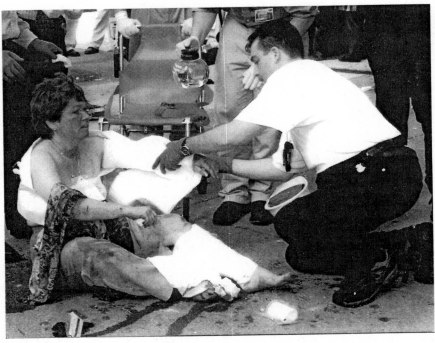

▲ **This photo of Emergency Medical Technician Mitchel Wallace** treating a survivor with a severe leg injury is one of the last taken of him before he perished in the collapse of Tower 2. Mitch is referred to by Tyree, who tells his story in Chapter 7. *Photographer unknown.*

▶ **Retreating office workers watch** in stunned disbelief as one of the Towers falls. *Photo by Philip Mattera.*

▲ **New York City police officer Carol** *(second from left)*, who shares her experiences of the attack in Chapter 1, and another officer lead a survivor through the heavy ash and debris immediately after the collapse of Tower 2. *Photo by Gulnara Samoilova.*

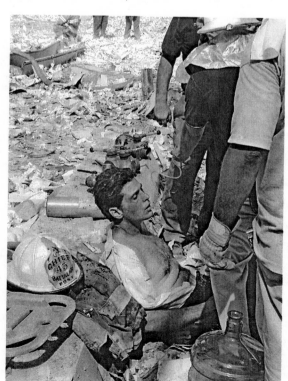

▶ **Responders administer first aid** to a survivor of the Towers' collapse. *Photo by Steve Spak.*

▲ **A survivor and a responder,** both completely covered in dust, walk north on Broadway toward safety. *Photo by Steve Spak.*

▲ **Vehicles in the vicinity of the fallen Towers,** including Ladder Company 113's fire engine, were crushed by falling debris, burned, and covered in ash. *Photo by Steve Spak.*

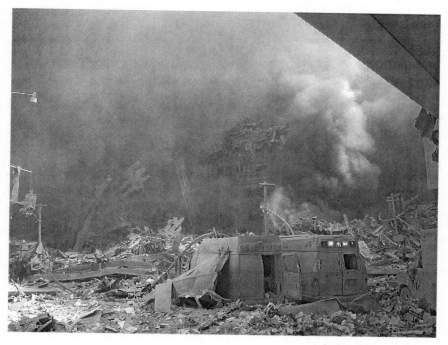

▲ **A ghostly scene of the wreckage** that includes the ash- and debris-covered remnants of two ambulances. *Photo by Steve Spak.*

CHAPTER 1
....

WE'RE NOT LEAVING

Carol worked for the Transit Division of the New York City Police Department. Assigned to a unit covering the World Trade Center, she was one of the first officers on the scene. Standing in the lobby doorway trying to get people out, she was blown violently away from the building as the Tower collapsed. Blinded, choking, and seriously injured, Carol continued pulling people from the rubble and looking for survivors. Most people she found were dead. Portuguese writer Fernando Pessoa wrote that, "To express something is to take away its terror." But Pessoa didn't witness Nagasaki, the Holocaust, or September 11th. Otherwise, he may well have agreed with Theodor Adorno that, "To write a poem after Auschwitz is barbaric." Mass atrocity overwhelms language's capacity to express the atrocity's magnitude and fierce evil. Carol and other responders often struggle to find words darkly and deeply rich enough to suggest the horrific. The same adjectives and comparisons recur—"amazing," "unbelievable," "surreal," "shocking," "like in a movie"—but the words seem anemic. One of the most piercing frustrations of people touched by violent mass atrocity is not being able to adequately relate it to others; they often feel trapped inside their heads with unbearable memories.

WHEN WE CAME OUT OF THE SUBWAY SYSTEM, people were frantic. They were running and they were screaming and there was a lot of debris. As I ran toward the World Trade Center, people were pointing, screaming, and shouting, "That way, that way!" As I came upon the buildings, I saw Tower 1; I saw the rear end of a plane sticking out, halfway in, halfway out, but I could only see the rear of that plane in the building, and a lot of blood and debris. People were frantic, people were panicking, not knowing what to do.

I called for assistance on the radio and confirmed that a plane had hit the World Trade Center, calling for other officers to respond, for assistance, for supervisors, and immediately went to Tower 2, which we were closer to. People were still coming out of that building. We tried to just get people to calm down and to evacuate, and we headed people uptown. That area needed to be supervised in some way, shape, or form—with the panic and the debris. So we just took it upon ourselves to just go into action.

Because the plane was so forward into the building, it did not look like it was a big jet plane. When I looked up, I saw the rear of the plane. A lot of people never even [saw] it sticking out because once the jet fuel dripped into the building, there was an explosion and you no longer saw the plane. But when I initially got there, I saw the back of the plane sticking out of the building.

More police officers came, ambulances came, fire departments came. My immediate supervisor, I never saw. We just continued to evacuate and tell people to go uptown and get out of the area. But everybody wants to know what's going on. It's human nature. They want to stand there and look up and see. It was very difficult to get people to move on. We didn't realize how bad that this was going to be at this point in time.

There were about ten police officers working the area with me. Big, big burly guy, FBI shield around his neck, came up to us and said, "You're not a coward. If you want to leave, there are more planes coming. We're under attack. You're going to die if you stay here." And this came from an FBI agent.

And I remember looking up at him and saying, "You're kidding me, right?" He said, "We're under attack. It's terrorism." He knew more than I knew.... The cops that I was working there with, we were like, "We're just going to continue. We're making a choice: We're not leaving; that's our job." It was more important to get all these people to safety. So we stayed and continued.

So now you've got two planes hit the Tower, you're just in this smoke-filled, debris-filled area where there's jumpers. I saw my first jumper. I had no idea what it was. When somebody just jumps and they're on the ground twenty feet from you, it's just an awful sight. It's like a tomato. You can't—it's unrecognizable. What do you do? You hear these noises and these crashes and you don't know what they are, but they were people jumping. I saw people actually hanging off the side of the building, as people saw later on, in the films, coming out of the buildings because of all the smoke. That was hard, to see those people up there and not be able to do anything for them.

I mean, body parts, dust, debris—people that were coming out that were injured, burn victims. I mean, a guy came out, his shoulder was like totally dislocated and—backwards. The side of his face was burnt off and his ear was missing.... You can't train to see that. I'm sure even a doctor would take a second look at something like that.

So we just continued to evacuate people. There was a woman down in the basement level that had cerebral palsy and couldn't walk. She was trying to get out of the building. I picked her up and carried her out of the building. I knew that we had to get her away from the area because there were more planes coming, because that's what the FBI had said.

I think that my personal adrenaline… I was in shock mode. My strength to help just blocked everything out. Did I throw a woman over my shoulder and carry her out of a building? Yes, I did. I was strong. Because you just do things with the adrenaline.

I walked that woman up the escalator—the escalators weren't working—and walked her half a block. And I saw a real tall man in Army fatigues—he was a National Guardsman—and I passed her off to him and asked him to continue, to take her to Downtown Beekman Hospital,[1] to triage her.

I had a real problem…with where these people were triaged. They were triaged at the base of the buildings and inside of the buildings. Which now … we don't do. The ambulance would pull up and we'd load six or eight people in, and off they'd go. But a lot of people were triaged underneath the tree areas and the seating areas. And all those people are dead. They didn't live. There's no *way* that they lived through that, because that building just came down and crushed and pulverized. So where did all those people go?

I WAS INSIDE

Tower 2 collapsed first. I was actually inside the building, near the escalators, when the Tower collapsed. When the building imploded down, it blew me out of the building. And I was able to hold onto the doorway with my left arm. People blew by me and under me and through me. Only with one arm, did I hold on. If you ever saw a cartoon with somebody midair, holding on for their life, I was actually holding on for my life. Not knowing what was happening, just knowing that there were explosions and that there were people coming past me and that there was utter terror. I was able to bring my other hand over because I was in shape. I worked out. I lifted weights four times a week. And that's the only thing that really saved my life, was me being strong.

I was able to pull myself down. And I heard somebody to the right of me, *yelling* at me, "Grab my hand! Grab my hand!" And I tried to feel for somebody, because I couldn't see anything. You couldn't breathe. I pulled and this person pulled back to me. I pulled myself over to them. We did the Chinese fire drill thing and held onto each other like we were taught when we were kids. Brick and debris and people and everything was coming

[1] New York Downtown Hospital, located between Beekman, Spruce, and Gold streets in Lower Manhattan.

down and it was very loud. We didn't know what was happening because you couldn't see; it was totally dark. And then there was total silence. I was lying under all of this debris with a guy.

I had no idea he was a police officer, or who he was. His name is Richie. He worked for Manhattan Traffic at the time. I found all this out afterwards. He and I crawled out of the building together. We were trapped. The only part of the building standing was a very small piece of cement, where Richie and I were. Everything else was down. Now, we had to crawl out. As we crawled out we saw people and we tried to help them and they were dead. It was very quiet. It was eerie. It was utter silence. I had no idea that the Tower collapsed.

I came out to Vesey Street, where the church is, where the Millenium Hotel was. This is a picture of myself and Richie, after we crawled out of the building [*see page 3, top*]. The woman on Richie's arm was standing with her hands up in the air. Her statement was, "Where's my pocketbook? I lost my pocketbook." She was in shock. She wasn't physically injured. Don't know where she was or where she came from. We just grabbed her and said, "You need to come with us. We need to get out of here." And she did.

We didn't know where we were walking, but I personally didn't look back to see the Tower was down. I didn't know the Tower was down. As we were walking through this big cloud of smoke, you couldn't see, you couldn't breathe. We were choking. I thought a nuclear bomb hit. Or I felt like napalm was dropped, like the Vietnam War. I really thought that we were just going to drop and die at any moment.

I kept hearing, "Holy Mary, Mother of God." And somebody just kept praying. It was a man's voice. They just kept saying it and it got louder and louder. Later on, I asked Richie, "Did you ever see anybody?" And he said, "No." "Did you hear that man?" And he said, "Yes." It was like a voice we were walking to. It was really eerie because my dad had passed away. I think it was my dad. So that was very difficult.

WHAT THE HELL HAPPENED?

Richie and I were vomiting. We were vomiting thick, black chunks of I didn't know what. I think it was a good thing, because we were trying to get that stuff out of our systems. We were both vomiting, and we couldn't breathe, and our corneas were scratched.

This woman, she left us. We helped other people. And then we started hearing the beeps.... We didn't know what they were. We thought they were car horns. "What are all those beeps?" We didn't understand. The cars were crushed, there were small fires, there was debris everywhere. And the beeps were the firemen's packs.

We walked down past this deli, and we went in and grabbed a bunch of water bottles, rinsed our faces off, tried to clear our eyes out. Just grabbed water bottles. People sitting on the side of the road, we were helping them, pouring water on them, telling them to get up and walk, just go uptown.

Richie and I walked down this one area and he saw a cop that he knew. This cop said, "Come into this building. Clean up. Come into this building. You're safe in here." I don't know where the building was. I don't know how far from the site it was, but we went into the building.

Now, mind you, I lost my partner and didn't know where my partner was. Beforehand, I had said, "If something happens, I'm going to meet you right here. You stay there, you wait for me." That never happened. There was no meeting. He [Richie] lost two of his partners.

Unless you were there, you don't understand how chaotic it was. People were running and pushing, and this big explosion and the building actually came down... How are you going to find where your partner is or where you were going or what's going to happen?

So Richie and I ended up going into this building. As soon as we got into the building, he falls down and collapses, clutches his chest, and I think he's having a massive heart attack. Two other guys come, grab him, take off his vest, his shirt, start giving him oxygen, giving him first aid. I'm yelling at him. "You can't die on me! I don't even know your name!" It was horrible.

You couldn't see outside; it was all black and dusty. Every once in a while you'd see somebody walk by. Our radios didn't work; the phones didn't work. I didn't have a cell phone. Nobody had a cell phone. I couldn't call my command; I couldn't look for my partner. We didn't know where we were safe, where we weren't. We didn't know what to do. There was no supervisor. There were other people here in the building asking us questions... We didn't know how to answer them. I still didn't know the building had collapsed.

A half hour later, you hear another big rumble. The other Tower collapsed—everything was shaking. We saw this big cloud of black smoke again, come through past the building. And fires in the back.

The cloud of debris was from the collapse of the second Tower. After it passed the building, Carol decided it was time to leave. She still did not realize that the Towers had fallen.

THEY'RE ALL DEAD

After walking to the West Side Highway, Carol and Richie hitch a ride on a truck that normally carries barricades. The truck drove up the highway and dropped them near Canal Street, where Richie met up with his command.

I told Richie's boss who I was, where I was from, and they notified my command. I told him I didn't know where my partner was, and they said that she was fine. Richie's two partners were fine... .

Hours later, an ambulance came. There were all firemen and cops, and I was the only woman. They took us up to St. Clare's Hospital. On the way, we're sharing an oxygen tank. What good is this really going to do us? There's nothing left in it. But we're passing it around like we were passing a bottle.

When they arrive at the hospital, they notice the triage area with nurses and doctors waiting for the arrival of victims. Carol realizes that nobody's coming.

They bring us in and start treating us. They did our eyes, and they interviewed us. Detectives came to talk to us. It was really funny because the one fireman, he was hurt pretty bad and he was burnt and he was injured. I was in a lot of pain with my shoulder and my back and my legs and stuff.

They said to all of us, "We're going to send you home." We said, "Treat us. We're here. Just take care of us. Please treat us." They said, "We have people that are more seriously injured than you are, coming." We're like, "They're all dead. Nobody survived that. They're dead. Treat the living. Help us."

They didn't believe us. They handed us all Valiums and water and stood there while we drank our water and took Valiums. They thought that we were all crazy and that we were acting out. One fireman was a little vocal. He said, "You've got to be f'ing kidding me. I'm hurt. You're going to send me home?" He needed attention.

WHAT I DID WASN'T ENOUGH

Eventually they took us over to Manhattan Traffic, where Richie's base was, over on 30th Street. I called my command and went off-duty from there. They had the TV on. Richie and I sat there and we held hands and we watched TV. We saw the Towers collapse.

Well, I still didn't want to accept it… I watched the TV and saw that all those people were killed and still didn't want to believe it. That was a big issue for me. I didn't accept the fact that the Towers fell. And I didn't understand that the Towers fell and that I was in one when it collapsed.

January of 2003 is when I actually realized what happened to me. They did an awards ceremony for the Police Department and I got the Medal of Valor for… for what? Saving all those people and all those people that died? *Whatever.* I took the piece of paper and I threw it at my commanding officer and I said, "You've got to be kidding me. I'm not accepting this." He said, "You have to." I said, "No, I don't *have* to."

I felt like what I did wasn't enough and that it was a defeat and that so many people died. I didn't feel worthy of receiving a medal when all those people died. He told me that I would be suspended if I didn't go. So I had to go. He said, "Dress blues, be there." Whatever. I went to the ceremony at the Winter Garden. They had FBI snipers all around the area.

And then I remembered. I remembered what happened to me. It kicked in and I said, "Oh, my God."

I worked for four doctors in the medical division. They're like, "Carol, the building fell on you. You were inside when the building fell on you. You crawled out of the building." I'm like, "No, no, no. That didn't happen. No, no, no."

I was interviewed for a book, *Women at Ground Zero*. I told them, "I got blown out of the building when the first plane hit." And that's not what happened. I was blown out of the building when the building collapsed. So, it didn't jibe. And they're like, "That's not what happened to you." "Yes, it is." And I was adamant about it. The doctors said it was a defense mechanism to push that off and repress those feelings.

AN INCH OF DUST

I didn't work the Pile. I didn't do recovery work. I blew out my rotator cuff. I had shoulder surgery. I had both my knees reconstructed. I had back damage, I had lung damage, and I had corneal abrasions. My physical injuries kept me from working the Pile. They put me on light duty, answering phones and doing what I could to help, while I awaited having my three surgeries. I was in the vicinity because I worked at Canal Street. So I was in the air zone [contaminated] area.

What was interesting to me was, if I drove in I parked down there on Canal Street where my precinct was. When I would come out, I kid you not, there'd be like an inch of dust on my car. When I brought my car home, I would tell the children and my friends, "Don't touch my car." It was impossible to wash my car every day, working sixteen-hour tours. They didn't care that I was injured and hurt and sick, they just needed everybody that they could. That's just the Police Department. Even after driving, that stuff stuck to my car.

THINKING BACK

I knew almost all the Port Authority officers that were killed, because I worked in the World Trade Center. The E train was a dead end and we'd take our breaks with the Port Authority police officers. We hung out with the Port. We backed the Port Authority police officers up. We'd take our lunch with them. I was there…a couple of the police officers that were killed were right there with me. The firemen that walked into the building, they went in, they never came out. I don't know what company they were or where they were from, but I held the door for them to get in and cleared the way for them to walk to their deaths, basically.

It really pisses me off that the communication system was horrible. You're really on four or five different frequencies, because Transit has their own line, NYPD had their own line, Housing had their own line, the Fire Department has their own line, EMS has their own line, Port Authority had their own line. Only supervisors could communicate with those people, so we don't know what's going on. I think that the communication problem is a very big thing that should be worked on. I really don't know if they've changed anything.

The other thing that I would change is that you don't set up a triage center at the base of a building that's on fire. Let's hope that we've learned that. Because I have footage of people that are actually dead, that were at the foot of the building, being triaged. That really pisses me off because those people really should not have been there.

Don't ever take your life for granted. Live each day to its fullest. Yes, we're a free country, but I do believe in more screening at the airports, more screening at the bus terminals, more screening at the buildings. I do believe it is going to happen again. I think the terrorists are out there.

We've recently put a stop to another terrorist attack. Our subway system is *totally* vulnerable. People don't want to put the money out to make it *not* vulnerable. We should be going through every subway station and checking luggage. All they could do is take a bomb through the subway station and let a bomb go on say the A train under High Street, or in between Brooklyn and Manhattan. You're going to make mass casualties and a lot of damage. It would be so easy to hit New York. As much as they say that they're taking security serious, I don't think they're taking security serious enough. I think there's a lot more that they could do. And the federal government should stand behind all the cities and put more money out to stop these things.

I think I did my best. I had a chance to leave and I chose to stay. I wish more people could've been saved. I definitely have survivor's guilt. I definitely have post-traumatic stress syndrome. I definitely have lung damage. My body hurts all the time, every day. I try not to give in to that; I just get up and I try to live my life every day to its fullest.

CHAPTER 2

RUN FOR YOUR LIFE

Philip is an inspector with the New York City Department of Buildings. What resonates so deeply in Philip's story is the description of his emotions as events were unfolding right in front of him. They are important to our story because ten years later he is able to still articulate his emotions—his feelings, his fears, his disbelief, and the way he coped in the face of events that had no precedent in human experience.

Philip elaborates on his sense of disbelief at the events surrounding him, even though it was clear that they were indeed happening. He describes his inability to reconcile what he was seeing with what he knew his reality ought to have to have been. We learn from him that when so-called normalcy is ruptured suddenly and violently, it is one of the most stressful situations people can experience. He demonstrates to us that what he saw and was caught up in defied cognition because it was so profoundly discontinuous with the course of everyday life. Philip's story stresses the complexities and contradictions associated with survival.

FROM MY BOSS'S DESK, OUT THE WINDOW, is the Towers. We could see what looked like a little hole and some papers blowing out the window. That's all it looked like. It looked like some papers were blowing out.

Philip and his colleague Ivan decide to take a video camera and binoculars to the roof to see what is happening.

There were these five guys doing facade work up on the roof. They spoke very little English. We asked them if they saw a plane and one guy kept going, "Yeah, big plane, big, big." I said, "What's he talking about, big plane?" It had to be one of those small little planes.

I'm looking with the big binoculars and Ivan is videoing with the video camera, and it looked like they were throwing furniture out the windows. I thought that was strange. As I was looking I said, "Ivan, why are they throwing furniture out the window?" He said, "Maybe they're breaking the glass for the fire or something."

Now smoke started coming out. When we first looked, it looked like papers. It didn't look that bad. He goes, "Give me the binoculars." So I gave him the binoculars, and I was videoing. I just thought it was strange.

And then he said, "Those are people. They're jumping out of the windows." I'm like, "No way. Why would anybody be jumping out the window?" He gave me back the binoculars and I looked. I could actually see people jumping out the window. For the life of me, I couldn't understand why anybody would be jumping out of a window. We hopped in the car and we headed down there.

We get to the building, we look up, we look around there. They had some things blocked off and it looked a lot worse now than a little plane. I still wasn't believing it. We went back to the Buildings Department and we told my boss, "This is something big. This is something bad."

Now reports were coming in and we hear people in the halls talking: terrorist attack, it was a bomb, all sorts of things. So we're getting ready to go back now to the Towers, and while we're waiting in the elevator, at the window, we see another plane coming.

So that's how much time?[2] I don't recall how many minutes were in between when the two planes hit, but we were at the elevator getting ready to go back down there and we saw the second plane coming and Ivan goes, "Imagine if another plane hit the Tower?" I said, "Yeah, but it looks like it's awfully close." Right in front of our eyes, the second plane blew into the Tower.

That was the first time I actually believed we were under attack. That was the first time I heard Bin Laden mentioned. Al Qaeda. I said, "Who's…?" Certain people that were with us, they seemed to know about it.

We weren't ready to go into the building. They were waiting for an engineer to come right outside the World Trade Center. From where I was standing, I could see into the lobby. I could see firemen in there. I could see people walking back and forth. We walked maybe a block away or so and we reconvened, and we were talking about what we were going to do, who was coming?

I kept hearing noises like *shhhhhhh, boom*. Sounded like glass was breaking or something. It sounded like something was falling and hitting the ground and making a weird noise. Someone tells me those are bodies that are coming down from the building and crashing and hitting things. I don't know what to believe. I don't see anybody hitting the floor and exploding, but I hear this bang and this noise and then I had the binoculars again in the car and I looked up and I could see people hanging out the window with flags…like *help me* type of things.

At one point, I saw a couple—a man and a woman holding hands—

---

[2] Seventeen minutes passed between the planes striking the North Tower and the South Tower.

and they jumped out the window. I thought "I don't believe this." Never knowing about the gas and they were trapped and they couldn't go through. It was very overwhelming. I had no idea what was going on, and it was obvious everybody around me had no idea.

By now the FBI was there, and the Police Department, they were putting up barricades. I even think I saw CIA if I'm not mistaken. We were walking toward the first Tower that was hit to make an assessment. Out of nowhere, there was a guy from the FBI, had a big blowhorn, and he makes an announcement that there is a report of a third incoming plane.

Actually, if it wasn't for that guy on the microphone saying that another plane was coming in, I think I probably wouldn't be here right now. I think I would've been inside—trying to go up with an engineer, take photos to assess the damage.

RUN, RUN, RUN!

All of a sudden, the building just started coming down. Everybody panicked. Everybody everywhere was just screaming, yelling, "Run, run, run!" It seemed like it took seconds for the building to come down. It didn't seem like it took long at all, but it seemed like time stood still a little bit and then the cloud came.

It almost looked like a tornado type of thing. It was swirling and coming at us. I thought that if we got caught in it, that we were going to die and that we wouldn't be able to breathe. I didn't know what to think. We started running.

I ran for my life. I remember hitting into people, knocking people over. There was a woman with a carriage and a baby and she was screaming, "Help me, help me!" I remember for years that it bothered me. I thought maybe she died because I didn't. Normally I'd help anybody, but I have a wife, kids. I thought I was dying. I ran. I didn't help anybody, and that's not like me not to help anybody. For a long time, I had a hard time dealing with the fact that I didn't stop to help people.

So now we're running to get away from this cloud, and everybody dispersed in different ways. The last thing I do remember when I lost the commissioner was he decided to run down into the subway. There were people saying, "Go in the subway. It's safe." I didn't feel the subway was going to be safe with that cloud coming. I thought you were going to go down the subway and the smoke was going to go down there, and I took my chances and ran.

We're running and you could see the cloud passing us on the next avenue. That's how massive it was. I just remember Ivan was with me a good part of the way when we're running. He decides to stop and pray. He just stops. I'm looking over my shoulder and I see him. He's on the floor and I stop. I run over to grab him to pull him and he pushes my hand away and he goes, "No." I just kept running. I thought he was dead. He decided at that moment to pray. I decided to run.

I didn't know what to do, where to go. We had no plan. I didn't know if it was safe to go back to 60 Hudson Street [where the Buildings Department was located]. The cloud was coming. What do you do? Where do you go?

I was alone and then I got lost. I tried to go from 60 Hudson Street to the Towers to go look for my boss, to look for the commissioner who was with us. He was an elderly gentleman, probably in his seventies. I felt bad that we left him.

I was so disoriented, I didn't know east from west, north from south. Nothing looked familiar. I was asking people, "Can you help me? Can you tell me which way?"

People were in shock. I may have been in shock myself. It was embarrassing; I was scared. I didn't know where to go or who was going to help me. I thought maybe people were going to come out now and start shooting us. People were talking and you hear all this chatter that is going on and I kept hearing *terrorist*, I kept hearing *cells*. I kept hearing a lot of talk.

NEVER WENT HOME

Philip thought about leaving downtown, but when he heard that the Buildings Department was convening in Queens he went there instead.

It was just like an instinct to help. I didn't think they needed me at home. [They] were safe in Long Island. I did call my wife right before we went into the Towers. I told her we were heading over to the World Trade Center.

She saw in the news that it fell, and she never got to talk to me until that evening. She said, "The last thing you said to me was that you were going into the Towers." What she must have thought.

I don't even think I slept that night. We were up all night. They had no sleeping facilities for us, and we just stayed there in case they needed us. I just want to stress that nobody really knew anything at this point still. Nobody knew anything—[there was] a lot of speculation.

LIKE I WAS IN A WAR ZONE

The next morning they put us in groups with inspectors, engineers, or architects in groups of threes, and they gave you a letter. You were group A, group B, group C, and we just went into Ground Zero to assess damage on the outlying buildings. We were doing a quick assessment, if there was a piece of glass or a piece of facade that was ready to fall and was going to kill somebody.

We went right into where the Towers were, Ground Zero. I was reluctant about what we were going to find there. I figured there was going to be bodies and dead people everywhere. That's what I thought I was going to see, but it wasn't like that. It was like everything was covered with soot. You really couldn't see anything. I couldn't make out anything when we were there.

The only equipment we had was those white dust masks. And after a few minutes of breathing in them, sweating, they were soaked. You had to take it off because you couldn't breathe if you had it on. They had given us Tyvek suits, but I had no real respirator for maybe almost two weeks, a week and a half. I was just using a white mask or some form of that white mask, with a little cartridge filter. As time went on we got fitted for actual respirators, but no gloves. We were really unprepared. But people were sending in supplies, and within a few days anything that you needed was there.

In the beginning, the first few days, it was very hard to get around. There were makeshift morgues around the place, and you could see people picking up body parts and putting them in bags and people crying. It was very sad and scary. I actually felt like I was in a war zone.

There were rumors going around that there were cells and these terrorists were going to come shoot at us and blow each other up. All sorts of rumors were spreading amongst people like *watch out*. We thought we were going to find people in the building, maybe trapped. And then they were talking about the buildings might be booby-trapped.

We used to go up and down thirty, forty flights checking buildings. One of the buildings in Ground Zero, reports kept coming in that this building was falling. I think it was 1 Liberty Plaza—I'm not even sure what address it was—and this building was always falling.

One day—like I said, communications wasn't the best—we were using little walkie-talkies that kids would play with because we didn't have anything. We were up on the 30th floor, the radio is breaking up and this is a serious report, this ain't like hearsay, this is coming from command center. They're telling us the building we're in is collapsing.

So we start running like maniacs. I don't remember what inspector was with me, and I got to the 15th, 14th floor, I couldn't run no more. I just started praying. I said, "That's it. We're gonna die." It didn't fall, and we came outside and we addressed the problem. "Why you keep saying the building is falling, and we're up in the building and you're telling us the building is coming down?" You have to be there to understand what it feels like. There's nothing you can do. It was just terrible.

Even though I was employed as an inspector to do the inspections, it was more like helping. Somebody said, "Give me a hand with this," and you'd give them a hand. They want to move something. I remember holding open one of the body bags—I don't know if it was for a fireman or who it was—and they were putting stuff in the bag. I really didn't want to do that, to be honest with you.

The closer you got to the Pile, the more of that you saw. When you were more towards the outskirts there was less, but we started going up into the buildings that afternoon—the outlying buildings. All the windows blown out, everything was covered with soot. There was a huge pile probably about three or four stories high easy, of debris, smoke everywhere, and everybody was dirty and filthy. You were in there ten minutes, you needed to change your clothes.

It was rough for the guys in the Buildings Department. The agency wasn't prepared—nobody was prepared—but for days I wasn't able to shower. We had no facilities to shower. We were eating whatever we could find to eat. They were making makeshift places to go eat, but the guys kept working. We were working twenty-four hours a day, seven days a week. We were sleeping on the floor at 60 Hudson Street. We just take a nap, get up, and…. It was taking its toll. A couple days without showering, everyone smelling, stinking, lying on the floor. I remember there was a McDonald's and they were giving out free Big Macs for breakfast, lunch, and dinner, and we're getting sick of it.

Within a week or so we found what everybody else seemed to know but us. You could go to a certain hotel, a certain school, you could get showers, baths, you could get a massage if your feet hurt, chiropractors …. There was all this stuff that was available that we weren't aware of. It was very upsetting. Here we are killing ourselves and we weren't privy to any of this stuff. I don't think anybody deliberately didn't want us to know, but nobody had the mindset to say, "We need to take care of these guys. We need to make sure they're okay." We needed places to eat. We needed clothes. We're wearing the same clothes, and they'd be soaked.

You start walking thirty, forty, fifty flights, and they might ask you to go back to the same building two, three times in one day. There's no elevators and we're doing nighttime inspections, in groups. We're not sure if the floors are going to be there when we walk out. It was very scary, but I think the adrenaline kept everybody going, and that hope that we were going to find somebody, rescue somebody. Maybe somebody was trapped in a building that couldn't get out. Stuck in a garage somewhere. We didn't find any of that the whole time I was there.

I don't think I went home for the first week.

WE GOT CLOSER

There was a group of us—Frankie, Ivan, me, George, Eddie, Mark. There was about eight of us that hung together. We actually got closer. There were certain guys there that I really didn't care for too much or really weren't friendly with them, but after spending so much time with them and they were in the same mindset as I was, nobody complained. We just went. And we just kept shifts, rotating, going doing inspections.

We're still friends to this day, all of us. We still keep in touch. We used to call each other on September 11th. That has died out as time went on. But the first four, five years, I would call all of them. "How are you guys doing today?" We're involved with actually seeing someone, like a therapist, through St. Vincent's, and to this day I still see them. I've been going there for seven years.

EVERYBODY IS A HERO, NO?

In the beginning the appreciation wasn't even a thought. You were just in work mode. Your adrenaline was flowing. You were just doing what you needed to do. But as time went on and days turned into weeks, I personally felt that what my agency was doing wasn't actually appreciated. I felt like if you didn't die, if you weren't a fireman or police officer, whoever died, or affiliated with someone that died in an agency, you weren't a hero.

It just seemed that what we did wasn't that important, and it *was* important. What every individual did was important. Just because a building inspector didn't die doesn't mean that what the Department of Buildings was doing wasn't important. We weren't the first guys to run in—the firemen, the police—but we were there right after them. That's how it goes. The hero thing was just really starting to get to us.

HBO put a sign up at Ground Zero that said, "HBO salutes our heroes." They had the little insignia of the Fire Department and Police Department. I used to see it every day, and it used to bother me. But people gave what they could and did what they could. So after about a week, I couldn't take it no more, and I noticed that Department of Transportation put a sticker up there, and then I noticed another agency did it. So I went back to my office, I got our letterhead that says Department of Buildings. I blew it up. I had someone let me stand on their shoulders; I went up. I actually have a picture of it.

While I'm doing it, a fireman comes over to me and says, "Hey buddy, it's a little disrespectful."

I said, "Excuse me?"

He said, "We lost a lot of brothers."

I said, "I'm not taking anything away from anybody, but there are other agencies here that are doing the best we can. Everybody is a hero, no?"

He said, "Well…," and just walked away.

SOMETHING WAS WRONG WITH ME

It was July 10, 2002. I got my first anxiety attack. I was working, and then couldn't breathe, and the next thing I know I pass out. I'm in the hospital. They tell me, "Too much sun. Drink some water." A few days later, the same thing happened. That was the beginning of a long road of panic attacks, anxiety attacks, post-9/11 stress disorder, whatever they call it.

I'm moving forward in mind and spirit. But my health… I have sleep apnea now. I have chronic sinusitis. I get bronchitis at least twice a year. I get four or five sinus infections a year. At one time I was on ten, eleven medicines—breathers, inhalers, steroids. I blew up to almost 300 pounds. [I was] very depressed. I felt like an old man.

I was always athletic. I wrestled in high school and college—All-American. I used to run marathons. I was always in good shape, and slowly but surely I was sick and depressed and not feeling well and on all this medicine. I thought for sure something was wrong with me, and it was only going to be a matter of time. I was refusing to take any more medicine every time I went to a doctor. I felt this wasn't working. The doctors don't know everything. They try to help you, but…

I tried a detoxification program. It was really for the firemen and the policemen that it was offered to. A friend of mine told me about it. He said, "I heard some good things about it, bad things about it. I'll get you a number. Why don't you try and see?"

I went down and I met with the guy who is running the program—his name was Jim—and I told him my story, told him what I did. He said, "You're a candidate. We would like you in the program." At the time they told me thirty days was the max you could stay there. I think there was one or two other people who stayed thirty-one or thirty-two days. They kept me for forty-four days. Seven days a week, minimum of four hours a day, and my job didn't pay for me to go. I had to do it on my own time, which I couldn't understand. To this day I have hard feelings about it. I worked for the City of New York, so why won't you let me? Nope. I had to use my own time.

So after work I'd go there at 6:00 at night and stay till 12:00 or 1:00 in the morning, because you had to give them four hours. Saunas, all sorts of supplements, exercise. And after the forty-four days I was off all my medicines—the majority of them I should say—95 percent of them.

A few years went by...it came back, the sinus infections. I have one now, actually, that I'm on medication for. I think it was a great thing, trying something different. I was willing to try anything they wanted me to try, but certain things didn't seem to be working anymore.

The weight gain was unbelievable. Now I'm just trying to lose weight. I'm eating better. I'm exercising. I still have sleep apnea, and I hate that I can't hug my wife.[3] I don't want my kids to see when I have it on. I keep the door closed because I don't want the kids to see their father has a tube hooked up to his face.

WE JOIN TOGETHER

We were definitely unprepared, everybody. We were the big boy on the block, never thinking anything was ever going to happen to us. And we got caught with our pants down.

I guess you could say a lot of people joined together. That's what this country is about. Americans in time of need, we do join together. I remember I never saw so many flags in my life. Six, seven months following 9/11, everybody had a flag.

In drastic times, this country does pull together. We can get through anything—as long as we stick together.

---

[3] Philip refers here to the CPAP (continuous positive airway pressure) mask he wears at night to treat his sleep apnea.

CHAPTER 3

AM I DEAD?

*Jack, the director of Emergency Medical Services at New York–
Presbyterian Hospital, brings a perspective of a manager and planner
to Ground Zero. His job was all about preparing to move into a disaster
site at a moment's notice and to receive the critically injured into the
hospital's emergency room. Plans had been in place to execute it all with
discipline, speed, meticulous organization, and professionalism. However,
airliners are not supposed to hit towering Manhattan buildings and
explode on impact, and 110-story landmark structures are not supposed to
collapse. What Jack encountered mocked his sophisticated planning and
strategies. People like Jack may escape being consumed by the flames, but
the experience of having been close to those flames marks them for life.
Regardless of what they do or where they go, hell goes with them.*

I HAVE TO TELL YOU, I THOUGHT THAT IT WOULD BE a small aircraft, where perhaps a pilot had a heart attack, or something like that, and actually went into the Trade Center. I absolutely did not think, at that point, that it was a terrorist event. We responded to the 1993 bombing of the Trade Center, so even with terrorism in the back of my mind, I felt that there was no way that it could be anything but a small aircraft.

In the communication center, they also have a small TV. We were hearing the reports of fire and police and EMS units at the scene, and somebody indicated that it was not a small aircraft; that in fact it was a large, commercial passenger plane. My mind immediately swung over to a terrorist event. They always teach us that in a terrorist event, you have the initial event and, traditionally, you have a secondary event that is aimed at the rescue personnel.

I ordered all available units back to the hospital to increase the amount of supplies, backboards, trauma supplies, burn dressings, etc. I was going over the scenario of another event occurring, never anticipating that it was going to be another jetliner, just another event that would be detrimental to the emergency personnel.

The Fire Department notified us that they wanted us to respond with mutual aid units. So at that point, my activities went from being in the communication center to going out and directing the preparation for the response. Our units were all packaged. Staff were on board and waiting. I got out on deck and we just took off down to the Trade Center.

The second plane had hit just prior to our arrival, so there was total chaos down there. I got my staff to start preparing their medical equipment.

I had two people already in the lobby of Tower 2 that had gotten there earlier. They were communicating their needs as well. Then we all started in unison to walk towards Tower 2, but with the jumpers that were coming out of the building it was obviously a danger to us. So we actually went out of our way to line ourselves up with the entrance to the building, which had a canopy. You could see when people were hitting the canopy; they were bouncing off and not penetrating it.

IT'S COMING DOWN!

We were taking a lot of time, keeping personal safety in mind, to line up with that canopy and sort of figure out how we were going to time and spot one another as we were getting in. It was at that moment that a Port Authority cop standing at the corner of Tower 2 started screaming, "Run for your lives! It's coming down!"

I looked up, and it looked like the top of the building was just falling over. Probably the top fifteen stories of the building. What quickly went through my mind was: Do we turn around and run back, or do we run into the lobby for protection? I yelled to the staff and we all ran, turned around and ran in the opposite direction of the Towers. There's the traditional line, "Run for your life!" I mean, we truly were running for our lives.

I was running next to one of my guys, Mike, and there was a female rescuer that was running between the two of us, with probably fifteen to twenty feet between us. The debris started getting bigger and bigger. When it first started out it was small stuff, and then it started getting bigger and bigger, and then the steel started to land around us, and a piece of steel came down and actually decapitated the woman that was running in between us. I guess if we thought we were running fast, we just ran a little faster and tried to dive under the stairs of the overpass, and that's where we lay as the debris continued to come down. When I went to dive, the force of the air just carried me. I would imagine that I was carried forty to fifty feet just by the sheer force of the air.

As we were running away, obviously we weren't looking back. It wasn't just the top of the building that was falling off, it was the whole building collapsing, and there was a *New York Post* photographer that actually wound up getting injured because he snapped a picture of us just as we were walking towards the Towers. He snapped a picture of us, and then when the Tower was coming down he snapped more photographs and he was badly hurt, getting buried in the rubble as well. I spoke to him afterwards and he said that the whole building was pancaking as we were running away, and that's what he was photographing. He couldn't believe this building was just coming down as it was.

I COULDN'T TAKE A BREATH

You couldn't see anything. Everything was pitch black. I actually thought I was in the process of dying at that point. My pulse was down in the low 40s, and obviously after you have just run the length of a couple of football fields you should be totally out of breath. I was just laying there numb. I was expecting that I was just going to fade away. I just laid there, pretty much at peace with myself. At a certain point I realized that I wasn't fading off, and then I started wiggling one hand and then wiggling the other hand and wiggling my feet and I said, "This isn't happening."

I tried to take a breath and I couldn't take a breath. Every time I went to breathe, I couldn't breathe. Then I lifted my head up. I must have been in so much concrete dust that I couldn't breathe. So once I got my head up, my heart started pounding. I said, "Okay, I'm not fading away here." My heart started pounding, and then I got a breath of air. At that point, I started to try to move out of the rubble.

I was crawling because I kept bumping into things. I couldn't stand up because there was something above me. I started crawling just down different avenues and then got to a point where I could stand up. I got over to an area where I saw a window that was blown out. It was in the World Financial Center. I was going to go to that window, and go in when I realized that between me and the window was a set of stairs that went down and if I actually had been moving too fast, I would have fallen down those stairs, probably about twenty-five feet. Once I saw that, I went down the stairs and there was a gentleman at the base of the stairs that had opened up the fire door, and I got in there and they had a little canteen inside there and there were a couple of Emergency Services Unit [ESU] cops and myself. My throat, my airway, was all full of the dust, so I wound up getting a bottle of water and tried to drink that.

I wound up vomiting up a lot of the dust and debris. Then one of my other men wound up coming into that same canteen...the guy's name was Mike. I said to him, "Let's go back out and see if we can find any of the other staff." We went out, back to the area where we had scattered, and that's when the second Tower came down.

Mike and I again ran for our lives and wound up inside a bank. As the dust kept rolling into the bank, we went deeper and deeper in, and we're just standing in the doorway because the ceiling was caving in. The light fixtures were falling in, and then the lights went out in the bank, and all you heard were dead clunks, which were the automatic door locks. We're like, "Oh, this is great. We just locked ourselves in the bank."

Later when we exited the bank, I met up with Charlie, who was the chief of the Fire Department. He and I had a little emotional exchange because he had just seen his brother-in-law on his way into Tower 2. He realized that the likelihood of his brother-in-law surviving was little to none. Then he told me that he had seen some of my staff down at the waterfront.

So we went down to the waterfront and all of the staff was there with the exception of two. The dispatchers had been doing a radio roll call to get people to respond. We went down there with twenty-three guys. Out of the twenty-three, thirteen of us were pretty significantly injured. I took the most seriously injured staff. We got on a police skiff and took them over to New Jersey, to Liberty State Park, where they were incredible. They had EMS agencies there, and I just handed off my staff members and took the skiff back across, so that I could go and see if I could find my two guys.

SEARCHING FOR THE MISSING

I returned to the site, at which point Andy, the chief of EMS for the Fire Department, asked me to take charge of EMS for that sector. He assigned me to a fire chief who was directing the firemen, and they were starting to go through the rubble, because at that point all you could hear was the firefighters' PASS [Personal Alert Safety System] alarms going off. Firefighters wear a PASS alarm so if they go down in a building, and there is no motion, no activity, the PASS alarm then sends off this high-pitched squeal so that you can locate that firefighter.

I remained down there until Building 7 came down, at which point I probably should have been out of there because of the fumes, the smoke, the everything... A couple of my staff members came over to me and they said, "You're out of here."

I was like, "No. I'm not going to leave. I'm still looking for Keith and Mario," the two that were in the lobby of Tower 2, who ultimately perished. One of my guys, Andrew, says to me, "Boss, I may be fired for this, but you're coming with me." And they threw me in an ambulance and carted me off. But it's the camaraderie amongst the staff.

They took me to the hospital. I had every specialty under the sun there to take care of me. I had ophthalmology; ear, nose, throat... . I'm not the best patient in the world, so when I got back to the hospital, they wanted to take me to the emergency room. I said, "I'm not going to be seen like this." So I went back to my office and took a shower, which they agreed to as long as they could send some staff to be with me. Then I went to the ER and they treated me, and as I say, I was pretty feisty. The attending wanted to do a blood gas.[4] I said, "If I can do one on you first, I'll let you do one on me."

I was in the hospital probably about an hour and a half, and then I said to them, "All right, I'm out of here."

I had to notify the families that we had been doing radio roll calls all day and that we were not getting a response. Their last known location was in the lobby of Tower 2 and that I would keep them posted. It was very difficult. The families didn't understand the size of the disaster. One of my guys,...his name was Mario Santoro. I spoke to his wife, Lenore... She didn't comprehend and she was assuring me that, "Don't worry. If I know Mario, he's down there, he's treating patients. He'll show up." I felt very frustrated with that phone call because I was trying to let her know the severity of the situation and I didn't feel I was getting the message through to her.

Then I spoke to the mom and dad about my other guy, Keith Fairben. He was an only child and his mom and dad were both involved with the Floral Park Fire Department. I told them and they thanked me and asked to keep them posted.

Ken, Keith's dad, came down to Ground Zero with the volunteer fire department with the intention of going in, finding Keith, and bringing him home. Ken left there very frustrated when he realized how large a scope we were actually talking about, he realized that his dream was not going to come true. He was not going to be able to bring his son home. As a matter of fact, we didn't find Keith until March. Mario we found the week between Christmas and New Years. It was a very difficult situation.

Lenore didn't want to have anything to do with news, media, anybody. She actually directed everybody to me. I was dealing with that. She actually wanted to just forget about September 11th. Diane and Ken, totally different dynamic. Diane and Ken actually came into the hospital the following day, met some of Keith's co-workers. The two of them were so inspirational. They were absolutely incredible people. They would speak to the media;

---

[4] A blood gas, or arterial blood gas (ABG), lab test measures the levels of oxygen and carbon dioxide in the blood and is used to check how well the lungs are able to take in oxygen and remove carbon dioxide from the blood.

they participated in any number of events. They really embraced it. Knowing that EMS was Keith's life, they wanted to honor him.

As far as the camaraderie goes, you gotta remember that with EMS personnel, your partner is your backup. You're the only two out there, so when something goes awry, you need that support from your partner, and I think that has a tremendous amount to do with the camaraderie that you see in the industry. When we found Mario's body first, I went to his wife's apartment and told her. I was at the medical examiner's office, obviously, and I took his valuables and went to his wife's apartment and spent some time with her and the baby. She had a very difficult time with it, but at that point, she was expecting it. After I notified Mario's wife, I came back to notify the staff and sent out group pages and announced it on the two-way radios and that type of thing.

In March, we found Keith's body. They thought they knew who he was because of his ID card. They called us and asked if we wanted to send down one of our units to transport his body to the medical examiner's office. So I went in with a couple of people and we removed Keith's body from the area and actually had to stay for the autopsy and for a positive identification.

Keith's dad was a funeral director. I went to the house to notify them and Keith's mom was there. We spoke to her and it was a very emotional time and she said that Ken was down at the funeral parlor, so we all went down to the funeral parlor and the second that Ken saw my face he knew exactly what was going on.

Both families were very fortunate because we were able to recover the bodies. I think that they truly appreciated that, having their remains back. It meant a tremendous amount to them. I think it brought closure to them.

THERE IS NO CLOSURE

There is no closure to 9/11, unfortunately. You can't get away from it. When you read the newspaper, when you watch the five o'clock news. Anytime. You just can't get away from it. It's always going to be that way. Is there total closure? No, but dealing with people who did not recover remains, it's very difficult for them. There's always that [thought], well maybe they weren't there. Or maybe they got knocked unconscious and they're in a coma somewhere or they have amnesia. It's just all of those scenarios playing through people's minds. I think that without a body, you can play tremendous mind games with yourself. I think that one of the things that bothers me is that 9/11 happened; it's probably going to happen again and I think that too many people have become very passive about it, and don't really have a concept of what it's all about. I'm not bashing the government or any particular party, but I sit there at night with my experience. I sit there at night and I look at the Gulf Coast crisis and what are we doing? We're doing the same exact things we did on 9/11. You had Christie Whitman standing there saying, "The air is fine; don't worry about it." And we've got guys out in the Gulf Coast right now that are cleaning up a tremendous oil spill that not only is oil coming out of there, but there are tons of minerals and gases that are coming out of that well as well. And we're doing it again; we didn't learn our lesson. It's one thing that 9/11 happened and what happened, happened, but when I look at my health, or the lack of my health in certain areas, ... if it was a lesson learned, that would be one thing, but we're doing it all over again. And that's very frustrating to me.

CHAPTER 4

THEY WERE ALL KILLED

NYPD Officer Michael was on the 20th floor of World Trade Center Tower 1 when it was hit by the first plane. The neighborhood was his usual beat, and that morning he was in the Tower to help a woman with a disability reach her office after her personal scooter was damaged as she exited a subway car. Together with his partner they made their way safely out of the building; however, they got caught in the mayhem that followed the Towers' collapse. Michael's story tells us about sacrifice, the professionalism and camaraderie among the first responders, the endless work they engaged in during the weeks and months following the attacks, and the psychological trauma that he suspects he will carry for the rest of his life.

YOU HAVE TO LEAVE

WE STARTED THE MORNING OFF with a bomb scare on Bowling Green. So we responded to that. Normally, those things turn out to be unfounded. Somebody leaves a bag or a package or something like that. Or some crank call. Which that turned out to be, a crank call. Then a couple more silly calls after that. But the kid I was riding with was fairly new. I told him, "This is normal on September the 11th, because it's my birthday." I said every time I worked on my birthday, weird things happened.

It was after eight o'clock in the morning, and the next call we get was from an unidentified person, a female caller had called 9-1-1, said she needed help at the World Trade Center subway station, on the E line. So we responded there and we found this lady. She was coming off on one of those handicapped motor scooters. And when she came off the train, the front wheel bent. So of course her motor scooter was damaged. And she was quite frank that she had no insurance on it and she wanted the TA [Metropolitan Transit Authority] to either replace it or repair it. She told us she worked on the 20th floor of 1 World Trade Center, the North Tower. I said, "Well, we'll go up to your office and we'll take the report and we'll get you settled down.

So we go up there and I'm taking the report. The next thing I know, [there was] a big bang and the building shook really bad, knocking myself and a lot of people down on our backs.

People were looking at us, "What's going on?" I said, "Who knows? Maybe it's the wind." Because up there—I don't know if you've ever been in the buildings—but the higher up you go, the buildings move with the wind.

People were looking at me like, that's no wind. So I'm looking around, I saw all glass around us. As I'm looking out the windows, I start seeing debris falling past us.

I still can't figure out what's going on. It hasn't dawned on me yet, until I saw a body go by. But the guy was still alive, and he was like flapping his arms like a duck.

So at that point, I know this is going to get worse, and I said to everybody, "Let's get out. Everybody out." The Port Authority started sending a message over their loudspeakers that everything was normal, everything was calm, stay at your desk, do not leave the building. I said, "Get out of here. Get out of here now."

They listened. We get into the stairwell. It's smoky and there's some debris coming into the stairwells. Dust and stuff like that. Nobody's using the elevators because of the first World Trade Center [bombing, in 1993]. They learned their lesson on that one.

Then we got knocked down again because [of] another explosion, the second explosion. I said to a civilian, "Do me a favor. We're going to go back. We've got to go upstairs and see if we can … make sure everybody's evacuated as far as we can go." To make a long story short, we went back up to the 29th floor. That's as far as I could go. Because I was having trouble breathing.

People were still coming down. So we went inside each one of those floors, 29th, all the way down, till about the 19th floor, made sure everybody was gone.

People were still working at their desks. Not too many, a few. I told them, "You have to leave! I don't know exactly what happened outside, but it's nothing good." "No, no," they're telling us, "we can stay in our office, and everything's good." I said, "No, I'm telling you right now, you have to leave."

When I reached the 19th floor, as I was going into that stairwell, I ran into a bunch of friends of mine from Engine Company 6. I told the lieutenant which floors I cleared. He said he'd have to check them again anyway.

They all got killed.

We got all the way down to the ground floor and onto the mezzanine. Most people were walking towards where the escalators were, under the North Tower. There's only one escalator, and it's a small one. So it was like a funnel going up this one escalator, and people were backed up. So I directed them. I said, "Well, go to the end of" whatever store it was over there. I said, "Make a right, and go to the end of that." Then there is the entrance to the subway station. There're eight staircases you can leave by. So, boom, a lot of people started going that way, which is good.

When I got to that area, I see another crowd of people off to my left, where the restaurants are, and there's an entrance that leads out to West Broadway. There was a crowd of people there. They were like in a fishnet because the Port Authority, in their wisdom, locked the doors. They didn't want nobody going out that way, so they just locked the doors and left. Now these people didn't know how to get in and out.

Not only did they lock it, they locked it after the plane hit. That was an exit. Why they locked it, I don't know. Maybe it was for safety reasons. So I told them to go through the subway station.

So I got to the street level, I saw the North Tower, the way it was on fire, and also the South Tower now. We're directing people that are coming out to go up to Broadway. "Don't look up!" There's no sense in looking up at this point with the glass and stuff falling down. People are jumping out the windows. You really don't want to stop here and make a crowd. This is going through my mind.

The first guy we run into was a city police sergeant. He was walking this African-American fellow out. But the guy was so badly burned on his arms—you could see the skin and everything just falling off his arms down to his bone. So we got water, cold water, poured it on him and got [him] to the triage center. They took him right away.

We went back in again. We pulled a couple other people out and brought them to the triage center. The last person we went under for was a woman that did some bad damage to her back or broke her collarbone, I forget which. One of the EMS guys took a door off one of the exits or offices, and we put her on that and carried her out to the triage center.

Michael takes a cigarette break and the North Tower comes down on them. They run.

I was body surfing up Vesey Street. You couldn't see anything with the cloud. I thought I was dead. I stopped. I said, "This is being dead. You didn't make it out." But then I said, "I can't be dead because I'm in pain." My back. I got up, coughing and choking. Couldn't see anything. My eyes were filled with dust. I heard a woman screaming for help. "Help me, help me, help me."

I worked my way over to the voice and grabbed her. I told her, "Look, I can't see you. I know you can't see me, but I am a cop." I said, "I'll help you. Just calm down a little bit."

And then I seen a flashlight across the street waving back and forth. "Over here, over here. We can get in here." So we worked our way over to there. I think the address was 27 Vesey. This plainclothes sergeant, he said, "Come in here. We got—you know, things are good." But it wasn't. People were in a broom closet, about seventeen, twenty people in like a broom closet, all coughing and throwing up. I worked my way back out of there and it had cleared up a little bit.

I saw glass doors from an office building. It was clean inside. But it was locked. I shot the door. We could get in there. It was bigger, and they had water. It was clean. Sergeant wasn't happy about that [shooting the door open], but what are you going to do? We got those people in there, and they were able to clean their faces up. They even had a working telephone somebody used.

We got ourselves composed again, we went back outside and started getting people up the block. My partner stayed with me there. Then, of course, the second Tower came down and knocked us down again.

Between that time and leaving to go home, I don't remember too much. It got to a point where I was half-blinded from the scratches I received, and exhausted. I decided we'd had enough. It's time to go back to the command, take a break. Clean up a little bit and then go back down if we were told we had to go back down. So we walked out, and my command is on Canal Street, so we walked from there to Canal Street. They told us that everything's supposedly contaminated.

We were told to take our uniforms and put them in garbage bags and to clean up the best you can and hang out until we decide what we're going to do with you. Eventually we ended up at St. Vincent's Hospital, getting treated for the injuries I received. About nine, ten o'clock that night, they released us, sent us home, and put us on the department sick list. I stayed there on that sick leave until the following Sunday, when I was ordered back in to work.

NEVER LOST CONTROL

Until I was out of the area and relieved of duty, I was just doing what I was trained to do. There was just so much to do. You didn't have time to think. I've been told by another doctor that you become numb and you just go on automatic. My wife also works in the city, in the Grand Central area. She knew what was going on because of TV reports. She called my precinct and she was looking for me, and the original desk sergeant was foolish, I guess. He told her I was reported missing, which wasn't true. We just weren't reported missing. So that was the wrong thing to tell somebody.

When I got back and I found out what he said, we had words. I finally got through to her by about three o'clock. I told her, "Everything's okay. I'm fine. Just beat up a little bit." I told her, "When I get home, I get home."

They released us later that night about nine, and I was able to go home. I took five or six other cops that were injured and lived out in Long Island. I put them in my car, and we took off. In the car, we were somber, I guess you want to call it. We didn't really want to talk about anything. I didn't want to think about what was going on, even though it was obvious. A couple of the cops from other commands said, "We got there after a lot of the stuff had happened, after the collapses." They were stunned. But I really wasn't paying attention. But I never lost control of myself. My partner didn't, either.

The department brought in some detectives trained in counseling and wanted us to talk about how we felt and whether we were okay. I thought, I got about fifteen more years on the job, more than you'll [the counselors] ever have. Do yourself a favor. Go talk to the youngsters, leave me alone. I did it the old timers' way. You go get a couple drinks. And it goes away. If you do go see somebody, don't let nobody else know. Especially the department. If you start talking about it to other people, they start giving you the funny eye. The next thing, you're red-flagged and you're shunned. You're done. You're finished. So you suck it up and walk away.

The firemen who died, I knew them professionally, of course. Their engine company is Beekman Street. When I was walking a foot post in that area, I was a block away from there. Any job that involved EMS or fires, obviously, subway fires and all that, it was always that engine company. So, I knew them quite well. If I was working Thanksgiving on that foot post, we'd go over to the firehouse and have dinner with those guys. Did we always go and knock on the door and talk to them and sit down and take a break and get some air conditioning? Yeah. Even on the job we were on a first-name basis. I would say, "Look, this is what's going on. This is what happened. This is what we did. There's no need for your guys to go down eighteen stories with all that gear. There's nothing going on. You don't have to check it out." And they would know that we weren't telling them fairytales, best way I could put it. They would say, "Okay, fine, no problem." This way, we saved them time.

Or, if I'd give them advice, especially for subway incidents, they would take it from a patrolman instead of a lieutenant, for example. We trusted each other, put it that way.

But that's the way it is. I was probably the last guy to see them alive. I didn't go to their funerals. No. I couldn't.

I tried to go to the firehouse once. I got inside, but that lasted about five seconds. I haven't been back since. I don't know what I could say to them. I still can't think about it. What could I say?

The fireman I passed in the Tower had been there about a year. It was his bad luck, I guess. I think he just got transferred in for his training period. I think, I'm not sure. But I still know what he looks like.

BACK AT THE SITE

I really wanted to go out sick. But if I did, I didn't want to be on restricted duty, I wanted to go back in the field. I got a call Saturday night. Now, the police surgeon, when I saw him a couple days after the incident, he told me to take the rest of my set of tours off and go back to work on Tuesday, because I was off Sundays, Mondays. "Okay," I said, "I'm satisfied with that." Saturday night I got a call from the administrative sergeant on my command, and he said, "You have to come back in by two o'clock in the morning Sunday."

For the first time in my career, I started giving him an argument. I didn't want to go back. "I'll come back Tuesday," I said. "I was told to take off till Tuesday." He said, "No, your tour of duty ends four o'clock Saturday. You'll come in." I told him, "You're going to have to order me back, because I'm not coming back voluntarily." So he said, "Mike, I'm ordering you back. I have to. I've got no choice." So I went back to work at two, three o'clock in the morning.

We worked ever since then, except for a couple of scheduled vacation days and regular days off when you got them. But they put us back down there for a minimum of twelve-hour tours a day. Then they started with the overtime after that. I ended up working seventeen-hour tours until I retired.

During those tours, I did a little bit of everything. On a regular timespan, you're supposed to work back in a patrol car and patrol the area. The first couple months there was nothing to patrol downtown because nobody was down there except the guys who were assigned to dig and the National Guard people. My partner and I would fill up the back of our radio car with bottles of water and sandwiches and pass them out.

Then they decided to give us these nice face masks. Had these two cylinders on the side. Because it was still burning and dusty down there. Then they told us we couldn't wear them. "You have to have them, but you can't wear them," they said. I said, "What's the sense of that?" They said, "Well, if you go down there with masks and we start letting these civilians back in, they're going to get worried, and they won't come back down. But if they see you're not wearing these masks, they'll think it's okay." I said, "What about us? What do we do with all that stuff—the potentially dangerous airborne particulates and toxins down there?" He says, "Doesn't matter, you have to have the mask because the department issued them. But you're not allowed to wear them." I said, "Alright." What are you going to do? So we threw them in the car and left them there. After a while, we just left them in the locker.

They didn't open Wall Street up till a couple weeks later. Nobody was allowed past south of 14th Street the first week. And then finally, they started letting people go further down. And once that opened up, then you had normal crowds. We'd interact with those civilians. Everybody's "Thanks a lot," "Appreciate what you've done." Things were still deserted from a policeman's point of view, it was still quiet down there. There was no crime.

GETTING BACK TO NORMAL

I wasn't—I don't know—I wasn't my normal self. I knew that. I was down at the time; I wasn't paying attention to what I was doing. I know my regular partner saw that. He told me to get my head out of my rear end. "It's over. Forget it. It's done." I would normally say, "Got to get back to your normal self." I would be able to do that, but I still haven't. I know one of my patrol supervisors, a sergeant I knew quite well—sometimes we'd carpool back and forth to work—he'd see what I said, and instead of putting me on a patrol area, he would take me as his chauffeur just so he could keep an eye on me. He'd say, "I want you working with me today." It took me a couple of months to figure it out, that he was doing this because I just wasn't paying attention half the time.

The department sent out these other people, the Early Intervention people, or whatever they called them. I resisted it. But then it came down to the point where everybody had to go. I've got to mention it, because this is how I felt about it at the time. They asked us, "Are you having problems?" Being an old-timer and a union representative—I was a union representative for about twenty-six years—I know what the department and the Early Intervention people were doing. They were trying to come in and pick people to yank out because they felt we couldn't do the job any longer. And then they would ruin our careers. If they forced you to retire, it would be under less-than-honorable circumstances. They would put you down as psychologically unfit to work any longer. And that would carry through the rest of your life. So, to me, that's less than honorable. I couldn't talk to them. I certainly wouldn't tell them what I was feeling.

The department has nothing, absolutely nothing, set up to maintain your confidentiality or your privacy and your privilege. They have two things. One is the Early Intervention, and the other one, it's called POPPA—the Police Organization Providing Peer Assistance. If you go to POPPA first, even as a retired person, ... they put you on a blue-line sick, they call it.

Then, you could take care of whatever you need, but the department has no way of finding out. If you go to Early Intervention, it's the opposite; they're required to tell the department what the problem is, and they'll take action against you.

I'm rarely able to go a day without the thoughts about 9/11 bothering me. Although since I've been going to see certain doctors and with medication, it's become bearable. I can function almost normally, like I used to. My wife told me the other day that I was becoming a recluse. That I would rather sit in the backyard reading a book than interact with other people anymore. And maybe she's right, because I do read a lot of books. I used to be an organizer of parties and getting people going. Now, I can't. I just don't do it. I can't. I'm not a happy person anymore.

I'm very loyal to the Police Department. I'm just disappointed at what they've done to certain commands, the original responders who took the first hits and the brunt of this.

What I do know is that word came down—not officially—that they're all dead anyway, so just keep them down there working, and just write them off. And that's the end of them. We were never relieved, we were never allowed to transfer out of the area. They worked us to death; they got as much as they could out of us and then they said, "You're on your own." And I'm very disappointed in that. But I guess that's the way things are.

CHAPTER 5

LUCKY TO BE ALIVE

Robert was a civilian who worked as an accountant in lower Manhattan and was also a seventeen-year veteran volunteer firefighter in his home community of Commack, Long Island. He was coming out of the subway when the first plane hit. He then quickly checked in at his firm and ran to the nearest firehouse on Liberty Street to offer his assistance. He tells us of the lingering physical and mental effects of 9/11, the difficulty of going into home-improvement stores because the Sheetrock reminded him of Ground Zero's ash, how the smell of bacon revolted him because it conjured up thoughts of burning flesh. Robert, and many others like him, carry 9/11 in their bodies—in the shape of a constant reminder of pain. He tells us that whether psychological or physical or both, pain is forever associated in his mind with 9/11's images and terrors, and claims that both memories and pain make it impossible to release him from that day. It is a part of him that he cannot escape.

THE GUYS AT THAT FIREHOUSE were out on another call. They were on a gas leak at the time. But the captain of the truck company happened to be in quarters, so I introduced myself and showed him my badge and said, "I'm a fireman. If you can use me, great. If not, I'll get out of your way." He just looked at me and said, "You're all I have. So you're in charge of triage."

By the time I got there, there were several walking wounded or other civilians who had been carried in by co-workers or strangers. It just became a big repository for people with all different types of injuries.

They were an engine truck company house—they weren't an ambulance-based house—so there really weren't medical supplies or anything that would really be useful. So then it was just a matter of what I could do with what was available and how I could make people as comfortable as possible until more resources were available. So it meant running up and down the stairs to the bunkroom, stripping beds and getting blankets, pillows, and just trying to get people organized. Who is really hurt, who is not so bad, and who just needed a place to be, because we had a lot of that too. I ended up with about forty people who were just looking for a place to go because they didn't know what to do.

Everything was just happening really fast. You could hear the second plane then fly right over the firehouse and hit the second Tower. The captain had a radio on and he said another plane hit the other Tower, and then we started hearing about Washington and about Pennsylvania.

There were a lot of civilians that were outside the firehouse. I could hear them start screaming, "People are jumping."

I said, "I don't need to see it." And when they land, there's nothing I'm going to be able to do for them anyway. So I just focused on what I could do. I just kept working. Then we got lucky because there was an ambulance that was going off its shift. They're like, "We gotta get over there." So they took the Brooklyn Bridge over from Brooklyn. Brian Smith and another Brian—they just showed up at out firehouse. They weren't assigned, they weren't dispatched.

This is pretty much what was happening all around the city. Anybody that was home had to come in. They were keeping everybody, and nobody wanted to leave anyway. Actual EMS help showed up with an ambulance. It was great. I remember we just started backing the ambulance up into one of the bays. This way we had a place to keep the rig and I could show them the priority patients, how things were sorted, and this way we could progress from there.

One man had a broken pelvis, another was a woman who had been on fire, another was someone complaining with hearing problems. A lot of people were more just bangs, bumps, bruises. The woman on fire I'll never forget, and the man with the broken pelvis. At one point when Brian Smith and I were talking, we made the decision to cut the woman's wedding ring off because the blistering on her was very bad. She was Japanese and she really didn't speak a lot of English. I love to travel and I did spend some time in Japan. I said a couple of things to her in Japanese and she smiled. That made her feel a little more comfortable.

The captain at this point was putting together a team to go across the street, and I said to him, "You're putting a search team together? I'm a truckee in the Fire Department." That means search is your bread and butter. I said, "If you're putting a search team together, I can be a lot of value to that if you want me to switch over." He said, "No, keep doing what you're doing." I remember watching them go. I remember part of me was like, I wish I was going with them 'cause this is what I'm trained for, and I knew there were a lot of people over there that needed help, and it's just the way things worked out. But it turned out to be a good thing for me, because I guess about ten minutes later I watched these eight guys run across the street, and the civilians out front started screaming again. I said, "What's the matter?" They said, "It's coming down." "What's coming down? The plane?" They were like, "No, the Tower." They ended up getting killed.

Later on it was just a lot of survivor guilt, because why them, not me? A lot of strange things happened. For example, when the first Tower came down, one of the jet engines actually came into the firehouse and destroyed the ambulance that we had. It came through the front, the open doors. So if we had put the ambulance in the other bay, it would have killed us as well. An ambulance is supposed to save lives, but not this way. So we were pretty lucky.

What happened was when the Tower came down, you couldn't get out of the front of the firehouse. They estimate that the wind speed where we were when the Towers came down was about 140 miles an hour. So I was in the truck room: I was about six feet away from a back wall, a cinderblock wall, and I got thrown into that wall, and Brian Smith was in a little more of an open area, so he was about twenty-five feet away from the wall and he hit the same wall.

Part of the back part of the firehouse had gotten blown out, and we ended up using that hole to pass injured people through. When everybody started running towards the back of the firehouse, there was a narrow hallway and everything went black. You couldn't see your hand in front of your face. You couldn't breathe—you were choking on all the debris.

So as we're going towards the back of the firehouse towards that door, I couldn't figure out why people weren't moving. So, like I said, you couldn't see and you're holding your breath now 'cause you're choking. I could feel a person in front of me so I pulled them out of my way, felt another person, I just had to keep moving, and again, you're blind, moving people out of your way so you can get to the back wall where the door is supposed to be. Feeling around, again part of my training, I'm feeling around where the door is, and I felt hinges and I realized that the door was an inward-opening door so the person who was all the way up against it couldn't open it because everybody else was pushing against them.

So once I felt the hinges, I realized what the problem was and I was able to pull the door open. Then I tried to push the door—the real door— out into the next street—the alleyway—but there was a lot of debris on the other side as well, so you had to force that and just keep muscling it until you got the door open and people could get out. What was tough also about that was you still couldn't see. Everything was gray and a few minutes later, you can start making out images of people standing, and I saw then what turned out to be a small group of police officers. I was able to call out to these guys and say, "Listen, we have a lot of hurt people in here!" We started passing people through the hole that was blown through the back section of the firehouse.

I don't know what happened with the woman who had the burns. I know because of her injuries, she wasn't able to run. From what I understand, there was at least one person that was killed in the firehouse. I just don't know if it was her. I didn't see her. It was hard to see. That is one of the things that still bothers me today. I spent a lot of time with her before that happened.

A short while later, the second Tower came down. Again, another whole blast of ash and everything else.

What happened then was the decision was made from dispatch to go to 2 Rector Street, and we were assigned to start evacuating that building. I stayed in the lobby and the two Brians went to the first three floors and said to everybody that we need to evacuate and that they'll see me down in the lobby. So we got everybody down in the lobby from the first three floors and it was a several-story building. We explained to them that our assignment was to get these people down to the Staten Island Ferry area, where they were lining up buses and they were going to be taking these people to Queens.

Basically, Manhattan was closed and we need to get these people out of here. So it was just strange because we were covered in all the white ash and everything that you see in a lot of the films, and these people came down in still crisp shirts and slacks and everybody looked clean. Our eyes were burning because there was so much ash in our eyes.

I don't think they got it until they looked out the window of the lobby area and they saw a couple cars go by kicking up all the dust. They were like, "Oh, wow." We explained to them that we were going to go single file down Broadway to the Staten Island Ferry. So we had about ninety people. I was in the front and the two Brians were in the back.

What's also probably worth noting was that on our way to Rector Street, we had the man with the broken pelvis. He had a suitcase with him and we had some medical bags. We had this man on each of our shoulders, so he was in the middle. It was like helping a football player off the field. He wouldn't let go of the bag. We were trying to carry him and we're getting hit in the head with this bag that was really heavy. We said to him, "We have to leave the bag." He said, "No, I can't. I can't." It's worth noting he's from China. And we said, "Please, it's heavy and it hurts when we get hit in the head with it." He said, "I cannot leave the bag." Finally we said to him, "What's in the bag that you can't leave?" It was a million dollars in cash. So he had just gotten a loan from the Chinese government and the government made a loan to him in cash. So we're like, "Okay, we're not leaving the bag."

So we're going single file now. I was in the front, ninety people in between, and two Brians and this man. His name was Fu. So we're headed south on Broadway and people were coming up to me because they saw me up front, and they saw I had some fire gear. They'd come up to me and say, "Where do I go? What do I do?"

I said you can come with us and this is what we're doing. You're more than welcome to join us; if not, you're on your own. I can't guarantee you anything. So we left with about ninety people and got down to the ferry area with about 125 people. Two of the women in the line were pregnant, so I said to them, "You stay with me. If you feel any changes, please tell me because I need to know as soon as possible." They did great.

We get down to the Staten Island Ferry and there was a police officer there coordinating everything and I said to him, "I have 125 people. You give me the buses, I'll get out of your way." He thought that was great, pulled up a few buses, loaded the people up, and they went into Queens. The only problem was when we got to the end of the line both Brians and Fu were missing. I said, "Oh my God! What happened?"

Robert tried to retrace his steps but he couldn't find the Brians and Fu. He ended up connecting with a command post being set up in Battery Park.

There was a restaurant down in that area in Battery Park, so I'm going to see if I can wash my face real quick. They were operating like nothing happened. They were serving lunch, the early lunch crowd. I'm still covered in ash. My eyes are absolutely burning.

I find the restroom where I can wash my face and get some water in my eyes and try to get a lot of the grit out, and a waitress comes in and starts yelling at me. She goes, "Do you realize you're in the ladies room?" I couldn't tell. I don't think they really got it. I don't think they really knew. Now you're representing the fire service at this point, so what I thought and what I said were two different things. I just told the lady that right now I really don't care where I am. I just washed my face and got out.

While we were waiting in this area trying to figure out what to do next, fighter jets started showing up. We didn't know they were ours; we thought it was just the next part of the attack. So the first plane comes in and it's coming nose in straight at us, and we're out in the open. There was no place to hide. We were just in a completely exposed area. At first we put our hands up trying to block ourselves, but we were like, this is a fighter jet. What are we putting our hands up for? And we just put our hands down and waited. At this point, the plane turned and we were able to see it was an American plane. I'll never forget because it was so close that the lead pilot had a white helmet on. It was right there! We were pretty relieved.

So it's now starting to get late, and I gotta start figuring out what I'm going to do. I can't get home. I tried calling a friend of mine who works in the city. He has his own business. I tried to get in touch with him to see if I could walk up to his business and sleep on a couch, but he didn't go into work that day. He was living in New Jersey. He said, "If you can get to Jersey, I'll find you." Okay, fine. My cell phone is almost dead, but I'll get to Jersey. It was around four when I started doing this because Tower 7 came down and people heard the rumbling. We knew what that sound was because we had been through it a couple of times already. Everybody started running except some of us. We all looked at each other and said, "What are you running for? It's only fifty stories." That's how messed up it was. We're used to a hundred stories coming down. Fifty stories? Oh, this is nothing. This is minor league at this point. It's how twisted the day was.

So I ended up again down by Battery Park trying to figure out if there was a way to get over to Jersey. Oddly enough, a fishing boat showed up and the captain of the fishing boat saw me. And, again, a lot of people were able to see me and know that I was in the middle of a lot of this. And he said, "Where do you need to go?"

I said, "I need to get to Jersey." And he said, "Hop on." He took me in his boat and we went over to New Jersey and the problem there—well, one of many problems—was his boat wasn't the right height for the docks on the other side. So we got to the wall and I'm trying to figure out how I'm going to scale the wall to get from his boat up the cement barriers to get onto land. So there had to be at least fifty New Jersey cops on the other side where the boat pulled up. So as I'm trying to figure out where to reach onto, I had one police officer here, here, here and here—I had four cops literally just lift me up and get me onto land.

Now I'm in Jersey and I have to see if I can find my friend. I called him up, and I told him where I was and he said okay. So I didn't move from that spot because at least now one of us has a fixed point and the other could work that way. I figure he's been living in Jersey, so it's easier for him to find me at this point. But like I said, he lived in Hoboken and I'm in Jersey City. So he made his way over to Jersey City to find my location, but because a lot of the cops were being reassigned, the cops who were working in the Jersey City area weren't from Jersey City so they couldn't give him directions, tell him, "Oh, just make a left and go down five blocks." So it became a lot of trial and error until about three hours later we hooked up.

I can remember I felt stressed. At my friend's apartment across the way there was a construction project going on, and there was an empty tractor-trailer and they were scooping up big parts of metal and dropping it in and it made a lot of loud sounds. I jumped out of my skin and my friend saw it. I guess I was a little shell-shocked. Loud noises were not a good thing at that point.

I was exhausted. I fell asleep about midnight. Twelve-thirty in the morning there was a big bang on the door. I go over and I open the door and it was the FBI and they asked if this was my apartment and I said no. I said, "Let me get my friend." He comes out and I said, "Frank, the FBI is here. They want to talk to you." He said, "What?" I said, "I'm not kidding. Please come out."

It turns out there were people on his roof while all this was going on, cheering, so people knew that this was coming. They used it as a vantage point to watch as it was happening. So they [the FBI] ended up actually identifying one car and impounding it and trying to see what they could get out of it.

On Wednesday, I heard the trains were running and [I was] trying to get back home. Eventually I was able to get onto a PATH train back to the city and then get up to Penn Station, but again, it was weird because I was standing on the PATH train as the train was moving, and I could only imagine what I must have looked like, because there were two women pushing eighty years old who both got up and said, "You need to sit down." So if they thought it was better that I sit than they sit, that probably wasn't very good. I had had nothing to change into. My friend and I are different sizes. I took a shower, but I had nothing else to put on, so I just went back into the clothes. Also I still had the medical bags and they were still covered in everything. So every place I went bags came with me.

I got onto the train, and there was a husband and wife that had worked that day. Again, it's certain, funny things that you remember like that. They were having their dinner. They had little individual pizzas, and they just decided they were going to share theirs. And they gave me one and a soda and I was really appreciative.

[After returning to Long Island,] I was able to get in touch with Brian Smith and Brian Gordon—I was able to keep in touch with him by email.

I can remember talking on the phone with Brian Smith, because it turns out that one of the medical bags was his bag, and it had his house keys and everything. I was able to figure out whose it was and how to find him. It turned out he was a volunteer fireman in Wading River. So I drove out there to get him his stuff back. Since then, both Brians left working for the city. Brian Smith is now a police officer down in Virginia and Brian Gordon is a train engineer for Amtrak out west.

About a year after 9/11, there was an article in a Chinese newspaper all about Fu. One of my colleagues came into my office—she was Chinese and read the Chinese paper—and said, "You're looking for Fu?" I said, "Yeah, how'd you know?" She showed me the Chinese paper, which didn't do me any good 'cause I'm not Chinese, and she said, "He's looking for you." We were able to put together like a reunion at Brian Smith's firehouse.

We got there at the same time and he recognized me right away, and he was walking with his cane because, like I said, he had a broken pelvis. There were a lot of hugs.

His wife, I remember, at one point came up to me. And she knew what everything was like through what he had told her, and there were a couple of times I said to Fu, I said, "I'm not leaving you; I'm just trying to figure out a place where I can get you to that is safe, so don't worry. I'm not leaving you. I'll be back." She had said to me that if I had decided to leave him behind, she would have understood. For me to be able to see him with his wife and daughter as a complete family, it made a lot of what we went through that day worthwhile.

I have a picture at my desk of my family with Fu and his family. People are always like, "Oh, who's this?" I say, "This is my family."

I've been back [to Ground Zero] a lot. After everything happened, I had lost a lot of friends there, a lot of my friends being in the fire service. I didn't lose any of the guys from my firehouse, but I do have friends who were killed there. One of the guys I used to ride the train with, Glen, was a police officer and a volunteer fireman. And the first time I called my firehouse, they had me not accounted for because they knew who was in the city. They had contact with all these guys and I was the last one with no contact. So when I called and they heard my voice, they screamed like my wife screamed on the phone. So that cleared our list, which was good to hear. I said, "How is everyone?" "Everyone is fine." But when you go into the firehouse and you see it, it looked like a telephone book. I said, "What's this?" They said, "That's the killed list." All the guys and what happened to them.

So they're trying to figure out all the memorial services and funerals and stuff like that. I remember one day I had four. I made it to the first one and the first one ran late, so I missed the second one. Made it to the third one; the third one ran late, and I didn't make it to the fourth one. I ended up missing Glen's service, but then you just did the best you could. We spent so much time in our dress uniforms going from service to service.

I'll tell you, when you work in the city, a lot of times you walk past a lot of the delis and they have flowers out front. And I couldn't walk past them because the smell of the flowers was just like being in another funeral home. So I remember I couldn't walk past the delis. I couldn't go to Home Depot. People were like, "Home Depot?" You gotta understand, ash was a lot like Sheetrock. And it had that same smell and I couldn't deal with that. I couldn't look at bacon for at least a year; again, it goes back to when the woman was on fire—that's what she looked like. I just couldn't deal with that because at the time, at thirty-three, I was afraid of the dark because everything went black in the firehouse. I couldn't see a hand in front of my face. So anytime—nighttime?—forget about it. Nighttime was awful because everything was just dark. There was a lot of time not sleeping, and I just kind of fall asleep during the daytime.

A couple weeks after everything happened, I found out there was an organization that was dealing with support for the rescue. The city pretty much had it under control from the actual rescue work. They don't want any outsiders; they don't want any freelancing. You can understand that because it was a dangerous situation, trying to figure out who's on site and who's not on site. So when I heard that this opportunity came up to be based out of Bouley Bakery on the West Side to deal with just getting meals together, I said, yeah, let me get in on that. So I was doing that once a week. By around Thanksgiving time, they were winding that part down.

From that position, I ended up working with a lot of people from the Red Cross, and I actually got a call from those guys saying, "Listen, Rob, we heard that your area got cut, but we saw the way you work. We'll take you." So I ended up hooking up with those guys and being based out of Saint Paul's Church, right across the street from everything. I [worked at Saint Paul's] until May 31st of 2002, because that was the last day that area was considered a rescue recovery zone, and June 1st it was considered a construction zone where they would start the rebuilding.

I was able to get a shift once a week. I would work in the city for my accounting job from my regular day, and then the shift at the church was basically from eight in the evening till eight in the morning. I would go in early. I would finish up at work at five and be across to the cathedral by five-fifteen, already changed and working. There was a lot of food prep.

Whatever had to be done. I can't remember how many thousands of meals a day, so we were dealing with dinnertime and then morning breakfast. But it wasn't a set time for breakfast or dinner, 'cause you had so many guys working down there that you could come and go as you wanted. Even if you just needed a fresh pair of socks or eyewash, or just a place to relax for a few minutes.

Some of the kids had Hershey's bars and they made their own labels, and so it was like little thank-you labels that they drew pictures and stuff like that. There were cots around the cathedral where people would sleep, so you'd find a Hershey's bar on your cot. I met a lot of really nice people.

It was always busy because you're trying to get out as many meals as you can and you don't realize how much work is involved, because basically nobody wanted to serve a bologna sandwich. Everything was a hot meal—a hot breakfast and a hot dinner. I remember meeting some guys from Alabama and we were serving grits one morning, and I asked them, "What exactly is grits?" Thank God I wasn't in charge of making it because I would have messed it up. One of them said to the other, "Check this out. Yankee boy here wants to know what grits are." It was good to find a way once in a while to laugh. Just meeting a lot of the people after everything—it was amazing.

There were certain things that didn't go so well, even there. I remember it was Christmas Eve and we had the food line and a bunch of the guys came in to have their Christmas Eve dinner, while they're working, and we did our best to make it as much as a home as possible. One of the guys had this plate and he just put it down and he said, "I can't eat." I said, "What's the matter?" He ended up pointing at his boots when he realized he had human remains on his boots. So it still was what it was. Like I said, you do your best to deal with things and you try to make people as comfortable as possible in a bad situation.

My wife didn't go to any services. She didn't want to think about it. And for me it was the exact opposite because of the connection that I had to the situation. It was pretty obsessive. In that February, I was getting really burnt out, and I ended up saying to her that I need to go away for a while and just take a vacation. So I ended up going down to Costa Rica for a while. It was the first time since that whole event that I just said, "I need to deal with me." I didn't mean for it to sound selfish, but I really needed to get away. At that point I didn't have any kids yet, and it was probably better that I didn't because I had enough trouble taking care of myself.

I think 9/11's had an impact on a lot of different parts of my life. Certain things I find don't matter and other things I pay more attention to. Here's a silly example. I travel a lot. Before 9/11, I loved the window seat. Get on a plane, sit down, close my eyes, the person next to me can get up and walk around as many times as they want. It didn't bother me because I was tucked against the window. Now I only take an aisle seat as long as it's available. Again, it's because if you think about what they went through in Pennsylvania, you always get one shot as long as you can recognize it. God forbid something happens, I don't want to climb over somebody's grandmother to get at that one shot. So there's that.

I still get a lot of emails from friends during anniversary time saying, "Hey, just want you to know I'm thinking about you." It means a lot. What's interesting is especially this past anniversary was also the time of year when Congress was voting down health care for the rescue workers. It tells you something.

CHAPTER 6

WHERE ARE THE PATIENTS?

Marvin was a paramedic on 9/11, working shifts at a number of New York City hospitals. His story is about the brutal awakening of emergency-service and hospital staff who expected to be taking care of a large number of wounded survivors, but ultimately found and treated relatively few patients because so few people survived. He delves into his own personal thoughts and fears when initially confronted with the results of the attack: his amazement at facing the chaos at Ground Zero, and his private prayers that his death from ash-induced asphyxiation would be fast. He darkly points to the government's failure to match politicians' rhetoric about heroism and "never forgetting" with sufficient funding to properly care for disabled responders. Marvin tells us that ten years hence, many responders feel forgotten; that they had already disappeared from the country's consciousness by the time the ash finally cleared. His story is not about wanting equal time, it is about preserving the integrity of 9/11's stories that capture what happened that day in September, and about wanting current and future generations to know about everyone who unhesitatingly served with pride, and who cared.

AS A PARAMEDIC, YOU HAVE TO GO through training—being in a classroom as well as being out in the field. So we had a paramedic student with us that morning—Anthony. If I work a day shift I got to have breakfast, 'cause otherwise I get very cranky if I don't eat. So as we are heading up to go to the deli to get something to eat, it comes over the air as a single forty, and I look at my partner Jimmy. He looks at me [and] we're like, "single forty," and the student's like, "Oh my God, that's a plane crash."

You have to understand, I have the type of job that people live for the excitement, the high—what's the word I want to use?—the high-intense calls. 'Cause if somebody said to you, "How was work today?" "Ahh, had a lady with a heart attack, somebody had some fluid in their lungs, there was another person was unconscious because of diabetic conditions." Or, "How was work today?" "Oh, it was great. We had a jumper down, we had two people shot, we had a person underneath the train." I mean, so you live for that high-profile type of a job.

A SINGLE FORTY

So when it came over that it was a single forty at the World Trade Center, you have all these units now jumping on the air to say, "Oh, I'm not so far away. I can be there in no time." 'Cause now they want to go on a hot job. But again, my focus was getting breakfast. So we really paid it no mind, 'cause it was a nice, beautiful, clear day out. We thought, "Okay, it must have been some sightseer got too close to the building."

So we parked. We go in there to the deli. I'll never forget it. I remember I grabbed my orange juice and as I went up to the counter to order my two eggs over easy, ham and cheese, salt, pepper on a roll, the next thing I hear is, "Four-six, Willy"—that's my unit number, four-six William—"I need you to go over to Citywide." Citywide is a special frequency when they have something big going on. Instead of tying up the regular traffic, they put you on a special frequency. We were told to meet at the 59th Street Bridge 'cause we're heading over to the World Trade Center.

Marvin left his orange juice on the counter and they headed to the bridge.

When everybody got together, we all went in the caravan. And I'm on the bridge, and I'm on the phone with my girlfriend at the time, Barbara. She was screaming. She's goes, "You're not gonna believe this. This big jetliner just went into the second Tower!"

When that happened we knew that this was terrorist—this was no accident. And about 30 seconds later it came over the air, "Be advised the second Tower has now been struck."

The caravan of thirty emergency vehicles made its way to the World Trade Center.

One of the things that's etched into my mind was how the people were standing on the streets. And they were just frozen. They had never seen so many emergency vehicles and they were all just heading downtown— lights and sirens blasting.

We pull up down there, near to the Trade Center. We parked on Chambers Street. I don't know what possessed me when I got there—I parked my ambulance on the sidewalk right next door to the Hilton Millenium. I don't know why I went on the sidewalk and parked up next to the Hilton Millenium, but thank God I did 'cause that's what saved our vehicle subsequently.

WE NEED A MEDIC

And it's just total chaos. You got people that are trying to rescue, you got people that are injured, and, of course, you got people sightseeing now— want to take pictures of everything. I remember this one gentleman had a camcorder and he put up the film, and I remember sticking my hand there and pushing his hand down telling him, "No, you really need to get out of here." And there were some ladies there, and I said, "Ladies, you need to get out of here. We need to clear the streets." The ladies [were] like, "You don't tell me what to do." One starts yelling at me, then another lady starts yelling at her, and they're going back and forth. 'Cause we are trying to clear the street. And I would like to see that lady today because subsequently, when the building came down, we had to move or she would've been dead.

It was total chaos going on, and they said, "We need a medic here, we need a medic there," and everything. And one of the things that I do resent with this whole 9/11 thing is—and no disrespect to the cops or firefighters, but just so we can make a point—everything was about the cops and the firefighters, and they act like the EMS [Emergency Medical Services] people were all on a fishing trip that day. And I did not hear anybody screaming for a cop or a fireman. All I heard people screaming for were medics. And even the cops and the firefighters were screaming for medics. But yet, the way the media plays this, the EMS people—especially the ones with the private hospitals—were constantly left out in the cold.

As I was walking up by the Hilton Millenium I see a paramedic I know, Carlos, who works for the city. We played in the EMS League. And I've known Carlos for years, and we were friends and everything, and I watched him and he said he had to find his wife, 'cause his wife worked in the Trade Center. And…I always get emotional at this point, because I watched Carlos walk towards the building, and he didn't know that his wife, Celia, had gotten out of the building. And he never came out. Carlos died. Yeah, he was a real great guy, Carlos.

I'm in the Chase bank and the people were crying. But everyone's like, "What do you need?" And I'm telling them, "All right, get this person some water." Thank God nobody was critically hurt. So I said, "Well, stay put. I'm going outside to get an ambulance and get you people out of here." And they said okay. And as I stepped outside the bank somebody yells, "The Tower! The Tower! The Tower!" And I look up, and you could hear this rumble. I said, "Oh my God."

You heard this loud noise, and it got louder and louder and louder and louder. And now it's on top of us, and all of a sudden the glass is starting to break and you went from day to night. Normally nighttime you could still see. Think of yourself as being blind. You couldn't even see an inch in front of you.

I just knew I was gonna die, and I said, "God, let it be quick." Then everything stopped. Everybody's crying; we're all covered. Thank God no one was seriously hurt. I got everybody out of the bank—had everybody just go up north, because if you wasn't unconscious and you was able to walk... keep moving, 'cause we have more critical patients all over the place.

YOU HEARD THE RUMBLE AGAIN

At that point, I went back down towards the Trade Center, where my vehicle was, to try and find my partner and the student. Because, again, the ambulance was parked right next to the Hilton Millenium, which is right in front of the Trade Center. I find my partner. I'm like, "Jimmy, you have the student?" He's like, "No, don't you have the student?" I'm like, "No, I don't have the student." And so we're like, "Wow, [the] student's dead." And at that point, we're like, "All right. Well, we gotta do what we gotta do."

My partner took patients down to, I think it was Beekman [New York Downtown Hospital]. I said I'd stay back and look for more patients. So, again, I had some supplies with me. As he was driving off, there was a woman who was bleeding and crying... . She came out of the second Tower. I said, "Look at me, look at me, look at me. You're gonna make it, you're gonna make it." And no sooner than I said that...oh, man ... you heard the rumble again.

Thank God I knew what the buildings sounded like from when it went down the first time. Without hesitation, I tell her we gotta go—'cause the building was coming right down on us. I took off, and she said, "Don't leave me, don't leave me!" I turn around and I look. I ran back. I grabbed her and we ran. Directly across the street from the Trade Center is the Hilton Millenium, and as we dove into the Hilton Millenium, we got covered with debris. I knew I wasn't going to survive again, to survive the collapse of both Towers.

Everything came into the hotel. It went from day to night. You couldn't see anything in front of you. Everything with the World Trade Center, depends on where you were—people standing to the left of you might've been killed; people standing to the right of you could've survived. It was just all [in] the positioning. You couldn't see anything. Everybody was shaken up. The hotel was actually closed for like eighteen months—that's how much damage the hotel suffered.

The way that we came in—we dove in the front of the hotel—you couldn't go back out that way because it was all covered up with debris. You had to come out through the side. There was a garage door and they hit the button, and due to all the debris that had fallen, they couldn't open the garage door. So a couple guys, we just physically lifted up the door.

Then when I crawled out, it was like I was the last man on Earth. There was nothing moving; there's stuff flying all through the air. It was like a ghost town. I didn't see anybody. The hotel was beautiful at one point, but now the hotel was just ruined. It was all dust, and you were covered. I mean, you couldn't even tell what race I was. I was literally white from head to toe.

There was these emergency vehicles, and I'm looking inside the emergency vehicles for anybody. I'm looking inside the fire trucks. Nobody is around. There's nothing. I'm here thinking my partner, who was just driving off with the ambulance, he's probably dead also, 'cause when the building came down, it probably crushed the ambulance. So I thought he was dead; I'm like, this is not good. I didn't have a radio. I had a cell phone. Cell phone wasn't working, so I had no communication with anybody.

This is when your mind plays tricks on you, 'cause it seems like you hear dead silence. I didn't hear sirens. I didn't hear nothing. Obviously there were more people still coming, but my mind, it totally blocked everything out. And, like I tell people, in my career I've had a gun to my head twice, I've been shot at once, and nothing compares to those Towers. Nothing.

And I remember in the pile of all this debris I look and I see something coming towards me that looks like an ambulance. And I'm like, okay, now I know what it's like to be in the desert with the whole mirage. I think that I'm hallucinating. I'm standing there, and all of a sudden this thing is getting closer and closer. And…wow. It wound up being my partner, and we just jumped out, we hugged each other.

Then we ran into a firefighter. And he was screaming 'cause his eyes were burning from all the stuff in his eyes. So we took him, we cleaned out his eyes and everything, and we were gonna take him to the hospital. But he's like, "No, no. I gotta stay here for my brother firefighter, my brother firemen." I mean, that's the mentality level that you always had. You don't care about yourself; you care about your fellow brother firefighter, or paramedic, or police officer—whatever the case may be. So we let him go.

Then we ran across a police officer that was in tears because his sergeant had been killed. So we took him with us, and then we found some other cops and we handed him over to them. And then at that point, everything around us was just blowing up. There were fires all over the place.

That whole scenario changed when those buildings came down. If the buildings had never come down, yes, it would have taken us a while, but we could have treated a thousand patients each. We would've gotten through. But when the buildings came down, the rescuers needed to be rescued.

The few masks that we did have, we had just given those out to the public. We didn't have any masks. We weren't concerned about any of that. We were just there to save lives.

REDEPLOY

Marvin and his partner were redeployed to the Staten Island Ferry Terminal, where a portable hospital was set up.

The thing about it was, we were there [at the makeshift hospital] and they're like, "Oh, you guys are a mess. Probably get some water," or whatever. So 'cause there was no food—remember, I still hadn't had breakfast—now I'm hungry, I'm starving. And, they said to us, "Well, where are the patients?"

And we said, "They're dead."

And they're like, "What do you mean?"

And we said, "They're dead. There are no patients. They're all gone."

And so they were like, "Well, you guys must be in shock, so you guys sit down."

Then another ambulance will come, and they said to those guys, "So where are the patients?" And they were like, "There are no patients; they're dead."

It wasn't until maybe the fourth ambulance came, and the exact crew said the exact same thing when it really dawned on them: "Oh my God, the people are dead." I said, "Yeah, there are no patients. They're dead. There's body parts and the few critical ones—they've already been taken. And everybody else is…they're gone, they're dead."

One of the other deputy chiefs said, "What, Marvin? What, Jimmy? You guys can go. You guys have been through enough now."

A NICE PAIR OF UNDERWEAR

As we went to leave, I got a call from my best friend and he says, "You gotta do something. Your goddaughter"—his daughter—"is trapped in the city." Well, I'm like, "Where is she?" Since I was in Manhattan I was able to go get my goddaughter, and she was at some apartment building that her father knew somebody lived there. The security people were holding her there. And she's kicking and fighting with the security people: "Let me go, let me go! That's my uncle Marvin, that's my uncle Marvin!" She ran out. She was hysterically crying and everything. I remember wrapping her up in some sheets, and now we're heading back to Queens.

Our vehicle had all this dust and debris. It was smoky. It looked ghostly, as my goddaughter would like to describe it. As we were coming across the Triborough Bridge, which is now the R.F.K. Bridge, we hear this horn beeping. We're like, "Oh man, what is it now?" And it's these three guys in a truck and they said, "Hey, guys." I don't know where they had came from, but they had this big cup of Coca-Cola with ice. I love ice. "Guys, this is all we got," and the guy leaned out of the truck and handed it to my partner and gave us a Coke. And we were both sitting there, and we were sitting there both sharing the Coke. I gotta say that was the best Coca-Cola I ever had in my life—'cause we were just dying of thirst.

So we're about six blocks away from St. John's and my phone rings. And they're calling me to let me know the student's alive. They have the student. When the building came down, he just ran. He said he just literally ran up from lower Manhattan to the 59th Street Bridge. He walked across the bridge, and then he just broke down 'cause he knew we was dead. He just went back to the hospital to see what was gonna happen with us.

We're getting back towards the hospital, and there had to be at least a hundred people out in front. My hospital is on Queens Boulevard, which is a main road there. And our vehicle is barely moving. We get back to the hospital [and] they give us a hero's welcome. They hug us and they're kissing us and everything else.

It's so true that you always wanna have on clean underwear, because the next thing we know they turn around and they stripped us right down to our underwear right there on the main road. Right on Queens Boulevard, so people were passing by. We had to take what they call a decon shower because we were so contaminated. The nurse is like, "Oh, let's see if he's a boxer guy or a brief type of guy?" So, I'm just glad I had on a nice pair of underwear. It wasn't holey or anything.

They gave us clothes, and they wanted to do a debriefing. We're like, "To hell with you and your debriefing; all I want to do is go home." I got into my car and I left. 'Cause the highway was shut down, you couldn't come into the city on a highway; you could only go out on the highway. So I took my goddaughter. Her father met me out on the highway, and I turned her over to him. Then, I turned around. I had to show my ID to get back on the highway and get back in towards the city, because I lived in the city.

And it didn't hit me till that night, and that's when I broke down.

I remember people were saying all the hospitals were waiting for patients and the patients never came. 'Cause most people, if they were alive, they walked home. One of the things I thought was so touching was how people walked home, told the families they were still alive. And then they went back to the hospitals and all stood in line to donate blood. Something I'll never forget.

I'M HAVING A STROKE

I came back to the site three days later, and I worked on the Pile that day—the day President Bush came. I took a picture because I went back by the hotel—the Millenium—and I took a picture. Because the exact way I left the garage door on Tuesday when 9/11 happened…it hadn't been moved. The space that I crawled out of was left exactly the same.

I was only there for two days. I was there for the collapse of the Towers, and I came back three days later. Voluntarily, I worked about eight, nine hours on the Pile that day. You were still looking for people, even though I knew in my heart that even if anybody were still there, they weren't going to be alive. But they kept doing the PR thing. There was still a rescue thing 'cause they wouldn't give up. We found some body parts the day we worked on the Pile. As a paramedic, I was in the business of saving lives. So anytime you see somebody, you wanna try to save a life. It becomes part of you. Even when you're off-duty, you see an accident, you stop. If at any time you see a situation where you can help, that's what you do.

My big mistake was going back to work the next day. I lived by myself; I didn't want to be alone. The week subsequent to that, the girlfriend said that the bed was soaking wet, because I went over to the girlfriend's house, and I was shaking and saying, "We gotta save the people, we gotta save the people." I cried almost every night for, I don't know, five, six weeks, or whatever. I'm sure I tossed and turned. I wasn't really sleeping well.

So mind you, now, this is a Tuesday, once again. We leave there. We're down to Jamaica and we head back up to my area. I tell Jimmy to stop. I want to go to the bank to get some money 'cause I want something to eat. While I'm in the bank, next thing I know, I start to feel numb. My arm got numb and then my leg got numb. Then all of a sudden my speech got slurred, and then I realized I'm having a stroke—at forty-one. I didn't want to cause panic in the bank, so I'm standing there at the bank and I'm holding on to the counter for dear life.

People are just walking by and walking by, and finally some guy realizes there's something wrong. He's like, "Mister, mister, are you all right?" I was aphasic. I couldn't get the words out, and I'm trying to tell him "Ambulance, ambulance." He's like, "Hang on there, buddy. I'll go and get your partner."

And God bless this gentleman 'cause he had a walker, so he's doing his best with the walker. I'm just standing there 'cause I didn't want to collapse in the bank and cause all this chaos and whatnot. And even though it would've been okay to collapse, I'm holding on for dear life.

Marvin's partner Jimmy rushes into the bank. He immediately recognizes that Marvin is having a stroke and begins treatment.

He got on the air and told the dispatcher, "Four-six William for notification." "Six William, you're not on a job." He says, "Be advised, my partner's had a stroke. " And the dispatcher's like, "All right everybody, off the air, six William, six William." He gives him all the information and everything and he says, "Be advised, I'm going to need help at the hospital." And then the other units—you hear everybody screaming over the air that they want to head back—and finally the dispatcher just said, "All the St. John's units head back to the hospital."

They did. They called a notification. Normally the hospital team waits inside the emergency room, but they were all actually outside the emergency room when we pulled up. They're like, "Oh my God, it's Marvin, it's Marvin." So, my speech was gone. I could barely move my hands. They bring me into the hospital; they're examining me. And mind you, at the time the only medical problems I had were colitis, which I've had since I was fifteen. I took two medicines. Otherwise, I ran like a deer. I could do anything.

So now, since I had a stroke, there's a medicine called tPA, but you gotta be careful. You gotta do a CAT scan, 'cause if they're having a heart attack or a stroke with a bleed and you give them the tPA, you're just gonna kill the patient. It does save people's lives, but you have to make sure there's not a bleed.

Anyway, they got me on the stretcher. They take me down for a CAT scan. And I'm down at the CAT scan and all of a sudden I'm feeling better. My speech comes back, everything is good. So I'm thinking, well maybe I had a mini-stroke—what they call a TIA. I knew exactly what was happening. And so I'm like, "Yeah, I'm all right. I'm all right guys. I'm all right."

And then all of a sudden I grab my head, and I started screaming, and I wound up stroking out in front of them. And here I'm having another stroke. I remember just lying there, and at that point they rush me out of the CAT scan. And I remember them just running down the hall with me laid on the stretcher. And they are giving me tPA, 'cause I've had a major stroke and I'm paralyzed. I lost the right side of my body, my hands. My right side of my body was gone. My speech was gone too. And so now I'm in intensive care. And the doctor felt it was the stress. The stress was just too much for me.

My medical career was over. The question now was, "How well am I going to be able to just function in life in general?" To everybody's amazement, I came back to full duty three months to the day. And my mindset was that if I could survive the collapse of two Twin Towers, I can beat a stroke.

THEY HAVE FORGOTTEN

In 2003 I went to the Mount Sinai program, and they examined me and diagnosed me with post-traumatic stress disorder. They found a few things wrong with me.

My health took a turn for the worse. I went from taking two medications before 9/11, to currently today I take anywhere between ten and sixteen medications, depending on how I feel. I've been diagnosed with post-traumatic stress disorder, major depression. I have the sinusitis that you can hear. I've got restrictive airway disease, and I have asthma.

I just pray to God every day that I don't get cancer, because so many people are getting cancer. Since they don't want to own up to anything …I mean, my father died of cancer. With me they'll be saying, "Well, your father died of cancer. You didn't have nothing to do with the Trade Center."

What I say to these critics, these elected officials, is [that] being a firefighter, police officer, or EMS person, we are required every year to take a physical. So if you have five years, ten years on the job and you don't pass that physical, you can't work. So my question would be: Why is it that people that do such physical jobs—why is it that such a high number of all these people are sick? And what is the common denominator? It's Ground Zero—whether you were down at the Trade Center that day or you worked on the Pile, you was at the morgue, or at Freshkills. Because there was a medical report that came out that said anybody who was there the day the building came down—our lungs have aged twelve years.

At the end of 2003, my breathing was getting really, really bad, and I kept going back and forth to the hospital. I spent five days in the hospital. They were about to put me on a respirator, and the doctor says, "That's it. You're done." So I haven't worked since January 8th, 2004. Major depression, post-traumatic stress disorder—that's permanent. So I'm permanently and totally disabled.

TREATED SO BADLY

There's a tremendous strain on how badly we were treated. And a lot of us feel that they're calling us heroes—they're treating us like zeros. I mean, this is what you do. You see somebody dying or something, you're gonna go and try and help your fellow human being. 'Cause one thing about 9/11

I have to say is [that] we, as a nation, as people, we became kinder to one another—patient—more tolerable with each other. And then a few weeks later we got back to the way we were.

For most of the country, 9/11 does not exist. Because most of the responders are here in the Tri-State area. And in the 435 Congressional districts throughout the United States, you have sick responders in 429 of them. So when you think about that, you have sick responders in every state in this country. However, it's just a small volume, a small number. And so the news media is not doing the stories about it.

Come anniversary time, all the politicians are going to be front and center at a 9/11 event saying, "This tragedy we are not going to forget. We're going to remember these heroes for what they did." Yadda , yadda, yadda. Yet when it comes time to put your money where your mouth is, you don't.

I'm proud of how I served this country. I used to say if I had to do it all over again, I would. Honestly, if I was right there and it happened, I would do whatever I could.

CHAPTER 7

SHE SAVED ME

"On the good days, we save each other. We usually don't even know it when it happens," says Tyree. But Tyree did know. He even knows the name of the person who saved him; her name was Doris. Tyree, a court officer working at the Supreme Court in Lower Manhattan, is retired now. Tyree tells us about his courageous acts, which saved the life of a complete stranger, Doris Torres. Ultimately his purpose and commitment to this stranger gave him meaning and strength that sustained him, while his other colleagues were crushed to death. At the time Doris was already badly burned, and Tyree evacuated her from the mall under Tower 2 while his team members treated other victims with less serious injuries. Doris died several weeks after the attacks. But as Tyree sees it, he only survived because his and Doris's paths crossed in the moments before the building collapsed. Tyree tries to give us a sense of what that day in September was really like, but he struggles to find the language to adequately describe it. What is remarkable about Tyree's narrative is his willingness to be explicit, to resist euphemism, and to avoid circumventing the most painful things. He shares his vivid memories of that day and offers a profound contribution to the preservation of first responders' memories of what had happened on September 11.

I WAS BORN AND RAISED IN ISLIP. I recently retired as a master sergeant from the United States Air Force Reserves. I'm married. Have three kids. The latest addition came a week ago…. We now have twins, a little boy and a little girl. And I have a daughter, Margaret, who's almost four. And my wife, Caroline, we've been married—we're going on five years.

My wife is a police officer. She's currently assigned, and was assigned on that date, to the 6th Precinct, in Greenwich Village. We both ended up responding. Separately, but nonetheless, we both ended up down there—different locations, had different experiences.

We work nine to five; our day starts at nine o'clock. I'm usually at work an hour early, since I'm coming from Suffolk. I was in the 14th-floor locker room having my cup of tea. I heard the first airplane fly by and strike the towers. Not realizing what happened, I ran to the window. We saw a gaping hole, flames, smoke, debris.

Then over the radio we heard one of our patrol sergeants and patrol lieutenants, they were mobilizing a team of guys to respond down to the Trade Center. So I ran across the street to the 100 Centre Street location, where they were getting together. We had our major, who was the commanding officer, a sergeant, and a bunch of officers. We boarded the jury bus.

We were somewhere in the vicinity of Broadway and White Street when we heard the second explosion. Then we heard over the radio, "Oh, my God, another plane struck the second Tower." With that, our major turned around and said, "This is fucked up, guys. One plane's an accident; two is terrorism." I knew we were in for more than we were prepared to deal with. We were probably in over our heads. We stopped in the vicinity of 7 World Trade Center and we got off the bus.

There was a woman who was just carried out with a severe leg injury. And Mitch—it was Mitchel Wallace—didn't bat an eye. Got down on his hands and knees and started treating her. There was a photograph taken during that. And that, as we later found out, was probably the last photograph that was ever taken of Mitch.

I partnered up with an officer, Tommy Jurgens. Tommy was a twenty-six-year-old Army veteran, saw action in Somalia. He was a captain; he was volunteer fire department. When he was in the Army, he was an Army medic. I had spent some time as a corpsman in the Navy, although I'm in the Air Force. So we partnered up.

We saw wreckage from the airplane, or one of the airplanes—landing gear, engine parts. Didn't realize at the time, but there was a lot of confetti, other debris. Some of that debris turned out to be people that were jumping. As we crossed the street, I remember seeing Tommy making the sign of the cross. I realized, holy shit, we're in it. So I also made the sign of the cross.

We came up to Building 5. They weren't allowing anybody to [help] evacuate Tower 1 and Tower 2, because of the debris and the people jumping. So there was a steady stream of evacuees. We started making our way down the stairs. I don't remember the order in which it happened. There was a woman clearly having a heart attack. We assisted her across the street to the front of the Millenium Hotel. There was a triage station there. We dropped her off.

We grabbed some supplies from the ambulances there, started making our way back in. There was a gentleman with a severe head laceration. He had trouble walking. We brought him back to the triage station.

On our third trip into the building, I was met up with Captain Harry Thompson and Officer Mitch Wallace. So it was myself, Tommy, Mitch, and Captain Thompson. There was another court officer, Sergeant Pat Maiorino, at the front door helping, guiding people out. I remember her telling us, "Heads up. There's reports of more incoming aircraft."

So we went in. Harry Thompson was a captain at the Court Officer Academy. Big, tall, six-foot, five-inch black gentleman, very spit-and-polish appearance—just commanded respect. And there was a calm feeling. It was like, alright, we're okay, we're with Harry, Captain Thompson. Mitch Wallace was an EMT, worked for EMS, and was cited for saving somebody on the Long Island Railroad about a year before. So it was the four of us.

We came in Building 5, started going down the stairs. There was a Port Authority police officer, and he directed us to where there were more injured people. We ended up in the mall area of the Trade Center, one level below street level in Tower 2. There were about six civilians that I seem to remember. There was a female, severely burned; I estimated over 60 percent burns to her body. We didn't talk much. We all had a mission on our mind and we were working like a well-oiled machine. I said, "I'll take her." Because she was the critical patient. Turned out to be the best decision of my entire life.

I put her in a stair chair and we started exiting the area. I got maybe a hundred feet away, somebody yelled, "Get down!" I heard this horrible noise. I thought maybe it was an airplane flying into the building. There was this tremendous rush of air, followed by this debris. I was thrown to the ground and shot across the floor about a hundred feet, with my victim. That was the building collapsing. Fortunately, we were just outside the collapse zone. It was the last time I saw Tommy, Harry, or Mitch.

I had no idea what the hell happened. I got on the radio and started yelling, "Mayday, Mayday, I'm trapped. I'm in the basement. Mayday." Which isn't court officer terminology—that's volunteer firefighter. I wear many hats. I'm a volunteer firefighter, I'm in the Air Force, I'm a part-time police officer. I reverted back to training that I had learned some twenty-something years ago. The chair she was in flipped back, but I maintained contact with it.

The individual, I later found out her name was Doris Torres. She had grabbed me by the shirt, had a death grip on me. "Please, please, don't leave me." I couldn't see her. There was zero visibility. I had to put my shirt [up] to breathe. Took out my little flashlight and it did absolutely nothing, I don't think. All I saw was like a little orb of light that didn't project. And I told her, I said, "Sweetheart, don't worry. I promise we're getting out of here."

I flat-out lied to her. I thought we were going to die where we were. If I didn't have her, I probably would've curled up in a fetal position and just waited to die. She saved me. If our paths didn't cross, I would've been with Tommy, Harry, and Mitch.

...[I] had no idea where I was—completely lost. Found a wall, started feeling my way out. I didn't know where I was going. All I knew was something really bad happened that way and I was going the opposite direction.

I remember telling her, "Okay, sweetheart, let's get the fuck outta Dodge." It was just us. Miraculously, we made our way back to the same stairwell and we were in that corridor. Then there was somebody screaming, "Anybody down here? Anybody down here?" We started screaming. And there was a Port Authority police officer, an FBI agent, and a civilian. We all grabbed a corner of the chair, ran up the stairs to where we were.

And it was a very, very different landscape. Where moments before there was chaos—people running, screaming, deafening sound of sirens close by, coming in the distance, people jumping—I came out and everything was gray. There wasn't a sound to be heard. There was just this deafening silence. The triage area that we'd just left these last two people, the ambulances were on fire, they were overturned. It was like the end scene in *Saving Private Ryan*, when Tom Hanks is by himself at the bridge and he has no hearing.

So we ran up Fulton Street to—I think it was a Citibank. That was a new triage station that had been set up within minutes of the collapse. I dropped Doris off there. I had a pager at the time, and my brother was paging me. So I called my brother Troy, who lived at home with my folks.

He was hysterical when I called and he said, "Ty, you gotta get the fuck out of the city. We're under attack. Two planes just flew into the Trade Center. Plane crashed in Pennsylvania. They flew a plane into the Pentagon. There's more coming." He said, "And the Tower, Tower 2 just collapsed."

And I very cavalierly said, "Oh, is that just what the fuck happened? I just climbed out of there. I was caught in the collapse."

We were on the corner of Church and Vesey streets when Tower 1 came down. What I remember from when the Tower collapsed was there were still people, like gawking, looking. There was a couple pushing a stroller. You got cops and firemen running for their lives; firemen, their helmets—dropping their air packs. A fireman never leaves his air pack. That's his way out when shit gets bad. We're running for our lives, and I just remember everybody grabbing the stroller. Parents can be assholes, but your kid's not going to die. Cops' guns fell out of their holsters; they didn't go back.

We regrouped at the courthouse at 100 Centre Street, and we were trying to find out what happened. There was a whole lot of confusion. And Tommy, Harry, and Mitch were never to be heard from again.

If I had to do it all over again, I'd do it all over again. The only difference is, those people that Tommy, Harry, and Mitch were treating, I'd have made sure we got them all out. Where they found the remains of Tommy, Harry, and Mitch was near a pillar, a big support. I'm guessing it was ten by ten, maybe eight by eight. There were other human remains found there. Tommy had the presence of mind, being a firefighter, if it collapsed, to go for something substantial, hoping it'd create a void. The speculation was that they were shielding other people with their bodies. When Harry Thompson was found, he was found intact, like in a crouching position, his knees were up towards his chest.

So these guys made a difference, right up to the very end.

RECOVERY

I didn't get home until eleven o'clock that night. My uniform was torn and I had blood and burnt flesh on it. I took the train to Babylon. My mother picked me up because my car was at the Islip station. Cried. First thing we did was we went to St. Mary's Church in East Islip, said a prayer, and lit a candle. I was lucky, I wasn't injured. I mean, I had grit in my eyes and stuff like that, but I was okay.

I went back to work. I remember the lieutenant, the patrol lieutenant, they were sending details of people down to the Pile. It was a rescue mission then. I wasn't allowed to go. He said, "You did enough already. You're not thinking clearly. You're exhausted." I don't think I slept for a week after that. I was angry as hell. Couldn't understand.

Nobody was giving up. Once the determination was made that it was a recovery effort, everybody was going to come home. We were going to make sure that everybody came home. The night that Harry Thompson was found, I came into Manhattan for an awards dinner. A friend of mine is an emergency service cop. I met him at their temporary command post and I was going to the Pit. I showed up and he introduced me to his lieutenant.

He goes, "Oh, you're from the courts. We just found your captain."

I'm like, "What? Harry Thompson?"

He goes, "Yeah, they just recovered….We're waiting for a detail of your folks to show up before we bring him out."

When they found a person, they put him in a body bag and they put him in a Stokes basket [a rescue basket], and there would be a flag placed over them. If it was a fireman, somebody from the Fire Department would stand watch until their company came. If it was a cop—till folks from their precinct got there. When they were ready to bring him out, all work stopped. Everybody got off the machines; they shut down the equipment. Everybody lined up the ramp, on both sides. There was a Fire Department chaplain there. They called everybody to attention, rendered a hand salute and they carried him up. They'd load them into an ambulance and take them to the New York county morgue.

I was there with Harry Thompson. I rode in the front of the ambulance. He was in a Police Department ambulance. Folks from the academy, who carried him out, rode in the back. We actually had motorcycle escort—west past the courthouse and to the morgue. When we got to the morgue, once again, all work stopped. Everybody lined up, stood at attention, rendered a salute and they brought him in. Then the identification process began.

For me, it was unfortunate. I was there when they opened up the body bag. [That's] something I should've never seen, but I was there nonetheless. Harry Thompson was still in uniform, still had his shield pinned to him, a little bent. They cleaned it up, they gave it to the academy staff. It now sits in a curio cabinet at the academy, with photographs of him, Tommy, and Mitch, and his sweater with his captain's bars.

We had some post-traumatic debriefing. I remember one of the officers— he's now a lieutenant—Ed, was very, very angry. Eddie was outside when the building collapsed, and he took refuge behind a column. There was somebody running. And he was helping them and it was coming down and they wanted to run in a particular direction. He said, "No, no, no. Come this way," when the building came down. He thought he had them with him. He just ended up having their arm, from the shoulder. That person perished.

When we did our post-traumatic stress debriefing, they had people from the courthouse and somebody [said], "Oh, I was watching this on TV and I'm traumatized." I remember Eddie, "Are you fucking kidding me?" He goes, "You're traumatized from watching it on TV?" He goes, "I ended up with somebody's arm in my fucking hand."

Everybody dealt with it differently, but those of us who were there were a support for those of us who were there. Not to diminish somebody who watched it on TV. Everybody knew somebody who got killed. I ended up knowing probably about ten people who got killed, between police, fire, EMS.

I did a lot of reflecting...wanted to know why I'm here. Questioned God. Suffered survivor's guilt, post-traumatic stress. Spent three months waking up on the floor trying to feel my way out of my room. Talking about it has helped a bunch. It was a horrible experience. Glad I did what I did. I know I made a difference to some people.

They haven't recovered the remains of Tommy and Mitch. They got bone fragments. But the DNA technology keeps evolving. They haven't been *positively* identified. They assume it's them because they found the slide to Mitch's weapon, and they found Tommy's shield.

FINDING DORIS

I ended up finding out who Doris Torres was a couple of weeks later. I went to New York Hospital's Burn Center on the 16th, and I didn't make it to the burn unit. When I got there to the desk, they says, "Oh, yeah, nobody can go in. The nurses, everybody's busy. They just had a code." Which means a cardiac arrest. And that was when Doris passed away.

I found out later on—I got bits and pieces from this representative from the hospital; she was very cautious, wouldn't give anything up because of the HIPAA patient privacy laws. I started doing Internet searches, and there was a thirty-two-year-old female from the 78th floor, and it was Doris Torres. I couldn't recognize from the picture that was online.

So the next time I spoke to this person, I said, "Did it happen to be Doris Torres?" She about fell off her chair. Doris's sister Mercedes worked at the hospital as a clerical person. She said she would try and reach out to her. I left my number with her.

It took her a good six months to get in touch with me. She called me. I met the family, had dinner with them. This was a year and a half later. We went to the cemetery. The family's a wonderful family.

Doris ended up having burns over—I think they calculated—53 percent of her body. She had facial burns, chest, arms. She had skin hanging off of her. Unfortunately, with the facial burns came respiratory burns. She was intubated. She couldn't talk, but she could communicate. She knew that her family was there. Her family was by her bedside the night she died. So they were very grateful that, because of my actions, they got to see Doris, that she just didn't perish, never to be seen or heard from again.

They got to lay their daughter to rest. When I was in Iraq, I sent them a flag that was flown over in Iraq. I sent, like, twenty-five flags home. We'd fly them at the air base. I sent it with a certificate that this flag was flown to honor the memory of Doris Torres.

I got a picture of the family from Thanksgiving dinner the year before and a great letter. They were shocked and appalled that I was over there. I said, "No, it's okay. I could have gotten out of it but I'm here by choice."

They have an empty place setting for all the holiday dinners, which is Doris's place. They said there's a seat next to her for me. I don't have to call,

I can just show up; they'd be happy to have me. I knew they meant that. I call her mother. She doesn't take phone calls on September 11th, from anybody. I'm the only call she'll take that day. So…there's a bond.

ACTIVATED AND DEPLOYED

October 21st of 2001, I got activated for a year from the Reserves. I was stationed at McGuire Air Force Base in New Jersey. I was going to be deployed to Afghanistan, but because of everything that happened, I had a choice. Normally nobody gets a choice. So I became the poster child for the Air Force Reserve and won the Air Force Reserve, United States Air Force, and Department of Defense Heroism Award, Firefighter of the Year—even though I wasn't on active duty, it was an Act of War.

And when I won the Department of Defense award, it was with three firefighters from the Pentagon that day. Met them for the first time—regular guys. We all said the same thing—if we had to do it all over. We also joked if we knew it was going to be like that, we'd have just banged in that day.

I got activated again January of 2008, to go to Iraq with the Air Force Reserves. I had my twenty years in; I could've gotten out. I could've not gone on the deployment. I could've retired. But we just got done training a bunch of kids, eighteen, nineteen-year-old kids, and I couldn't very well send them to war, say, "Hey, see ya later. Good job. I'm proud of you. Bye-bye, I'm retiring."

I went over with them. I ended up doing a PowerPoint presentation on why we're here. I had some photographs from 9/11. The base commander was there and a lot of bigwigs. The major from life skills support, which is mental health. When it was over, everybody was crying their eyes out. Because there was a picture of my daughter Maggie, and I said, "That's why I'm here, to make the world a better place and do my part."

Afterwards, the major from Life Skills Support came up to me and said that I was a textbook case of what to do and how to deal with your post-traumatic stress. Take something negative and turn it into a positive and tell people about it.

The base commander said, "That was really great. You're helping people keep their eye on the ball and why we're here." You're away from home, you're in a foreign land. Almost everybody gets to go home; some don't, and it's hard. But I believe in everything we've done.

It wasn't just serving; now I'm defending. I was in fire protection; I'm a firefighter in the Air Force. I was a crew chief station captain in 2002, and when we deployed to Iraq, I was a station captain, assistant chief.

We had some young guys with us. One of the guys that was with us was going to go to college. His father was a retired city firefighter. He lost uncles. I mean, he had a lot of friends that they called uncles. So this was his way of paying back.

It's become politicized. It's not, "Well, the war in Iraq, the war in Afghanistan, we need to pull out." You can't cut and run. Those who've shed blood for us overseas, to do that is a slap in the face to them and their families.

Our whole country was drawn closer together and there was definitely a surge in patriotism, which I think has dwindled. I'm going to say this for the record: I think it's a complete travesty, building a mosque at the Trade Center. I know that's contradictory to what our country was founded on, freedom of religion.

RENEWED FAITH

I know for a fact that there are people out there that I work with, both as a court officer, my job as a police officer, volunteer fire service in the military, who will die for me. On that day, if I had been trapped, there were people that would've died coming to save me. It's a shame it takes a tragedy like this, but it renews your faith in mankind.

When I heard that fall that Father Mychal Judge got killed, that really shook my belief in God. I couldn't understand how a priest doing God's work could be the first person to die on that day. When they had the memorial service for Harry Thompson, Mayor Giuliani was at the church and he got up and he spoke. He said that God took Father Mychal Judge because there were just so many people that he needed to minister to. He couldn't possibly have ministered to them. So by Him taking him, he could minister to everybody now and do God's work.

I got a lot of comfort from that. It renewed my belief in God.

PART TWO

LOOKING FOR SURVIVORS

Although the devastation from the collapse of the Twin Towers was profound, the belief that there were survivors trapped under the tons of debris motivated thousands of responders to rush to Lower Manhattan and aid in the rescue effort. The hope that some people survived in stairwells or pockets of building materials resonated with the responders for days, and in some cases for weeks. It provided meaning and purpose for the workers who needed a focus when faced with such inexplicable destruction and overwhelming grief. For many responders, it was extremely difficult to accept that thousands had perished, and even more so, that the remains of many victims would never be found.

◄ **Dust and debris fall like snow** as construction and metal workers prepare to remove large sections of iron and huge concrete blocks from the Pile. *Photo by John Bombace.*

▲ **Construction equipment is dwarfed** by the huge scale of the wreckage of the three buildings that fell on 9/11. *Photo by Roy and Lois Gross.*

▲ **Scores of firefighters** congregate at the scene of the disaster. *Photo by Steve Spak.*

▲ **A billow of smoke and ash rises** from the Pile as firefighters, police officers, and emergency medical technicians search for survivors. *Photo by Steve Spak.*

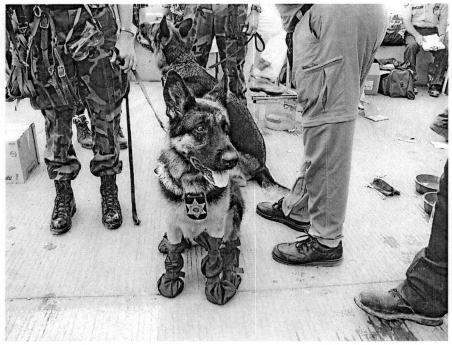

▲ **A search and rescue dog** wearing protective footwear to avoid burning and blistering its paws on the hot and smoldering Pile. *Photo by Roy and Lois Gross.*

▲ **A view of the iconic steel skeleton** of one of the fallen Towers. *Photo by John Bombace.*

▲ **Responders survey the destruction** through a heavy veil
of ash after nightfall on 9/11. *Photo by John Bombace.*

▲ **Sunlight breaks through** a plume of smoke and dust
rising from the smoldering site. *Photo by Steve Spak.*

▲ **Construction workers begin** dismantling and removing the large-scale concrete and steel debris from the Pile. *Photo by John Bombace.*

▲ **Three firefighters rest** on a debris-filled street before continuing their search for survivors of the Twin Towers' collapse. *Photo by Steve Spak.*

CHAPTER 8

SEARCHING FOR MY BROTHER

Devotion to the brotherhood is a fundamental and important mindset of police officers, firefighters, and military men and women. When confronting dangerous and uncertain situations, they need to know they are backed up by their brothers (and sisters). James was born in Jamaica and moved to the Bronx at the age of twenty-five. Shortly after, he became a U.S. citizen. The allure of firefighting and the desire to serve his community drew him to serve as a volunteer firefighter on Long Island. When the Twin Towers collapsed on 9/11, James and his fellow volunteers joined in the rescue effort. James's dangerous search for his missing friend and fellow firefighter, Linc, shows the power of these bonds among brothers. Even in death, these men and women did not want to abandon their own, they didn't want to give up the fight. Their strength to endure the horror they witnessed was rooted in this brotherhood and the belief that their brothers would do the same for them had the situation been reversed.

I WAS AT WORK IN THE FIRE RESCUE GROUP at the Brookhaven National Laboratory when one of the guys shouted and said, "We have a plane into the Tower, the World Trade Center." I said, "A little plane, a big plane?"

Nobody had the answer. It was like something out of the movies that shows how the Empire State Building was hit by a plane during the war, a private plane that just got lost somewhere. As we continued to watch the television, we saw that this was unfolding into what could be an act of terrorism. Right before our very eyes, you saw the camera, you saw the second plane come in and hit. At that point, we knew it was an act of terrorism.

It's very hard to explain the emotions. We are firefighters, and we handle emergencies very well. Some of us do break down and cry sometimes, but when something like that happens, initially your response is, what are we going to do? We gotta go help. We gotta do something. We can't just sit here.

I couldn't leave work when it happened. But I went home that evening, still watching on television, and then went down to my firehouse in Brookhaven to meet with a bunch of guys and we devised a plan. At the time, you weren't allowed to respond just carte blanche. You had to have some controls.

WHERE IS LINC?

My friend asked the question, where was Linc? Was he home? Was he working? So we called his house, and his wife at the time said he was working. She didn't know where he was, and that was our motivation to go in there. He was part of our community. He worked in New York City at Rescue 2. He volunteered in Brookhaven as a firefighter and he was one of our brothers. And he was missing. It was our job to go get him.

Communications were very bad. One of the big findings in the 9/11 tapes was that communications went to hell at some point in time. It was so chaotic and things just didn't work. The Towers were down; the antennas were on the Towers. Radios didn't work, cell phones didn't work, a lot of things didn't work. There were not enough frequencies for all the people in the departments to handle, to get their message across, so we didn't know where Linc was. We decided—we gotta go in.

The Towers went down on a Tuesday. It was either Wednesday or Thursday that we decided, "Let's go find Linc." Our fire districts are governed by the commissioners. Five people who write the rules for us and how we operate and how we do. The commissioners at the time said "no one will respond without our permission." Well, being the rebels that we are and the firefighters that we are and with our friend missing, we just took the gear and got in our private cars. I asked to use my Chief car, but I was told no, so we took the private car. Five of us piled into one car and went into the city.

I called my wife at work and told her she's going to have to fix dinner because I'm going into the city. She said, "For what?"

I said, "To go find Linc."

She said, "What, are you crazy?"

I said, "No. I'm going to look for my brother."

At that point she just said, "Do what you gotta do." Was it hard for her? Probably. We never discussed it. For the time I was there, which was probably about a week, we never discussed it. My youngest son, he was home and I said, "Kyle, I'm going into the city to help. We know it's dangerous, we don't know what's going to happen. If we're back, we're back. If we're not, you're the man of the house."

He said, "Just be careful, Dad." And then we left.

We drove the Long Island Expressway. We went to the Ladder 24 house, which one of our past firefighters who passed away from cancer worked out of. It was in Midtown and we figured that was a good jump-off spot. Plus, they could give us T-shirts that we could put on, so we would look like city firefighters even though our thing said Brookhaven on the back. We went there and stopped and they welcomed us with open arms. They gave us all T-shirts and they recommended that we drive to a certain point, park, and then walk the rest of the way, which was okay for us.

THE RAIN COULDN'T WASH AWAY THE GRAY

I'm not sure how many city blocks we walked with our turnout gear, but we got down to World Trade Center, and oh my God—that is something I will remember as long as I live. Picture yourself on a set where there is no color. As we got closer and closer to the actual site, everything went from green street signs and red billboards to everything just gray. It was gray, we realized later on, from the dust that settled. Nothing was colored anymore. Everything was just gray.

And it started to rain, but the rain didn't wash away the gray. It just stayed very drab and gray and as we approached the scene, there were a lot of lights. The whole place was lit up. Where we expected to see two tall buildings, we just saw a skeleton. Wow. That was the reaction.

How could this happen to the most powerful nation in the world? How could this happen? Why would anyone want to do this? Why would anyone want to bring a giant to its knees and prove a point by killing innocent people? Not just firefighters. We expect to die at some point in time, in a tough, mean manner, because that's the nature of the job. I don't think firefighters are really afraid of death, but these were innocent people who got up, went to work to earn a living to put food on their table, men with wives and children and grandchildren.

EVACUATE TO WHERE?

So when we got there, there were no controls, no place to report to, nobody to check in with. None of that was set up yet, not like two or three weeks later, a month later. You just got in and started digging. You found a spot that you figured was okay.

We went down to the Ten House, which is Engine 10, Ladder 10, right at the base of the World Trade Center. Just south of it, I think. We went in there and the guys there welcomed us. They thought we were from Ladder 24—they didn't know we were from Brookhaven, Long Island. They gave us packs of gloves. It was pouring rain; everything was soaking wet. They gave us gloves and dust masks, the little painter's masks, the throw away things. That's all they had. They gave us tools. Screwdrivers, whatever we needed. I had some water and we shoved our pockets with extra bottles of water and went to work on the Pile right outside the Ten House.

We brought our gear. I made one mistake, though: taking my white hat. Chiefs wear white hats in the fire service. I took my white hat and every time I turned around some firefighter was asking me for orders. I said, "Dude, I don't know what to tell you to do. I'm here just like you trying to help out." And then I realized. My buddy Mark said to me, "Chief, you got your hat on." He said, "Chief, it's a white hat. They're looking for orders from you."

At that point I had to swap my hat out for a black hat. I didn't want to be in charge of anything. I just wanted to go find Linc.

We started crawling through nooks and crannies and caverns. It was still smoldering. There weren't flames, but there was a lot of smoke. It was hot. We were like gophers, moles. We found holes to go under the building, to look for him.

You think every step you take is going to get you closer to finding your brother, so you keep going. I'll never forget when we were down there. A friend of mine, I was leading him through and we're talking each other through it and we're going down through cavernous areas, just metal, and we see computers. We didn't see any bodies, strangely enough. All of a sudden we hear a voice from above—it wasn't God—saying,"Evacuate! Evacuate, take cover!"

I turn around and I look at him [my friend] and I say, "Evacuate where? Where are we going to go? How we going to get out of this? We're twenty, thirty, forty, fifty feet deep in a hole. It took us half an hour to get here. We're not going to get out in five minutes. Whatever is going to happen is going to happen."

What was happening was the clouds were moving in the sky, and the Brooks Brothers building is right next to the World Trade Center. They had a flag on top of the Brooks Brothers building. A lot of the buildings in the surrounding area were not checked for safety. These buildings were compromised at some point. We couldn't tell whether the building was moving or if this was an optical illusion from the clouds moving. It looked like the building was shaking, but there were times when the buildings did shake, and they had a guy watching for that. He would watch the flag and the building, and if it looked like the flag was moving too much, not from the wind, he would put out an alarm: The building is shaking. If the building shakes, the building is going to come down and you gotta run like hell.

It's funny now that you think about it, but down there in the hole you don't know: You gotta do what you gotta do. When we were topside, I remember the guy shouting, "Run! Evacuate!" And we evacuated the Pile and we took off like bats out of hell to clear the area. Five to ten minutes later, they gave the all-clear and we came back and started digging again. But down in the hole, what do you do? Where do you go? So we continued down the hole to see where we would end up.

I know at some point in time we came out and we went into Brooks Brothers because we were freezing cold. All the gloves they had given us from the Ten House were all soaking wet. Our turnout coats were the only things keeping us warm; it was a little chilly. We went to the Brooks Brothers place because somebody said there were gloves in there and T-shirts. We went in, took our T-shirts off, put a dry T-shirt on and put some dry gloves on, and then put our turnout coats back on. At that point, I think it was around 3:00 or 4:00 in the morning, whichever morning it was. We decided to take a little nap, and then went back to work.

I remember one thing about sleeping there. We were trying to nap, each of us propped up against each other, and…I woke up to a flash and there was a guy taking flash photography. He asked us where we were from and we told him, and he said if we want the picture, he'll sell them to us. We almost beat the crap out of him. The nerve. We're down there doing our job, and you're trying to sell us pictures?

It was a free-for-all. Everybody was coming in, including us. We shouldn't have gone in there unannounced, but hey—we were there and we were working. The guys were glad to have us.

THE BUCKET BRIGADE

It was organized chaos. Firefighters work very well together when they're under pressure, so at one point in time on the Pile, we formed lines. There were a few guys down in the hole somewhere and they would pick something up and pass it. We were looking for anything that would lead us to a person. What they call a Bucket Brigade. They would scoop something out, because if you found a tip of a finger, it's very possible the rest of the body might be there, close by.

There were times when we were alarmed because somebody found something and says, "Hey, I found a ring." Okay, the rest of the body might soon be there. So we'd work frantically trying to get something out. We had a few dogs there at the time, but it was always one guy in charge. With firefighters, you put one guy in charge and you listen to him, no matter who he is or what he is. You put him in charge and you take orders from him. We were very organized.

One guy would scoop the bucket up and pass it down the line to the Bucket Brigade. Then you'd empty the bucket out on a flat surface before the bulldozers came and scooped everything up, and we'd go through and separate. Kind of like a manual sift. You'd separate everything, looking for anything. And if you found nothing, then you sweep everything back to the side and the payloaders come and pick that up, and the next bucket comes down.

After we searched for Linc for quite a while, we were put on the Bucket Brigade. We thought maybe this is what we can do—maybe we can find something belonging to him. Not that we forgot about looking for Linc; we just did what we were asked to do as part of the team.

A GRAND SENDOFF

We never found anyone alive. Not one. We didn't find Linc, but our brothers did. We had a couple of guys working with Rescue 2 that kept in touch with us, that lived out here in Long Island. He was found sometime in November of that year. We brought him home and put him to rest. We organized the funeral here. He lived in Sayville. Gave him a grand sendoff.

We couldn't stay out there for as long as those Rescue 2 guys did because we're paid by a different entity. So we had to go back to work. We wanted to stay. We wanted to stay until the whole thing was done. Unfortunately, finances wouldn't allow that. Gotta pay the mortgage. Also, my wife would kill me—nobody home to cook.

We were very sad and unhappy that he didn't make it, but we knew after a month. We didn't hear from him, we didn't see him. He wasn't around busting our chops as usual. In the middle of winter, Linc would walk up and from under the truck you'd see these skinny legs and say, "What do you want?" And he'd say, "Your best friend is here!" I still do that today when I go down to the firehouse. We were glad his body was found, but we were unhappy he was not with us anymore. We missed his comedy, his jokes. Every summer we had a duck dinner and we would cook, and Linc and I would be out there shucking clams and eating them with hot sauce and having a grand old time.

WORKING AS A TEAM

I actually went back down to Ground Zero afterwards, because at some point in time, I think in January, February, or March of the following year, being Second Assistant Chief of my fire department, I organized a move. They needed equipment, so I organized a move to donate our rescue truck to the cause, and the commissioners approved it. I said, "We have two rescue trucks." I said, "These guys down there need equipment very bad." Our rescue truck had lights on it, a generator, and everything.

We took the truck down to the Javits Center and we passed it on to a California Urban Search and Rescue team down there, Task Force One. We exchanged T-shirts, and they used our vehicle for quite a while down there, but I was pretty pleased and pretty impressed with the controls they had in place by then. You couldn't get in, the bridges were shut down. All access to the city was controlled, which was good, a lot different than when we went there and just walked on the scene and jumped on the Pile. But it was good for us that we weren't challenged. I don't think anybody would have challenged us anyway. We had our turnout gear on. We looked like we knew what we were doing, even though we had no idea where we were going.

There wasn't anger. They were there doing a job. Let's get this Pile down to a manageable point. Let's hurry up and get this Pile done, so we can find people. We had steelworkers there, we had ironworkers, and these were guys who just came in, volunteers. Urban search and rescue teams across the nation showed up a little at a time, but I think a lot of credit should be given to the guys, the metalworkers, guys who were on construction sites in the city, building a bridge or a building or digging a hole in the ground to put in a new drain or something. These guys came on the Pile with their heavy equipment and their lights and their skills and knowledge, and started picking up pieces of metal the size of trucks with their machines, moving them out of the way, so we could get into the holes, into the caverns, into the crevasses, and try to find people. It was organized chaos on the Pile, but we were getting the job done—we were making the Pile smaller. That was the job. That's how we find people, all working as a team.

On the Pile the communication was very good. We were shouting, but people talked to each other. One guy would shout, "Hold everything! I got a piece!" And you would hold everything because he thought he might have seen a body part or something humanoid, and everybody would stop and make sure it's not there. We were very meticulous. We were going through things with a fine-tooth comb. The same way they did over in, I believe it was Staten Island, when they went over to the Freshkills Landfill over there, going through stuff. After we went through it, they went through it again because we only did a quick go-through of stuff.

DEAD SILENT

Having to leave was difficult. I think the decision to go down and find Linc was not a difficult decision, but the difficulty remained with not finding him and the disappointment of searching and not finding anything or anybody. There were guys that were there after us and guys that were there before us, and they found people and found things. Our group, we never found anyone. That was difficult. We knew people were there, based on the numbers we heard about how many people were in the building and how many people they'd found so far. We knew there were people there, but we couldn't get to them. You didn't hear any screams. Every now and then, the Pile would stop. Everybody would be dead silent because someone thought they heard something. And it would stay dead silent for a minute or so to see if that sound would come back. A cry, a scream, a moan, a groan, something. It never happened. We kept going. We would spend a minute to listen, but we didn't hear a second groan, so we kept digging and mulling our way through the Pile.

It wasn't until later in the game, months after, that they brought in respirators. I mean, people donated a lot of stuff. There was no want for clothing, for warm gloves, or heavy equipment-type tools, but respiratory stuff came later. We were wearing these little dust masks, and wearing the dust masks gets very uncomfortable. SCBA [self-contained breathing apparatus] equipment, you can't wear that stuff for more than thirty minutes. The bottle is done. You don't have any more air. So you'd be going through a lot of bottles of air. The dust masks they gave us started to irritate us around the nose after a while because of the dust and the dirt. Water and grime gets into it and it just becomes unbearable, so you take it off. Do you have another one to put on? Maybe. If you don't, you keep working. This is what caused a lot of the problems today, where people just never wore them and breathed in a lot of the stuff.

We have goggles that we wear, too. Some guys had them on, some guys didn't, because again, over a short period of time these things work very well; over long periods, it's like having a contact in your eye, but it's not an extended-wear contact and you start to feel grainy, so you want to get it out. So most of the guys took them off completely.

SOMEONE WAS WATCHING US

At one point, you looked up and every piece of metal started to look the same, but you learn to distinguish the different areas by the way the building has collapsed. I'm not really religious. At one point in time there was a piece of metal that looked like a cross, and I said to my buddy, "That's inspirational. Let's go. Something's gotta be down here." And that piece of metal was on one of the sides of the building, and it's not important whether somebody put it there or whether it just showed up there. So that inspired us to keep going. Someone was watching us. Had to be.

9/11 made me more aware of our vulnerability in this world and how anybody can cross the border. We have to be ever-vigilant. We have to watch our guard and make sure it's up. Nobody is above suspicion, even the guy next door to you. I always looked at people and took people at face value. After 9/11, I think twice about my neighbor if he's a new guy moving in. I watch him cautiously. I don't profile people based on your class, your color, your religion, or your creed, because we're all in the same boat. There is everybody doing everything. It doesn't matter what nationality you are. 9/11 taught me to be more aware of people around me and my surroundings, and to protect my civil liberties and my freedoms, and to fight for them. 9/11 made me more aware of what's going on in the world, made me more cautious about terrorism and people trying to take our freedom of life and our liberties away from us. It made me a lot more cautious. Spiritually, though? I always believed in a supreme being of some kind.

I get a little emotional every now and then when I think of things, but physically, mentally, no. I don't have the nightmares that a lot of people do. I look at life a little bit different. Like I said, I was there doing a job. I think the people who have the nightmares might be the guys like the metalworkers, who were not used to seeing body parts and decapitations and blood and guts. They're just not used to seeing that. As firefighters and EMS workers, we see that. Fortunately for me, I don't think I have the physical disabilities that a lot of guys do. I do have some restrictions with my health that could be attributed to 9/11, but I don't know. I'll never know. Do I let it bother me? Not really. Life goes on.

IT'S IN THE BLOOD

Anybody who has ever done any emergency service work—it's in the blood. You're just not going to stop these people from responding. I think people are cut out to do certain things. Whatever life has in store for you. I'm a firm believer in fate. I think being a firefighter, being an emergency medical technician, being an emergency service worker, is a calling. You do it because you love it. You want to do it and you want to help people, and not because you get paid to do it.

A hero is someone who in someone else's eyes has done something great or fantastic. If you have kids, you are your kid's hero. They look up to you. They look for an example from you. I didn't do anything that any red-blooded American who wanted to help out wouldn't do. I'm not a hero. I think the guys out there in Afghanistan putting their lives on the line every day—I think those guys are heroes. What we did at 9/11, we did because we had to, because we were forced to by some group of people who felt like our way of life and our freedoms are different than theirs. We did what we had to do to defend our freedoms and I'll do it again. Except I'll be there the first hour it happens instead of a couple of days after.

Ever since I got back from 9/11, no one has ever asked me how it was. I had one dear friend of mine, her son asked if I had anything I could share with him, because he wrote me a letter saying he saw the devastation. Like I said, I had a piece of glass and I had a piece of the black fascia from the building. And a piece of marble. So I cut those three items in half and I shared it with him. He's the only kid that has ever asked me, "How did you feel? Why did you go? What was it like?" I think people forget. People don't remember what it was like. People don't remember the tragedy. People go on with their lives. It's human nature.

When our freedoms and our way of life are disturbed by foreign entities who see us differently from them, I'm not sure if it's envy or if it's just because we are different from them, but when they see these videos, I think maybe they'll realize that we are truly one nation under God, indivisible, with liberty and justice for all, that we are a very strong nation, and we will prevail even though they think their way is the right way. They will realize that as Americans, we are free. We earn that right; we are very strong, and we will fight for our freedoms.

CHAPTER 9

DIGGING WITH OUR HANDS

John is a retired captain with the New York City Fire Department. He was near the tail end of a thirty-four-year career when the planes hit on September 11th. John is grateful that he and his two sons (a firefighter and a police officer) survived the attacks; all were on duty that day. Although the rescue effort seemed futile, even in those early days, to this day he finds it hard to accept the fact that he never found a victim alive, or at least an intact body. Despite his dedication to the Bucket Brigade and the sacrifices he made for the sake of his devotion to his job as a NYC firefighter, John does not consider himself a hero; he rather loathes the term and modestly refers to himself and the other responders as "the cleanup men."

I WORKED IN FOUR OF THE FIVE BOROUGHS over my career. The only borough I didn't work in was Staten Island. I started out in the Bronx, in the late sixties. I'm retired now. I was diagnosed in 2007 with pulmonary fibrosis, from my work at the Trade Center. I had been retired since 2002.

It took me most of the day to get assigned to the Trade Center. I had to do a little dancing around. Most of the companies in outlying areas were just held. So I was calling the dispatcher every couple of minutes, trying to talk him into assigning me to the Trade Center. Finally, he said he could get me in as far as Long Island City. When we arrived there, there was a convoy of about twenty heavy rescue vehicles from Suffolk County and Nassau County.

At about four o'clock in the afternoon, we arrived. Coming over the Brooklyn Bridge, you couldn't see Lower Manhattan. You were riding from the light into darkness. There was so much dust still in the air at that time. It was almost unbreathable. We were using paper masks. But they clogged so fast you had to keep taking them off, go get another one. But I remember how dark it was. I was really surprised by how dark—how much dust was still in the air.

We arrived at Broadway, right by Pace University. The Fire Department doctors, Dr. Kelly and Dr. Prezant, were setting up a triage area in that location. When I spoke to Dr. Kelly, I asked her what she needed. She said, "Patients. Nobody's coming out." Then I knew that it was even worse than I had thought. I thought there would be some survivors, but there were very, very few from the collapses.

Then it was just a matter of getting on the Pile and digging. Before we left the firehouse, I made the guys grab every tool that we had. You know, crowbars, whatever. I was thinking it didn't matter what kind of a tool it was, we would take it with us in case we needed it. But quite frankly, most of the digging was done by hand. Everybody was on their hands and knees, digging. It's just that's the way it was, quite frankly, most efficient.

What we did was form lines. We had those ten-gallon buckets from Home Depot, the orange bucket. The guy at the front of the line would fill it up with the debris and the bucket would be passed, like an old fire bucket brigade. It got to the end and they just kept feeding buckets—one line, putting empty buckets back up the hill, and one line going down the hill, full buckets.

Between Tuesday and Friday, anybody that wanted to be on the Pile could be on the Pile. They just came in and started digging. Friday, everything was cordoned off. There were entry points and you had to show that you were supposed to be there. No more volunteers just walking in. We needed the construction workers. They were amazing. I remember at one point thinking to myself that these guys are all new immigrants, because they only spoke two terms: "What do you need?" and "You got it." Those are the only two things they ever said.

At one point, I had to move an engine company, the engine itself, down Broadway. The avenue was blocked with debris. A guy pulled up in a payloader, said, "What do you need?" I said, "I need to get down Broadway." He led me down Broadway, just pushing debris out of the way.

It was amazing how organized [the] chaos…was.

BECAUSE OF THAT DELAY

I arrived at four o'clock in the afternoon on the 11th. And I got off the Pile at about eleven-thirty on the 12th— eleven-thirty at night, on the 12th.

I had worked the night before; I was scheduled to work the day tour, nine hours. Then at six o'clock at night on the 11th, they instituted a twenty-four-hour on-duty and twenty-four-hour off-duty….

It just so happened that my group fell into the chart—the group that was starting at six o'clock. We didn't sleep. Thirty-something hours, we worked that first night. They kept a twenty-four-hour on, twenty-four-hour off, for approximately a week, maybe two. Then they went to a three-group system, where if you were in A group, you worked in a firehouse; and if you were in the B group, you worked on the Pile; and if you were in the C group, you were off. They just kept rotating that.

The end of October, they made it a thirty-day detail, where you were detailed to the Pile for thirty days, but you worked the regular chart: two nine-hour days, and you were off for forty-eight hours; and then you worked two fifteen-hour nights; then you were off for seventy-two hours.

I was exhausted, I'm sure. We all were. But it didn't register until you got home. When I got home, sometime after midnight, I had to be back ... the following six o'clock.

That first night I had managed to contact my wife, who had spoken to both my sons. One son was at the Trade Center. He had just arrived when the second building collapsed. And my other son, a police officer, was working in Brooklyn, and they kept him in Brooklyn, at the bridge, keeping traffic out and letting emergency vehicles in and whatnot. We were assured that they were safe, at least.

I knew my oldest son would be there because I had heard his company, on the radio, being assigned. Actually, he got lucky because his company was diverted while they were responding. The dispatchers asked them to stop at the Fire Academy, where Matt's service unit was, and pick up all the spare bottles.

Because of that delay, they weren't inside the buildings when they came down. So he was lucky.

WE KEPT FINDING SHOES

There was just so much to do, you really didn't have a lot of time to think about how bad it was. We knew from the beginning that there were going to be a lot of firefighters dead that day. Once that first building collapsed, there was no doubt about it.

In the three months that I was there, we found very, *very* few victims. We found pieces, but not bodies. I remember shoes—kept finding shoes with feet in them. You say, "Oh, well, there's a body here." You would dig and dig and dig and there would be nothing else. Just a shoe with a foot in it.

I couldn't understand why there wasn't the rest of the body. I mean, if the foot is here, there has to be something else...there wasn't. You would dig and dig and [there] simply wouldn't be anything.

After two days or so, you started going by smell, from decomposition. You would get in an area and you could smell it. That's where you would start digging. Someone uncovered a spinal column. Intact. But that's all. Nothing else. Everybody ran to that spot and started digging.... we're going to find some remains. But you didn't. It was just pieces. They were just thrown all over.

Whenever you found something, you had to call. Each side of the Trade Center had a chief in charge, a command post. You would call back to your command post. They would send out somebody with a GPS unit, so they can mark the location of the remains for a record. Then the remains would be bagged and carried offsite to the morgue.

To me, it was like a reward. You were doing something right. You found somebody's remains, whatever they were, and you were going to return those remains to their family. So you did get that sense of accomplishment. It's just that you didn't get it that often.

I worked a total of about eight years in a row in Manhattan and was very familiar with the Trade Center. I was there almost on a daily basis, when I worked. So I did know a lot of people. And also, back in about '83, I was an instructor at the Fire Academy, so I knew some of the people that died were students of mine.

SO MANY PEOPLE CAME TO HELP

You were dealing with dust, instability of the Pile itself, with shifting and whatnot. You were dealing with smoke from the fires. When you were finding remains, you were dealing with blood-borne pathogens. There was some danger in everything you did.

I can remember—oh, God, I don't know how long I had been on the Pile. I was really tired. This wasn't in the first couple of days. It was maybe, maybe in about four or five days. I was really, really tired, and I was passing a bucket. I was saying to myself as I passed the bucket, "When I give it to him, I'm going to get off the Pile. Go and rest." As I turned, I'm handing the bucket to Boomer Esiason, who was a football player; he had retired, and is now a sportscaster. But he was on the Pile. So now I couldn't go and rest. No way I was going to let Boomer see me leaving the Pile. So I went back to work.

There was *so* many people, from all over the country, that came in to help. All of the Red Cross workers, from every conceivable state in the union. I have a friend who is a podiatrist. He volunteered at Ground Zero for months at a time. You're walking in that debris, you're going to injure your feet. He was at St. Paul's Church, treating people's feet, and now suffers from a lung disease.

I have a collection of little teddy bears. Every time you really got looking really whipped, some young girl would walk up and give you a teddy bear. "Hey, here's a teddy bear." It would perk you up and you'd go back to work. So I have about eight teddy bears ... over my computer at home.

THE TRADE CENTER COUGH

I believe we used the paper masks at least two weeks. I would say we were well into the second week before we had a respirator. Then the respirator they issued us wasn't the right one. The canisters weren't right or something. The filters weren't proper. So they had to take those back and give you different respirators. But quite frankly, by the third or fourth day, what they call the Trade Center Cough had emerged. The Fire Department issued every member a steroid inhaler.

What they did was they set up staging areas in Shea Stadium. You would get on buses, and the buses would take us down to the site. You didn't even have to go and see a doctor. They knew you were going to get the cough. If you didn't have it yet, you were going to get it.

If I can see the air I'm breathing, I know it's not good for me. So we expected that there were going to be side effects. I don't know that I thought mine was going to be as bad as it turned out to be.

It got to the point where you really couldn't be on the Pile without a respirator, because the ironworkers and steelworkers were constantly cutting steel beams. The smoke was really bad.

WHO YOU GOING TO TALK TO?

For me, it seemed safer to be on the Pile or in the Pit digging than going to a funeral. I did attend a few, but not hardly as many as most other guys attended. I just—I knew it wasn't going to work for me psychologically.

My sons? No, we don't talk about it much. He saw what he saw and I saw what I saw. Talking about it's not going to change what you saw. Quite frankly, this is the first time I've talked about it to *anybody*.

It's not that it was so horrific. It's just that who you going to talk to about it? The people that you talk to about it, most don't understand. Not that they don't understand, but they can't relate to what it was.

I do a lot of work with John Feal and the FealGood Foundation, and the New York City Firefighters Brotherhood Foundation, Kenny Specht. If you're out at a fundraiser somebody might come over and ask you. The further we get away from 9/11, the less people remember.

I wouldn't go to a memorial that they're going to build at Ground Zero. I just can't go back there. I prefer to remember the hole in the ground that I climbed out of on that last day as it was.

THERE WEREN'T GOING TO BE ANY RESCUES

The hardest thing would have to be not being able to find a whole body. I have a friend whose son died there and he was identified through a tattoo.

You just worked so hard and didn't find enough people intact. You found a foot here, a foot there. A piece of flesh.

I knew that there were 343 firefighters and EMS personnel that were buried there. I wanted to bring them home, as many of them as I could. And we did. We managed to find some of them, not all of them. Unfortunately, there are still a lot who haven't been found. There are no remains at all.

ON HEROES

Quite frankly, don't like the term "hero." We didn't do anything heroic that day. We did our jobs. Those men that died, died doing their jobs—it was what they were trained to do. The people that came in afterwards certainly were no heroes. We didn't rescue anybody, we didn't save anybody. The people that were the heroes were the guys that were there first, those 343 people from the Fire Department that died, those police officers, the Port Authority police officers that died, they were the heroes.

We were just cleanup men. It was the right thing to do, not heroic. There's nothing heroic about doing the right thing.

If it happened again—I know I'd be on that Pile. I know I would. It's just ingrained after all those years of firefighting.

WHEN—NOT IF

The world was a terrible place before 9/11, and it hasn't changed since 9/11. We're always going to find an excuse to kill each other. So I always laugh. I'm sixty-six years old, and in every decade of my life, this country's been at war with someone. I'm not saying it's *our* fault. But man will always find an excuse to go to war.

I don't see any positives out of it. We're, what, nine years out and nothing's really changed. There's no major change that's going to prevent another 9/11. I think most of us just argue about when the next time we're going to get hit, not if.

We can blame it on religion, you can blame it on politics, you can blame it on whatever you want—whatever you want to hang your hat on. But they'll find an excuse. It's just human nature, for some reason. And people talk about Islamist extremism. And they're trying to kill us. And they're killing each other. I mean, Sunnis and Shiites don't get along.... They war with each other, different sects.

There are places in this country where doctors have to have armed bodyguards—because they perform abortions. Because somebody thinks, well, I can protect that life by taking a life. I'll go kill that doctor. So I don't—I don't see any great change in the world since 9/11. I don't think we've learned any great insight. I would like to think that the average person was more aware, but I don't think they are. I think the average person was enthralled with 9/11 until the Super Bowl came along. Then after that, the World Series whatever else could occupy their minds. I don't think that the world is any better or any worse before or after 9/11.

I would love to see those people that lost their lives that day remembered in some fashion. But I don't ever see society as a whole remembering them. We'll put up monuments, we'll build a memorial. The people that want to go see it will go see it, but most won't.

It would've been nice, on September 12th, had world leaders got together and said, "We can't have this anymore; we have to get peace, we have to get along." Well, it's a pipe dream. It wasn't going to happen.

Maybe that's the lesson I've learned—that I'm disillusioned. I don't have a lot of faith in mankind, let's put it that way. I see it from the charity work that we do, how hard it is to get people to come out, how hard it is to get even the bare minimum of media coverage. We go down to Washington and meet with the senators and congressmen and their aides, and you're totally amazed at how little support there is sometimes for 9/11 issues. If by doing that, they manage to help 9/11 survivors who are sick and hurting, that would be great. I think we can do that. I think we can garner enough support to get a bill passed. Hopefully. But again, history will tell.

CHAPTER 10

IRONWORKERS DESPERATELY NEEDED

John was a union ironworker with Local 36. Together with his crew of 60 union members, he was escorted to Ground Zero by members of the New York City Police Department the day after the collapse of the Towers. The role of ironworkers in the rescue effort can be overlooked, but John makes certain that what they did is documented. By moving huge sections of iron and blocks of concrete with their heavy equipment, emergency workers could look for people who, they hoped, were trapped in the rubble. He describes the World Trade Center recovery effort as "a disaster turned epidemic," because of the resulting illnesses that he and other fellow responders suffer. He laments the fact that he and his colleagues seemed to have been forgotten by the government leadership after not being warned about the toxic qualities of the air at Ground Zero. After 9/11, John became entrenched in the fight for health benefits and compensation for 9/11 workers, especially the union members.

WE WERE DOING THE RESTORATION PROJECT on the Marine Parkway Bridge, so our best avenue of approach would have been through the Midtown Tunnel. We were told that even though we offered to go in immediately and they needed ironworkers desperately, the City of New York Department of Engineering and their specialists had not validated or verified the structural integrity of all the bridges and tunnels going in and out of New York City. So we did not get there until the morning of September 12.

The first thing we did as ironworkers and the laborers and painters who were with us once we came out of the tunnel, some of us got down on the sidewalk and said a prayer because some of us had never been in a disaster that was apparently an act of war, or warlike in nature.

When you're at home and you hear the phone ring or the doorbell ring, what do you do? You answer it. When an ironworker hears a building collapses or a building is gonna go up, that's our work, so we respond to that like it's a doorbell. So we were adamant once we got the approval to be there and we got the escort; we weren't going to let the National Guard or the Reserves stop us from entering this site, and they were armed.

There were at least sixty, or maybe eighty of us. We had all our heavy equipment. No one else had a hydraulic lift. And on our flatbeds, which we use to deliver iron or road sections, we have a hydraulic loader or unloader called a Palfinger. And this rides on our trailer.

So I was one of the big mouths that told the Guard that we're going in there with or without your permission. We're going in there. They didn't give us a Police or Fire Department escort for us to come down here to do what we do best for you to stop us. So we just made believe that they weren't there.

It was total devastation on West Street. The road was totally impassable. There were crushed fire engines, there were ambulances. Later on, we found out that there was a police car under the wreckage. They say that the police officers were inside there. I didn't see that, but that's what we were told.

We backed up to the first obstruction in the road, and the operator, who is also the Teamster, put the outriggers out so you could stabilize the entire rig and swung the boom toward the crushed vehicle, which was a fire engine.

There was all kinds of debris on the top of it. We slung the front of the vehicle, knowing we're not going to pick the whole thing up. Picking up one section at a time, we were able to get it far enough to the side of the road. The manpower that was there prior to us, they were forming these huge lines, makeshift lines of moving bucket brigades, or moving buckets of debris from the site. We're looking at each other like there is a better way here. We got this equipment. This is what we do. Just let us in there to do this and we'll get it done.

And we did. We moved these enormous sections of iron that came from inside the Towers. Some of them still had these huge blocks of concrete attached. We were able to move that out of the way with our equipment the first day, then came the cherry pickers, because now we opened up an avenue of attack for all the emergency rescue and heavy equipment.

Once we proved ourselves, it was like we became heroes of the day. The only thing I can tell you that I and others had in our minds was that if it was us or our family member or a friend or just anybody being stuck in that Pile, they're not going to last long with these little fires going on here and there and these fire hoses soaking the area. They could wind up drowning; they could wind up burning. We could have a further collapse, another building could come down. So all you had in your mind was addressing that immediate spot you're at and removing the debris.

They saw how beneficial we were, and we were given carte blanche to go wherever we needed to go to get the job done. And that's what we did.

WE WERE MISLED

I blame nobody for not having the proper equipment there, up to that point, but I blame the government and the administration for misleading the population and utilizing certain detectors that did not show the eminent danger of the fallout. I blame them because they knew what, as Dr. Stephen Levin[5] said, "toxic mixture" or "toxic cocktail" that we ingested. For them to have Christine Todd Whitman, George Pataki, and Rudolph Giuliani, among friends of George Bush, who was our president, stand on that Pile and tell us the air was safe to breathe and the water was safe to drink, was a total misleading of the public. If it wasn't for operating engineers who provided respirators later on as the job continued, we would have suffered even worse breathing problems.

When you breathe, especially in a hot environment—I'm going to use the term "tropical" because it was warm—and with all the steam and smoke and everything else coming off the debris, the heat was immense in some locations, especially if you were downwind of this disaster, so when you're trying to breathe in this type of environment, what comes out of your mouth but perspiration.

The perspiration doesn't take long before it saturates this type of a fiber or particle mask. Once it becomes damp from your exhalation from this perspiration, there was so much particulate matter floating around that it would stick to the damp surface. You're constantly moving around, dust is always coming up, smoke is always hitting you in the face, and there's the smell of burning debris.

I witnessed gases, the color of gases that most people have no conception of what it was that was burning. I was told that because it was a green coloration it could have been the computer screens or the computer components. So you have all of this emission coming at you and it sticks to your mask, and it wasn't long before it was a weight and you couldn't breathe out of it, so most of the people would take these things off.

You're constantly talking to people next to you, you're receiving instructions, people telling you what to do. There were people from [a federal agency] down there, they wanted to find any of the debris from the planes that were left, so you're talking to them, you're talking to search and rescue people. You couldn't have something like that over your face.

I believe, and from what I saw and what I witnessed, there was only one group that had the right health equipment, and they were either the EPA or FBI or something of that nature. They had these Tyvek suits and a self-contained battery pack that provided power for breathing apparatus.

---

[5] Co-director of the World Trade Center Worker and Volunteer Medical Screening Program.

I GAVE OF MYSELF

I have a recollection of being there twenty-nine to thirty-two days, and that was starting on the morning of the 12th. We worked until they legitimately said the search and rescue effort was over. From what we were pulling out of that Pile, only one body I saw came out intact, and that was a fireman who was stuck in a stairway; everything else was bits and pieces. So after viewing this, after experiencing carrying what was left of a man's head or another man's torso, body parts, intestines, people's brain matter, you probably made the determination that nobody else was going to come out alive.

I guess I would like to have it known that I suffer from post-traumatic stress syndrome, and I went through a bout psychologically where I felt that I gave of myself, and unless you were there, you can't tell me that what I've been through. So I was very hesitant to think that anybody could experience these kinds of psychological feelings that I was getting.

I became abrasive to my children and I became verbally aggressive toward my wife. I pushed them out of my life. I was suffering from nightmares, the same nightmares over and over again. I was going to counselors. I went to F.E.G.S. [Health and Human Services System] for nightmare therapy. I had to replay them, and I had to make these nightmares work out with a good ending, instead of the ending that was giving me a nightmare.

I went to the State of the Union address after this, and the only thing that ex-president of ours George Bush was kind enough to mention at the State of the Union address was the reason why we were in Baghdad was because of the attack and devastation of the World Trade Center site.

Would I do it again? I'd do it tomorrow. I may not be healthy enough, but it's what I'm made of. When I spoke before Congress and Senate, and I've done it many times, I always ask them: What's the one thing that almost every responder had in common? And they still to this day can't answer the question.

The answer to the question is that the majority of us belonged to a union of some shape or form. What people don't understand is that it's thanks to the unions we have a five-day work week, a forty-hour week at that. We have holidays, vacation. This is all thanks to the union, but that's old hat. Let's forget about that. What do unions have today? Well, they provided 80 percent of your responder population.

What else do they do for us today? Well, wherever union presence is strong, they demand in their medical systems that they support, they demand occupational and environmental health counseling for members such as me.

Do I receive the proper care? Yes, and that's because of unions. I also want to say that I am nothing special, but you can hear in my voice that I have a breathing problem. I have been listed as having a 37 percent breathing loss through Mount Sinai with the ingestion that I made at the World Trade Center site. I was a long-distance runner in school. I have excelled in track, wrestling, I could play football, I was a gymnast, and for this you need proper lung capacity. I never had a pulmonary problem prior to 9/11. I've been through a lot of wakes and funerals to prove that people who suffered like me did pass.

Has my expectation of government changed as a result of 9/11? I grew up in a military family. My father was captain of Kings Point Merchant Marine Academy in Great Neck. My uncle Al, my mom's last surviving brother, served in nine campaigns under General George Patton. My entire family was involved in the military. I was raised not to question but jump to when you're given an order. I was taught never to question my government.

We saw parameters set by Pataki and Giuliani about allowing OSHA to run the job site at the World Trade Center site. We heard George Bush stand on the Pile and yell we will never forget, when yet in all honesty the first thing they did was forget about the financial and health responsibilities and obligations that the federal government had at the World Trade Center disaster.

I can't live with that. I can't live with a regimental way of life knowing that what I'm told is all right in one aspect but is not all right in another. I'm sorry. I was also told by my union that we're all equal and what's fair for one is fair for all. So no, I don't have a good taste in my mouth for government, even though the first person to come to the aid of the responders was in government; does anybody know who it was? A Republican by the name of Congressman Christopher Shays from Connecticut. Though a Republican, he had the heart to stand forward against the Bush administration, and he did the right thing. And then Vito Fossella followed up. So there is good and bad in all parties, but still I feel that because some don't want to cross party lines, they commit acts against the American public that I can't accept....

My family members gave everything for the freedoms that we have left that we were supposedly granted by our Constitution and Bill of Rights. We have a doctrine that provides you a life of no equal anywhere else on this planet. Don't be bullied, don't cower. Persist. Do what's best for you, and most of all your future generations, because you're the one who is obligated and responsible for your future generations. You're going to be bringing them here to life. I'm trying to do the best for mine.

CHAPTER 11

CUTTING AND TORCHING

Demetrius, a young sheet metal worker, witnessed the second plane hit the World Trade Center from an Upper Manhattan rooftop on September 11th and immediately headed home to Long Island to check on his family. Being a certified welder, he knew he could help, so he volunteered to return to the Pile to search for survivors. However, he tells us that what he had found was utter devastation. He is angry at the fact that he was allowed to work on the Pile with no equipment to protect him from the harmful dust and fumes. He sadly informs us that he himself discovered six bodies, all of them dead. He admits that the reality of what he saw remains with him to this day. He frankly describes the danger of the elements and the interdependence of the workers (firefighters, police, and tradesmen like himself). He is still amazed at the generosity and kindness of the community that sustained him and the other responders.

I WAS WORKING UP ON 100TH AND AMSTERDAM or Broadway at the time. The project we were working on was a bus terminal. I think it was like seventy floors. At that time, I was working for a company called AC Associates. We were putting all the metal deck on top of the steel on the roof of the building. We were just about to take a coffee break, and someone said there's a plane crashed into the World Trade Center. When the guy said that, people were yelling and then they were all coming up to the roof to try to get a visual. We had binoculars on the roof. I said, let me get the binoculars. We were just in awe. We had a clear view downtown and you could see everything.

While we were watching, I remembered seeing this second plane come around. We seen it and we're like, "Where is that going? Why is there another plane so close? What's going on?" As we watched with the binoculars and a clear view, we watched the second plane go right into the World Trade Center.

LET'S TRY TO GET HOME

Recognizing that a terrorist attack was taking place, Demetrius decided to get out of the city. The subway wasn't working, so they walked from 100th Street to the 59th Street Bridge to walk into Queens.

It took probably six hours to get home. I took the L.I.E. and I'll never forget that day, just watching all the fire trucks and the ambulances and rescue vehicles going westbound. I was wondering where they were going and what were they going to do. What's there? What's happening? How bad is it? I was relieved to see that they were going in instead of staying out there, because there wasn't really anything happening out in Long Island, which was a relief.

About five o'clock that night I think we got in. My wife was there with my children. They were relieved that I finally made it home because I was trying to contact them, and at points of the day we had no reception on the phones. But they were panicking because they were worried about the schools. Everybody was screaming that they were trying to blow up schools in Long Island. There were dirty bombs out on the Island. It was all hearsay.

I just sat by the TV and I made phone calls. A lot of friends were on the Fire and Police Departments. A lot of them were already in the city. Just talking to family members, their wives, or girlfriends to find out where they were and what they were doing, trying to find out if I knew anybody who was down there at the time. But it was crazy, trying to find out who was where, and where to help anybody was my next step. I told my wife I wanted to go back that night. She said, "You can't go. Just stay here and let's find out what's going on." As I made phone calls, I found out where we could go the next day, where we could help.

THIS IS SOMETHING I WANT TO DO

The next day, I called the guys and said, "Are you going into work?" And they said, "Yeah, we're going in to do work." I said, "I heard the jobs were shut down." All the city jobs were shut down because they needed everybody who can work with construction tools. I'm a certified welder. Back then, I was certified for torch welding. I did all that stuff before I got into the union. They said, "They are looking for torchers and guys who can weld." So that's what we did. I went into the job site that day. I drove in. It was closed, but they let us come in and get the equipment we needed.

We went to the 59th Street Armory, or 65th Street, to sign in and then be told where we could go downtown. We had six of our guys from AC Associates, but three of us went down. It was on a volunteer basis. I went with a fellow named John and a gentleman called Paul. Paul was a Vietnam veteran—older man—at the time, I think he was fifty-five years old. I said, "You guys don't have to go. This is something I want to do, something I want to help with." They said, "Well, if you go, we go." I said, "John, you got the kids," and all this. He said, "No, I'm not gonna let you guys go alone." Unfortunately, some of the other gentlemen didn't feel that way and they stayed. And I understand that.

The armory when we arrived—I felt like I was voting. It was odd. They had all these different stations. It was hectic. No one really knew where to go or what to do. Standing on line, people were getting real antsy because they wanted to go down and help, but it was more "fill out this form and fill out that form; we don't know where to send you yet." Meanwhile, we felt like we could be more helpful if we were on the job site instead of just sitting there. We were there for about two hours before we were able to move. Once we had our badges, we went down there in our truck. But they was just picking up guys and throwing them in buses. City buses, yellow buses: everything was there and they were just bringing us down. We were escorted down by a police escort.

I was expecting to see the worst—definitely something I'd never seen in my life, something you would see in the movies and you'd say, "Wow, can you imagine that really happening?" I was nervous, very nervous. I had told my family I was going down there, and my wife was very scared. She said I'm not the one for blood, guts, and gore. I said, "I really want to do this. I feel like I'm needed there." My main motivation was to see if we could help recover people alive. I wasn't even thinking about finding people that had passed away. I had heard that there was people trapped, firemen trapped.

WHEN WE GOT DOWN THERE

When we got down there, we were seeing a lot of dejected faces coming back—people that were there all night, just worn down, covered in the white substance and looking beaten up. There was a lot of smoke in the air at that time. There was still pockets of fires in the area. We were seeing parts of the engine. Matter of fact, I seen on Varick the engine and some of the pieces of the plane. As we got closer, just smelling and seeing the destroyed vehicles as they were pulling them out. They just started taking all the fire trucks and police cars and everything that was in that area, pulling them down the block so they could get more personnel in.

We parked the truck, and the entrance I first went in on was over by where Century 21 is now—the clothing store. I guess it's called the Millenium Hotel. So I went in that area. I wanted to go somewhere I felt I could help a little more. I'm not going to be on the Bucket Brigade. I started talking to some firemen and asked them where could they use more guys who could cut steel.

I remember in the beginning hearing the horns about every hour, every maybe two hours. I didn't know the reason why the horn was blowing, just that when they started hitting the horns, people started running. So the horn meant to evacuate the area. They would blast these horns because they were supposedly worried about the Millenium Hotel coming down. Then there was the building that was brought down that had all the problems with the firemen that got hurt. They were worried about both the buildings collapsing at the time. You just try to run off the Pile and find somewhere to hide. I was about seventy-five feet from hitting the street the first time we ever heard the horn, and that was chaos because guys were getting trampled, guys were getting hurt. The gentlemen I went down with was a fireman. His son got severely cut across his leg running off the Pile. Tripped, fell, and a piece of steel just ripped his whole leg wide open. Watching guys getting impaled on steel rods when they fell, that was an issue.

I did it once and then we went back the second time. I was with a couple of firemen and they said, "We don't move. We'll wait until I get the call from someone else telling us really that that building is coming down." Because they were watching everybody run so crazy. Unfortunately, a lot of people got hurt for no reason. It was very intense, and the first five or six hours, not knowing what was going to happen above you, on the side of you, the holes and pockets as we started going into the Pile. Every time we got set up, we felt like either they were pulling us off the Pile or they were trying to detour us to a different area. There were so many things going on at the time that I didn't know about. There was supposedly money underneath the piles they were looking at. There were some areas they didn't want touched, so they wanted to clear people out—fires in some areas or something they found underneath and they were worried about guys being near. So we were moved around a lot in the beginning.

I wound up talking to a lot of the firemen. Their brothers or sisters were a part of the Fire Department or worked in there. They were looking for their comrades and family members. I was trying to tell them who I knew growing up in the Fire Department in Long Island and in my neighborhood, trying to talk and get to know the people around you because where we were going—into that crater—was dangerous. It was deep, dangerous, and it was on fire. Just trying to get to know the guy around you as quick as possible, so you could have a little trust. Especially if you wanted to be able to say, "If something happens, I'm there for you, you're there for me." We help each other.

CUTTING THE BEAMS

We had dust masks going in—that was it. We had five-foot flames shooting in this one area. As we were cutting, there were respirators running out. It was hot that day, trying to cut, weld, and torch. Then you would have a fire next to you, and they would put it out next to us. We had firemen bodies underneath us, so they wanted to preserve the area. When we were cutting the beams out near them, they were worried about the bodies. So we gingerly cut some areas out, work on it. Fire would shoot up on us and they would put it out. So much was underneath us burning and just coming up in our faces the whole time.

Cutting the steel beams was a lot of work. It was heavy and we were cutting them in small pieces so we could pull out and just try to get down lower and lower. The torch was small. They had lines just running so far—thousands of feet of lines running everywhere. Then you would be in a groove and you cut and all of a sudden, someone would drop something and it would cut a line. Now you're worried about the lines, worried about it blowing up and going into the big cases they had in the street. So they would flip—put in that area and evacuate or shut the lines down and get new lines put back up. At times we had no water to put out the fire that was shooting up underneath us. They would get better pressure and come back in again.

I felt I was prepared to do what I had to do in those days I was there. It was emotional, what I was doing and finding what I was finding. The hardest part for me was that I felt unsatisfied that we didn't find anybody alive. Everybody we dealt with was passed away. I wanted to find somebody...they kept saying all these people were alive underneath. Then you would hear guys cheering. They thought they had found somebody and they thought they heard somebody at the times we were there. It didn't happen. The hopes of finding and doing my job made me stay.

One of the things that bothered me in the beginning is that you go there and you're working. I remembered seeing guys standing there taking pictures of everything. And I'm like, what's there to take pictures of? A disaster? Carnage? People that are mangled? That was wrong for me, and I'm looking at guys, asking, "What are you taking a picture of a person that has passed away on the floor for?" Guys picking up things—that bothered me. Guys were cutting steel and taking it. The other thing that bothered me is guys just standing around talking like it was a meeting, at one point not doing anything. Some guys were hearing about the free things that the Red Cross was giving out—taking souvenirs. Hearing about all the looting—that was out of control to me. I said, how can people do that? Unfortunately, I had to see it firsthand—people taking valuables from people they were finding. I don't know how they could do it. To me, that was my low point of everything. I didn't really want to take anything, see anything. I mean, to me, it was a disaster. What am I going to save? I understand people wanted something to remember that by. To me, I'll always remember what I did and what happened—something you can't forget. I didn't need a piece of steel to remind me. I was down there.

I was down there for three straight twelve-hour days. After that one of my bosses said, "Listen, I'm glad you guys went down there, I'm glad you helped out, but we have a job to take care of, so you got to get back to work." There were people out of work that were going to go and work and help out. He said, "You can go work for them or you can stay with your job. What do you want to do? I have no problem; you just tell me what you want to do." He knew I was really into helping out there. By the third day, they were saying they were not going to find anyone. So I went back to work eventually after that.

PEOPLE KNEW I WENT DOWN THERE

As far as my family goes, my wife was more worried about something happening to me there. My daughters were fine, my son was fine with it. Just be careful. You're doing something positive. They felt proud. They know I'm not used to being around disasters and they always thought I was squeamish. They wound up having a party for me for helping out. They wanted to show their support of us. So that was nice of them.

There was community support, too, but I wasn't a part of that. I stayed to myself after that. My biggest thing was just doing what I could do for those three days. I wasn't trying to take anything from anybody or just let anybody know I was out there doing anything. I was very low key about it. People knew I went down there. They had seen it and, unfortunately—well, I don't know if it's unfortunate—but I wound up being on Channel 5 News, a live interview at 5:30. So that put us out there because everybody had seen us on TV.

I honestly think that right there is the high point of the three days I was there. To walk down Manhattan, get interviewed by Mike Sheehan. The guys didn't want to be interviewed at all. They were like, "No, no, no." I'm like, "Get over here," and they were like, "No." I said, "Come on guys; we'd do this together, we go together." He asked us who we were, basically, what do you guys for a living, who are you with, what union. I was very happy. Very nice gentleman. He asked us some cool questions: Where were you? Where were you working? How long have you been here? So we told him we were down there for twelve hours. I think that was our second day they were there.

When we were done with that interview, we didn't even go down a block before people started coming up to us saying, "I just seen you on TV." Oh my God, and hugging us—strangers just hugging us. "Can I buy you something to drink?" "Are you thirsty?" We were very dirty with all the stuff we had on. The first day we went down, you see the people look beat up after twelve hours of doing what we were doing. We were shocked, but to get that hug, that kiss, that handshake, that praise, made it for them. I honestly can remember them saying, "Oh my God, I'll never forget this day."

Going back to the job, I remembered each day we had to report to that job up on 100th Street. I remembered going back the second day, and one of the guys that works in the union of mine walked up to me and handed me two pictures. And he says, "I'm missing my sisters, my wife's sister, and a cousin of mine," I believe it was. He said, "Here's pictures of them. If you happen to come across them, please—here's my number. Tell me if you see anything." I said, "You can come down." He says, "I can't." I said, "What do you mean, you can't?" He said, "No, I'm not allowed to leave. My boss won't let me leave." So I went into the boss's office and said to him, "What's going on? Why would you do that?" He said, "No, we're not going to go down. My guys are either going to work or they can go home." I was very upset about that because I felt like some guys didn't want to help out. To see a guy cry and say, "If you see these people, please call me up. If you hear anything, please call me." I took the pictures and I went down. I never seen anything they were looking for.

THINGS HAPPENED THAT WE COULDN'T CONTROL

Being down there opened my eyes to how much people out there and on the other side of the world really don't like Americans. So as far as seeing somebody wanting to come into our homeland and hurt us and kill hundreds and thousands of people if they can, to me it's mind-boggling—that there's hatred for us and that they would want to hurt so many people that way. That bothers me a lot.

Since 9/11, my opinion on the government is not good. That's something I'll keep, especially with my son going in to the Army right now. I praise him for that. I really do. He's always wanted to do that since he was twelve years old. Me, personally, I believe that everybody in America, as a young adult, should contribute to the services: two years, three years that program would be—like they do in Europe. But then, after that, to go in to fight in Afghanistan and Iraq, to me is a problem. I don't have a military background, but my father was in the military, my grandfather was in the military, plenty of friends were in the military.

My thing was, the way I grew up is helping out. If you see someone down, you help them out, and I guess that's why I ran down there on 9/11—to help out. I just want to help, and if I can help somebody else find somebody else, or get whatever we need to get done, to clean up, or whatever we could do. Whatever we could do for them.

Still to this day, I wouldn't change my mind on going back. Unfortunately things happened that we couldn't control as far as healthwise, but I wouldn't change anything. I would definitely respond. But I'd do it differently. I wouldn't go down there without a mask or respirator. After the first three days I heard they started getting what they needed. I mean, it was a disaster; I understand that. It would've been nice if it was there. It would have helped a lot of people out. If you look at it now, I guess FEMA and everybody else had everything, all the supplies. We were able to bring our torches, our gear, and everything we needed. Whatever they needed they got.

Walking around in the street when I got down there, I took a break watching guys walk around with SCBA packs, masks, and everything. I'm saying to them, "Are you working on the Pile?" They're like, "No." And I asked, "Why do you have an SCBA pack? Why do you have that?" They were like, "'Cause they were there." I said, "Well, you should be up there for guys who need it because you're not near the flames; you're not near the smoke. You're down here." Lo and behold, they knew something better then we knew.

NO MOMENT OF SILENCE
Now that it's all over, I wish it was a national holiday. I think that's a day we should all take off. I had gone and moved to Florida a couple of years after 9/11, and my thing is when the 9/11 anniversary came up each year, I felt that a lot of people outside of New York forgot what really went on. I would ask my daughter, "Are they doing anything in the school?" She said, "No." I said, "No moment of silence?" "No." "No talking about the event? Anything to do with 9/11?" "No." I had a problem with that.

Where I worked at the time, I said, "Fellas, are you going to do anything for 9/11? Are you going to stop work, take a moment of silence?" They said, "For what?" And I asked, "What do you mean for what?" They said, "It doesn't affect us." And I said, "Well, it affects me, fellas." They said, "Oh yeah, you're from New York." I said to them, "I don't know about you, but from 8:15 till 9:15 I'm going to sit back and I'm going to relax. When both Towers went down, I'm going to have a moment of silence." I said, "I hope we don't have a problem here, because I'm going to do what I feel is right. You guys down south don't care about what really went on up north. It doesn't pertain to you, but I'm going to do it." I just started working with these people, so I was trying to do it cordially.

I went to my daughters' school and talked to the principals. I said, "I'm hoping next year when 9/11 comes, you can have a moment of silence or you can educate these kids down here that aren't a part of it. My daughters were a part of it and they seem to gather plenty of other kids from up north who were a part, especially New York City or the area." The principals were like, "Yes, we're sorry. We didn't know. We haven't had a lot of people from up north." So they put it down in their curriculum: moment of silence. Add a little thing. They asked the kids if they knew anybody, because it wound up being a lot of firemen from New York wanting to move in that area.

TO SEE ALL OF US BOND TOGETHER

Out of the three days I was there, we took out a total of eight bodies. I found six myself. So to deal with the guys and deal with the situations that we found in front of us—being a regular woman, a businessman in a suit, fireman, etc., that we took out. All of us staying together, crying. Watching the guys who knew somebody or found someone. Watching family members on the Fire Department come in. To see it all shut down in front of me. To stop work in an area because they found a fireman.

I understand the firemen. After the first World Trade Center bombing, we worked in a building joining the World Trade Center, and I happened to make friends with people in the firehouse right across the street from the World Trade Center. I believe almost all the guys in that firehouse disappeared. I just wished they gave everybody the same respect as far as the man or woman we found. The firemen had their own way of taking out a body. We would cut and they would say stop and they would bring them in. To sit there and cry with the gentlemen, hold hands and all of this prayer when they found someone they knew. That was important to see all of us bond together.

CHAPTER 12

THE RESCUE DOGS

The son of a former New York City police officer, Thomas has worked for the Suffolk County Police Department for over twenty-one years, and has been a K-9 (canine) handler for the department for more than sixteen. The day after the World Trade Center attack, search and rescue dogs were brought in from all over the country to help in the rescue effort. Thomas reveals the challenges these dogs faced and the deflation of their spirits— paralleling those of their handlers—at finding only remains. Consequently, the dog handlers asked some volunteers from the workers on the Pile to allow themselves to be buried and let the dogs find them. The dogs did, and this game cheered the dogs and the responders immediately. Thomas's dog became depressed and had to stop work after only three days.

THE PRIMARY PURPOSE OF THE BOMB DOG is to locate the device before the explosion, but they're all trained to track, locate, even do building searches if people were hiding or in a building somewhere. Our primary goal was to get to New York City and help locate trapped victims, but on the date of the 11th itself, we couldn't do much of anything to help. The fires on the first day were too intense for dogs. New York City called us and told us they couldn't even get their dogs in there. It's too hot. It was too dangerous. So those of us with police dogs could only do the bomb detection work.

THE COMMAND TO SEEK

On the morning of the 12th, the other half of the unit that had not gone to stage at Floyd Bennett Field now responded to where the city Police Department had set up a command post on Chambers Street at a high school—I think it was Stuyvesant High School. We responded there—all of us in the K-9 unit. They would pair us up with groups of city police officers or city firefighters that were going out to search on the Pile.

It was somewhat organized chaos downtown. I guess people were trying to take charge of the situation, but it was a hell of a situation to try to take charge of. A lot of the people who take charge of these situations had already been killed. The city Fire Department command post had been crushed, so we knew a lot of their chiefs who would deal with this type of thing weren't there. So it took a little while, but they did an outstanding job in a short amount of time. Every day, you could see when you went back it got more and more secure. They started keeping the public out because the first couple days, it seemed like everybody and anybody could just walk through there, but then as the city police took control of everything, the perimeter got bigger and you started to need identification cards. Only uniformed police and fire and construction workers were identified with ID cards, and it became more of a secure site.

To allow the dogs to rest, another K-9 handler would leave his dog in the car and would accompany me with my dog. He'd bring a couple of tools—a shovel, a pry bar, whatever—and a body bag. He would follow me. Or when my dog needed to rest, I would put my dog in the car with the air-conditioning on and then I would follow him with his dog. We would just give the dog the command to seek, and the dog would sniff around, and anything they indicated we would pick up and put in the body bag.

Whatever group you went out with, they would be replaced by another group. So let's say I went out with the city firefighters for, I guess, maybe three or four hours. Then a group of New York City police officers, or even Suffolk County's emergency service or Nassau County's emergency service would come in and begin where they left off. And then those fellas would get a break. Not that you're exhausted after four hours, but the heat on top of that was so intense, especially for them in their fire gear. There were certain spots, especially on the first couple days, where flames were coming up from the debris. So it was very hot, so you would be really drained just by that, so [after] three to four hours you really had to get out of there. I just wore my regular police uniform and I was melting. You were a puddle out there.

Same thing with the dogs. They would heat up even quicker. By the third or fourth day, people had donated boots, but by that point, my dog's feet were all blistered. Nothing could be done about it. Blisters on his feet and the work still had to get done. They weren't used to wearing them, so we tried duct-taping them on so they wouldn't be able to yank them off. Suffolk County Society for the Prevention of Cruelty to Animals [SCSPCA] brought in a mobile hospital, and by the second or third day when you came out, they'd actually give your dog an IV because they were really getting drained out there. They would examine every dog that came off the debris pile. They would examine them and give them intravenous fluids, and it made a big difference.

When we located the body of a firefighter or a police officer, everybody in that area would stop. We didn't have the same radio frequencies as the city, but one of the city firemen or police officers that had the right radio would say, "We found a firefighter's body. We're gonna line up." If it was a firefighter, we'd get a group of firemen to remove the remains and we would all stand at attention. We'd actually form a chain. Once they would remove the body that was found, we'd go back to what we were doing.

FOCUSING ON THE TASK AT HAND

I didn't really hear anyone discussing their feelings of the events. We were busy, and that's what kept our feet on the ground. We were just so busy, and when we got a break, you tried to close your eyes for a few minutes, but nobody really did. When we got out there, safety was a priority. There was always a concern of something else falling, so you had to be alert, and there really wasn't much discussion other than the task at hand.

By the next day or two they had published the names of police officers and firefighters that were killed, and one of the police officers that was killed was in the Academy with me in 1985—in the city Police Academy. Another was a friend that grew up in Deer Park. He lived a few blocks away from me.

Well, maybe the third day I'm there, I'm on the steps of one of the stores right across from the Trade Center waiting to go out to begin another search session, and up comes this fellow who I thought was dead. He said, "There are two of us." Two of them in the same unit with the same name. I said, "I thought you were dead." [He said,] "I know. A lot of people did." Just to run into him, I thought that was pretty strange. I think he thought it was just as odd to run into me. That was a nice relief. I got on my cell phone to call my father because he knew the family.

[My father] took a great interest in all that was going on there. He was born and raised in New York City, in Queens, so he had a lot of strong feelings about it all. If I called anyone on the cell phone during the breaks, I would call him because I could tell him. I didn't have to worry about upsetting him. I didn't want to upset my wife or my son. It was a nice, calming thing to be able to talk to him.

Now we have all kinds of equipment should something similar happen, but we only had some equipment on September 10th. One of the guys in our unit actually had to go to LIPA [Long Island Power Authority] because we didn't have hardhats. LIPA graciously gave us 15 hardhats. We went to the one LIPA office out here and just asked, "Can you help us?" Somebody got a box of work gloves, but that's about all we had. And when I left at the end of my twelve-hour shift, I would give my LIPA hardhat to another guy because we just didn't have the equipment then. By the third or fourth day, people were making donations, and they would come around and offer paper [air] filters. Somebody must have donated socks, too, because our feet were killing us and we were standing in puddles or whatever. People were smart enough to come around and give you a dry pair of socks, which made a big difference.

They set up an air horn system when they thought that maybe one of the adjoining buildings was going to come down. When we went out, they told us, "When you hear that, run." On the first day it went off. I was so far out on the Pile. Everybody ran. They were moving quickly, but the dog couldn't leap from spot to spot. Dogs are faster on grass and dirt. I actually got to a point where it was just sheet metal, and I had to run up the sheet metal. I could have done it, but there's no way the dog was running up sheet metal. A fireman turned around and saw my predicament and just said, "Throw me the dog." It's a big German Shepherd and I give him credit. I don't know if I would have been so willing to help, but that's what I ended up doing. I actually picked the dog up as much as I could and threw it up to him. He grabbed the collar and we were able to get out. Nothing fell at that particular time, but I guess they were watching the adjoining buildings, and if they swayed or something, you were told to clear the Pile.

After our shifts, we'd go home, maybe hose the dogs off 'cause they were covered with all kinds of nasty stuff. The dogs work with one person and then come home with us. We also bring the police car home because it's designed with no back seat, a special containment unit for the dog to be transported.

My wife was a police officer. She's now retired. She knew exactly what was going on, so they actually made it very easy for me. I'd come home, they didn't ask too many questions. They knew I just wanted to get some sleep and go back. I'd wake up, she'd have some food ready, she'd make sure the dog was taken care of. They were supportive, but I didn't want to tell them everything that transpired in there. Especially my son at that time. He was only six. I told her, "Don't let him watch TV." She told him Daddy's in there helping at the Trade Center with a lot of other police and firemen, and he was watching the news and it was a replay. Six-year-olds don't know that it's a replay, so he watches this and thinks I'm in there. That was a little traumatic for him, but she did a good job explaining that it happened, that's why he's there. But when he first saw it she said he was hysterical. I think he slept with me every day. If I went into bed and fell asleep, he would just climb in there, and I'd get up and shower and be gone before he woke up the next day.

We would switch shifts, though. The twelve-hour shifts could be eight at night to eight in the morning, or vice versa. You didn't go everyday, and it wasn't so much for us. We would have gone every day. We just wanted to be in there and try to help, but the dogs couldn't do that. They couldn't work twelve hours every single day. So I went the 12th, 13th, and 14th, but then the sergeant decided my dog couldn't work another day. I thought he was depressed. If a dog could look sad, they did. They sense, our dogs are exposed to a lot as police dogs: They see blood, they see death, they see injuries. No one outside of the military has seen something like this. We didn't find an intact body. They're animals, but I think they had some idea of what was going on. The saddest dog you ever saw. That dog is no longer alive. He was eight or nine at that time, and he retired in 2002. When the dog retires, the County offers it to the family that he worked with, and everyone always takes the dog. So he lived as our pet for three years before he just died of natural causes.

So I was there for the first two weeks. At the end of two weeks, New York City really didn't need our help any more. It was no longer a search and rescue. It was a recovery operation. So at the end of two weeks, all the outside agencies were thanked and returned.

THE COMMUNITY CAME TOGETHER

We didn't save anybody, but we brought closure for a lot of people [by] finding the remains of their loved ones. We knew after a week we weren't going to find anybody, but if it were me, I'd like to have a funeral for my loved one. That's the most we could do for people, and that's what we did.

I was really thrilled to see the way the community came together. The whole country, really. Watching the news, you saw it, but firsthand I got to see it. There were people on the overpass cheering all the way into New York City, just because we were going in there to help. Offers to my family from people in my community calling my wife, saying, "You need anything? Make you dinner?" I thought that was great.

Appreciate your life, your friends and your neighbors, 'cause they could leave for work one morning and you'll never see them again. It sounds dramatic, but no one thought that morning that this was going to happen. It happened to almost 2,800 people that day.

I was very proud of the response by what we consider our first responders, the police, the fire. When I left the New York City Transit Police Department and came to Suffolk, I never thought there'd be an incident where the New York City police or fire needed help from anybody. They are always regarded as the pinnacle of law enforcement and fire departments. And this left them needing help. I'm proud I had the chance to go in there and help them.

CHAPTER 13

IT WAS THE BEST SUNRISE

*Richard, a member of the Nassau County Police Department's Emergency
Service Unit, arrived at Ground Zero soon after the collapse. Richard
soon became part of the rescue team, digging Port Authority Officer John
McLoughlin out of the rubble. This rescue was arduous and complicated,
and the extrication tools were too large for the confined space. Richard,
focused and calm, spent three hours himself digging with whatever tool he
could find. The risk to his own life is not a part of this testimony; his concern,
it seems, then and now, was about the mission: to extricate John alive.*

WITH THE WORLD TRADE CENTER, we were involved
because we do confined-space rescue. Prior to me being
employed by Nassau County, I was a New York City
police officer for twelve years, where I was also assigned
to Emergency Services. I was born and raised on Long Island. I'm married
and I have two sons. My oldest son is currently in the U.S. Marine Corps,
and my younger son goes to SUNY Maritime College. I've been a police
officer for twenty-nine years.

I just got up that morning and turned on the news. The first thing I saw
was the first plane hitting the first Tower, and immediately after that the
second plane. My brother at the time was a New York City police officer
also assigned to the Emergency Service Unit. He evidently was watching
the news also, and called me and said, "You see what happened? I might
get called into work." He had his kids so I said, "Well, drop the kids off
here." I said, "If I get called in we'll make arrangements," and that's what
happened. So he evidently responded in to the World Trade Center site,
and I was called a little later on.

Obviously, when you see one plane, you think it's an accident, but the
second plane, you know it's not an accident. But who would ever think that
we would get hit in New York City, hit the World Trade Center like that? You
always think of a bombing or something like that; you don't think of planes

going into buildings. I knew many of the guys who were there that day. A good buddy of mine died in Tower 2, Ronnie Kloepher. I worked with all those guys because I was in their unit, and we worked side by side with each other all the time. Ronnie was a high school buddy of mine.

I saw in the news the guys I knew getting dragged out from under rubble. Obviously, it's emotional seeing people you don't know, but when you see co-workers you used to work with, experiencing that, it gets emotional. My nephew and niece at the time were in early elementary school, I guess first or second grade. You don't really explain to them what's going on. As usual, you say Daddy's got to go to work, and that's it, and I was off and doing my thing too. My wife eventually came home—I called her, I said you have to come home—and she came home and watched all of them, and off I went.

AMAZED BY WHAT WE SAW

Our building is in Bellmore, in Nassau County, so my unit mobilized there, and got all our equipment together and our vehicles, and sometime around noon we were deployed. Highway cars gave us an escort to Floyd Bennett Field, which was the main base for the New York City Emergency Service Unit. The Suffolk County Police Emergency Service Unit also responded with us, and we basically staged there for quite some time until they were ready to use us.

Walking up to the site, we had to carry everything. So we're carrying extrication tools—a big Jaws of Life type of tool—[and] grabbing carts that were pulled out of buildings and stuff to put the equipment in and push them like shopping carts. Carts that janitors would use to put equipment in, because the vehicles couldn't get through because all the fire hoses that were stretched, vehicles were blocking the street, and the soot that was in the street was approximately five inches deep from the dust from the building, which went [on] for blocks. Everything was coated with it.

We all got there, and they asked us to go to a certain area and start doing a search and rescue, so we went to that area, but when you first get there we all just stood back and in amazement just looked at the mass debris pile. For about five minutes we just stood there. Probably with our mouths wide open and our eyes wide open. We were amazed by what we saw and we just looked at each other and said let's get to work.

Obviously, number one, doing the job I do, is to see if you can find anybody to save them, and—unfortunately for the people who are deceased—to recover their bodies. But also a more motivating factor for me was knowing that thirteen of the guys that I worked with prior were missing, one being my good friend Ronnie. That was my motivation to really keep going.

I was with my partner and two other guys I worked with, and we were walking on the steel and amongst the broken concrete, seeing what we could find, if we could find anybody....basically working, crawling through that stuff, climbing over it, working by flashlights. Just trying to find a limb, listen to a sound, somebody yelling, whatever to try to find somebody. There was a rescue operation going on that my brother had told me about. They had a guy trapped, they were trying to extricate him, and they were all taking turns. It was going on for quite some time. I was able to personally get involved in that rescue, and there came a time when I actually did go into the debris pile to do the rescue.

On the side of the debris pile it was like a cave. The opening started out at about five feet high, and it went in approximately 20 feet. As it went in, it got a little smaller so you had to crouch down, and then to the left it dropped off about another six feet, and then there was a little area where three adults would be able to stage. To the right of that was an opening in the elevator shaft, and to the left was where the actual operation was, which I later learned was a Port Authority police sergeant, John McLoughlin.

TRAPPED

There were still active fires going on down there around us. Firefighters were basically misting the whole area with water, so you're actually walking through the water because they're trying to keep the dust down, the smoke and the heat. There were mini-explosions happening all around you while this is going on. It was dark. You're working with flashlights, but there was some lighting set up already. Prior to going in I learned that John was trapped, and at this point he was still trapped by his legs, and the plan was ...in order to save his life, if we couldn't extricate him they had doctors standing by, and they were going to amputate his legs if they had to.

I worked my way down, and when I got down to John I was by myself. Another police officer who was [with the] New York City Emergency Service Unit [and] who was also a paramedic came down and gave John some morphine for his pain, and then he left me. Basically John was laying lateral with his head towards me, feet buried in, and it was in an area where you didn't have much room to work. So I was able to start talking to John a little bit. He was in and out of consciousness. Obviously in a lot of pain, getting weak because he was trapped for so long. I was just talking to him, asking his name and so on. I said, I'm going to do my best to get you out.

I had to crawl on top of John so his head is facing me. I had to crawl in head first, so I'm laying on top of him, trying to hold myself up on my toes and knees and elbows to not put pressure on him so I wouldn't prevent him from breathing. I had to take my SCBA mask pack off because there was not enough room, so now I'm working without any of that on. I just began removing some of the debris that I found was trapping his legs.

One thing that I felt was trapping him was a big piece of concrete. I was still by myself at this time doing this, so I was able to make some radio communications out and I was asking for some extrication equipment, hand stuff we used in the old days—Porta Powers and stuff like that—so maybe I can free up this concrete. I was digging for a while with anything I could dig with—my knife, I was digging with pieces of rebar—anything I could get in there to try to free him.

I was later joined by two New York City firefighters. We introduced ourselves and went to work. John was asking us, whatever you do, don't leave me here. We told him that we weren't leaving until he came out. So we took turns again over him, removing debris. We were finally able to get that big piece of concrete out. It took some time. We put some webbing that we use for rescue under his shoulders and around his chest, and the three of us said, let's give a pull. So we pulled. He let out a grunt because of the pain, so we took a rest and let him rest, and we did it again. By this time we felt him give a little bit, so we all looked at each other and said, I think we got him. Pulled again and he broke free. We all together pulled him out and called for a Stokes basket. We called for a backboard and a cowl to put on him, put him in a Stokes basket, and we passed him up. At that time other firefighters came into the cavern and we worked him up. When I went in that hole it was 3:30 in the morning, and it was now 6:30 in the morning.

When I came out of the hole, John was being passed down. The sun was coming up. One of the best sunrises.

You could see from the debris pile hole where we were, all the way down to the street, a line of rescue workers, and John just got passed down to everybody. He went to the hospital. We worked our way out, retrieved some of our equipment. Me and the two firefighters at street level all hugged each other. A job well done, I guess.

It was a long day. We were all exhausted. We went back to Floyd Bennett Field, we had a quick breakfast, and then we went home. When I got to my house I was called by my work to come back in, you've got to do an interview. So I went back in, and then I finally went home. My unit basically for two weeks afterwards continued to respond there while the rescue operation was going on. Once they called off the rescue operation we ceased going, and obviously they continued recovery operations and cleanup later on down the road.

I have seen John several times afterwards, and each time I see him he's recovering after many surgeries. Obviously he was in the hospital for quite some time. Only he would be able to tell you what he experienced and what he's been through, but based on my visits with him from seeing him on different occasions, I know from when he started out—being in a wheelchair, to going to walkers, to going to two crutches, to going to a cane—and he walks without the cane now. He's been through a lot, but only he could tell you that.

EVERYBODY GETS CLOSURE

The drive was knowing that obviously you want to help the public, that's what we do, but the little extra drive was knowing that possibly some of my buddies were missing in action, and to try to find them and not only them, but the firefighters, civilians, everybody. You want to do the best you can to either bring somebody home or, if anything, give closure to some family.

I think over time everybody gets closure. I think on the anniversary dates everybody revisits that day. I know I do, but like I said, I think about it when I'm driving to work; if I'm stopped at a light I'll think about it just briefly. I think about my friend Ronnie just briefly. I don't dwell on it, but everyday it just comes to my mind and I think about it. I was fortunate out of that whole experience to experience something positive. I was able to help rescue somebody.

PART THREE

RECOVERY, RECOVERY, RECOVERY

After days and weeks of working incessantly on the World Trade Center Pile, at the Freshkills Landfill, and at the New York City morgue, responders began to feel numb. Part of the detachment that occurred was due to the mechanical and monotonous recovery process: the digging, the sifting, trucks hauling debris away, and the conveyor belts. As one responder puts it, "I became part of the machine." Perhaps this reaction was protective at the time, a self-defense mechanism. The question became: How much continuous horror and gore could a person see, day in and day out, without completely breaking down? Curiously, for some of the responders, the recovery process became routine, disturbingly so. And yet, others were able to overcome the detachment and the degradation through the human bonds they had formed with each other.

◄ **A police officer finds** a pair of pants while searching the Pile for remains. Photo by Steve Spak.

▼ **The cleanup of the site** and the recovery of remains and other clues to victims' identity, such as clothing and other personal effects, were slow and deliberate. Materials recovered from the site were also meticulously reviewed by responders at the Freshkills Landfill in Staten Island. *Photo by Steve Spak.*

▲ **Police officers and firefighters surround two of their fallen,** whose recovered remains are each draped with an American flag. *Photo by Steve Spak.*

▲ **Police officer William, who tells his story in Chapter 20,** contemplates the enormity of the recovery mission on the back of a truck headed toward the site. *Photographer unknown.*

▲ **Responders standing at attention and saluting** to honor the remains of a police officer or firefighter found in their area of the Pile. *Photo by Steve Spak.*

▲ **Two search and rescue dogs and their K-9 handlers** work alongside police officers and firefighters to locate remains. *Photo by Steve Spak.*

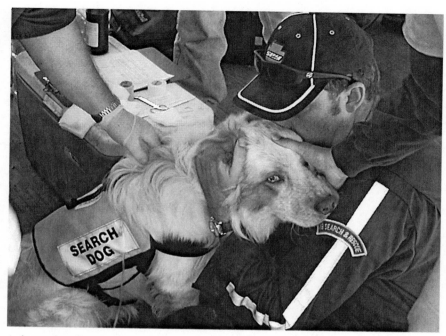

▲ **A search and rescue dog is praised and comforted** by its K-9 handler after working on the Pile. Many of the dogs became depressed because they found no survivors, so volunteers hid in the rubble to motivate the dogs to continue searching, which in turn boosted the responders' spirits. *Photo by Roy and Lois Gross.*

▶ **A police officer on the Pile** outfitted with tactical equipment: flak jacket, helmet, and gas mask. *Photo by Steve Spak.*

CHAPTER 14

I DIDN'T DESERVE THANKS

William was not a police officer or firefighter—he was a corrections officer. He explains that he spent his life in law enforcement on Long Island, so it was natural for him to pull together a team of his colleagues and head to Ground Zero. He cannot clearly explain what motivated him to rush to Manhattan that day. He did what his conscience told him to do. While working at Ground Zero he had a tough time with his emotions, because every day he was going to a place that was all about death. He tells us that it is hard to describe, but he would never be able to forget it, because it was just the "smell of death" that permeated everything and engulfed him. But amidst all the death, there was a lot of life: in the people who were so dedicated to the work, in the generosity of the community, in the overwhelming thanks he received that he didn't feel he deserved. It is this feeling that he is chasing today, the camaraderie and patriotism, which he had never seen before.

SO I'M TALKING TO MY FRIEND ON THE PHONE, and he's like, "What are we going to do? I'll call you back." I said all right. So we're watching the news and they're saying stuff like it may be a terrorist attack. It can't be two misplaced planes. They're saying first it was a small Cessna, and then they realized it was two passenger planes.

As time went on, there were more reports that it was definitely a terrorist attack. Then came news that there were more planes they couldn't account for. We thought we were going to be attacked and wondered what would blow up next. Some guys were going from the job. They were getting a team ready, and they were going into the city, and we just got prepared. I figured my friend and I were going to go, and we wanted to go right away. We were just going to go in on our own and try to do whatever we could.

Our wives thought we should just stay and go when they need us. That was a good idea. So we got our stuff ready; we put our guns on. I remember loading my gun. I didn't know what was going to happen. I figured I should at least have a gun. You don't know at the time. It was a weird sensation, then, a couple of hours later, you find out what was going on. Then the building collapsed. Never thought in a million years that the building would come down.

We watched it as much as we could, then got my son ready and took him to school. The attacks seemed like isolated incidents. I know it sounds weird now, but I thought we should try to keep as much normalcy as possible. I figured we were relatively safe. My wife and I went shopping after dropping my son at school. I remember going into the supermarket, and everybody was just shocked. In the store, it was as though a snowstorm was coming. People were grabbing milk.

THE DESTRUCTION WAS JUST AMAZING

We waited and waited [for a call to go to Ground Zero], and still nothing. The next day I watched the whole thing unfold, and news reports were saying 10,000 people may be dead. So two days later, my friend and I finally got to go in.

It was worse than what they showed you on TV. The destruction was just amazing. It looked like a ghost town. It was just closed down. You could see some of the smoke rising. But, when we got out, I'll never forget the smell. It's hard to describe, but I'll never forget it. It was just death.

Paper was just everywhere. Some was cleaned up and pushed off to the side. I don't think there was any anger right away because it was just so shocking. I think it was more shock and surging adrenaline. We found out where we were assigned to go, and we needed to write it down. One of the guys in charge said we needed a piece of paper, so he reached down and here's all this paper from the World Trade Center. He picked it up and wrote where we had to go. We got the truck to a firehouse where we were assigned.

We got to this one firehouse, it was Rescue 1. They lost eleven guys and their truck. The only guy there was a house-watch fireman; the others were down at Ground Zero. You just knew it when you walked into the firehouse. You just knew. We found out that they lost the truck and those eleven men. That was when it hit you. I didn't realize the whole sense of loss yet. I didn't realize yet that they had pulled everybody. One minute, these guys were here. The place was just how they left it.

A lot of the firefighters' wives greeted us. They were like, "Here's food. You'd better eat while you can." They told us not to worry. One woman said her husband is still here and that we shouldn't feel badly for her. She was trying to reassure us that it was okay to be there.

I remember sitting there eating at the table of the house, and another fireman came in. I asked, "Oh, how is Brian doing?" His name was Brian Hickey. The fireman asked me, "Oh, you don't know?" I said that I didn't.

He said, "Oh, he's missing." That was it. It hit me. I couldn't believe it. He was gone. Well, he said he was missing, but later on you realize what he meant. That was the wakeup call. Right there. That firehouse felt sacred. That was the place they left only a short while before. Now, their trucks were gone. They were gone. Everything was gone. Their names were up on the board. But that was their last call.

So we secured the firehouse and talked to the neighbors, who started bringing flowers and lighting candles. They walked up and hugged us. I'm nobody, but I guess I was a symbol for the people to say thanks for the firemen, but I felt guilty taking those hugs that didn't belong to me. You could tell that some of these people had nothing. There were some children and a husband and wife, and they wanted to donate what was probably their last dollar to the firemen. A lady donated her first paycheck, and she had been at her new job for only a week. It was an amazing time, people donating food and people coming together.

TAKE ME DOWN THERE

The firemen's wives were so courageous. So many of their husbands were lost, but at the time we didn't realize how many. The wives took care of us, they talked to us, they welcomed us into the firehouse. The firemen weren't there, except for the one house-watch guy. You could see he was numb.

I'll never forget when they asked me and my friend to use our car from the sheriff's department to take one of the wives home. She said her husband was fine, and I didn't second-guess it. As we're driving and talking a little, she suddenly asked if we'd been down at the site. We told her we had. She grabbed me from behind—she was sitting behind me—and she grabbed me, and she said, "Take me down there. Take me down there." She's clawing at me from behind. "I gotta find my husband. I'll dig with my hands." This lady would have done anything to get down there to find her husband. We never saw her anguish until that time.

THEY JUST LET THEM DOWN EASILY

We worked down there a short time, maybe a week, a week and a half. After that, it seemed there was less and less we could do. The machines were coming in and there wasn't any hope of finding anyone alive. So I volunteered to help victims' families who were bringing in things that may hold traces of their loved one's DNA—their toothbrush or comb. They needed DNA to identify the bodies the rescuers starting finding as they began clearing the wreckage. I volunteered to bring the family members down. Some of the guys picked them up at the airport or from different areas, and we went down to Chelsea Piers, where they'd set up the first part of the identification operation. I brought them in, and I'd go with them from one station to another as they provided different kinds of information. Here I am playing with this fireman's kids, and now I know he's most likely gone. After a while, you just become numb to it.

I'd go home at night after fifteen-hour days and look in on my kid sleeping. I am so lucky. It was a tough time with emotions because every day I'm going to a place that was all about death. And I'm trying to hold myself up and bring these people through this process and let them down as easily as possible. There were all kinds of organizations there. I saw all kinds of badges, people in civilian clothes, but they were law enforcement. I don't know if they were FBI or what. They had people working at these computers and they would check the name first, and after a while, after a couple of families, I realized that was the process. They just let them down easily. They had to. You can't just walk in and say, "Most likely he's missing. It's been a couple of days, and the news reports weren't good."

I talked about things with my wife, mostly late at night before washing up and going to bed. But, mostly, I didn't really say what was going on. She was worried. She wasn't sure I should go. Things were still going on. We're realizing that more people were lost, more posters were going up, people missing. She didn't want me to go back. My friend's wife didn't want him to, either. They were afraid of losing us. I felt that I had to go and do what I had to do. Part of that need to help comes from being a corrections officer, plus I used to be a volunteer fireman years ago. You have to do a job. If you have to go into that cell and protect that inmate from himself, you do. That's what you do. I felt we had to do [that] at Ground Zero, and we did it.

What should happen to that space is a very tough subject because that's hallowed ground. It should be for the people whose souls were lost that day. I believe that it should be preserved because I saw both parts of the spectrum. I went down there afterwards, and here I am, sitting here, having a cup of coffee on the same spot where we were working.

It's good to see people rushing by. It's like a construction site to most people now. They're rushing off to work on the other side. But I believe it should be more preserved. I think it's being more commercialized now. I understand things have to go on, but I think they should preserve the area more than they are. Maybe that will happen when they build the museum.

HONORING THE DEAD

I went to some of the funerals, and it was really tough. I met police officers from Arizona, from all over. They were strangers. There were so many funerals that, after a while, I realized there weren't enough people to attend them because most people were down there [at Ground Zero] working. I attended some of the funerals. There were SWAT teams on the roof protecting the funerals because we didn't know what to expect.

It was a hard time. I went to my friend Brian Hickey's funeral. When we got in there, his helmet was sitting on his casket. That's all they found. I said to myself, "That's the destruction. Here we are, we have a person, and his helmet is what's left of him." I couldn't believe that that's all there was. I heard later that they might have found a little, or part of—I'm not sure what it was. But, at the time of the funeral, they only had his helmet, which was in pretty good shape considering two buildings came down on it. It's just amazing.

Another one of my friends who died, a guy I used to work with, was Timmy Haskell. I found out later that his brother was lost that day, too. He was a New York City fireman, and I used to work with him when our overtime would overlap. We talked about the city fireman's test, and I took it, too. But my mother became ill and I couldn't finish the physical, but he did. He took the physical and he passed. He said, "What do you think I should do? Do you think I should go to the Fire Department?" I said, "Yeah, I would go. I would definitely go. I'd kill for the chance to be a city fireman." I always think of that now. Maybe I wasn't the swing factor. Maybe. I don't know. You feel a little guilty. He was getting off work that day, but he went and he was lost. It hits home.

I think the biggest thing was how everybody came together. That's what I remember of the time. How people were just kinder. It's the way life should be. I still chase that today.

Almost every day I think about it. Sometimes it's harder than others. Time has gone on, and I'm moving on, but you don't really move on. It's always there. Every memorial I go to. In Bethpage, by the fire-training academy, we have two steel beams, and I always leave pictures of my two friends, Brian and Timmy. I leave them down there every year. I make new ones. Some flowers. My little memorial for them. It's tough.

CHAPTER 15

AM I A GHOST?

Steve lived a quiet life with his wife and children in Suffolk County, Long Island, fifty miles east of Manhattan. He worked in telecommunications, keeping humidity out of phone cables. He learned about the attacks the same way most Americans did—from news reports and phone calls from concerned family members and friends. He describes how a call came for volunteers from the phone company, his employer, to work at Ground Zero. He leaped at the chance to volunteer, despite attempts by his colleagues to discourage him. The grinding work affected him emotionally. He became angry at the tourists who came to gawk and mistook a crane for metal beams of the Tower. "They were completely oblivious to the agony and the destruction." When he thought about it, he realized that the tourists really did not know what the workers were going through. It made him feel like a ghost living in his own private hell, though he was sustained by the kindness and the spirit of the other workers around him.

I ARRIVED DOWN THERE ON THAT SATURDAY after the disaster. I was down there sixteen hours a day for fifteen days. When I was driving down there, I was on what was the West Side Highway past the Javits Center, which was FEMA's headquarters. I would drive down there from that point. It was like a gauntlet, people on both sides. Everybody was holding up signs: "Thank you, our heroes." I didn't feel like a hero. I just felt like I was down there to do a job. So no, I could not imagine what I was faced with on the way down there.

IT WAS SO SURREALISTIC

When I did get down there to the main staging area, the first thing I saw was a lot of vehicles that were crushed, a fire truck that was crushed. Then I looked up, and where there was a street it was all blocked off. It was like something out of a movie. It was so surrealistic. It was actually the debris that formed in between the two buildings and took up all the space of the street. I walked around, and then I was faced with my duties.

They gave me a Tyvek suit, a protective white garment. Initially, they gave me only a cotton mask. It was about three days that I was there, and I finally went in for certification for the masks that the mayor's office provided. They were fairly professional masks like the military would use. The cartridges had to be changed every once in a while. But they didn't tell me that in order for this mask to be properly sealed, I should've shaved off my beard. Because I had a full beard. I really don't like to criticize anybody, but the EPA was down there, and they put monitoring devices all around the place. Then they actually lied to the people about the air quality and whether it was safe, which it wasn't. The worst of it was seeing the agony of the firemen on the Pit itself.

The ironworkers, of course, were dismantling everything, and the truckers were taking everything out. The firemen and the police officers from the Port Authority were working diligently on the Pile. A lot of them weren't wearing masks or anything like that. I could see the agony that they suffered. Every once in a while, they would blow the horn and everybody would stop working. All the firemen and the police officers and the civil authorities, they would all line up along a path that they made on both sides of the Pile all the way to where the Medical Examiner's trucks were waiting to remove the remains. Every once in a while, they would remove a police officer or a fireman and they'd drape a flag, an American flag, over the stretcher. Everybody would stop and [we would] remove our helmets and hold them over our hearts. They would take the remains to the Medical Examiner and drive away and everybody'd go back to work.

Then FEMA was down there. They would come out with human remains in plastic bags. It became so surrealistic to me. It was like going on a fishing trip and carrying a bag of fish. But it was actually human flesh. They were see-through bags.

It didn't bother me that the firefighters and police officers were treated differently than civilians. While I was down there, I felt that I was in the presence of true heroes, men and women who sacrifice their lives every day. I felt not worthy to be there. But I did make a lot of friends down there. They worked the night hours. My hours were like from four o'clock in the afternoon till almost nine o'clock in the morning. So there wasn't that much of a hustle and bustle as there was in the daytime.

It was just amazing the support units that were down there, from doctors, psychologists, animal psychologists [for the K-9 units]. They had triage centers all fixed up over there. There were a lot of volunteers—kids, teenagers, and senior citizens—who met the call. The Salvation Army, the Red Cross, and others gave out bottles of water or tended to general needs, even just giving responders somebody to talk with, things like that. Silvercup Studios donated the Hollywood lighting to illuminate the Pile at night. Hollywood studios also donated rainmaking machines, so it was very wet. The Sanitation Department came around periodically and watered down the streets. But the rainmaking machines kept dust from rising from the Pile, which it still did anyway.

The air down there was bad and didn't improve. None whatsoever. A little technique the firemen taught me was to use Vicks VapoRub: Just put it in your nostrils so the putrid smell isn't so strong. You could smell the decaying flesh mixed in with everything that was burning. Even the steel melted from the intense heat. Everything was a twisted, mangled mess. A lot of times I'd sit there and tend to my machines, which ran off of diesel fuel and gasoline and produced a lot of exhaust fumes. So, there was a constant smell of exhaust and fumes and that putrid smell.

It was incomprehensible to see what I was actually looking at. After a while, I felt like I was in a Salvador Dalí painting. It just became so surrealistic to me. Even the Windows on the World—that was the only thing left standing when the top of the buildings came down. That was it. And, after a while, it looked to me like a fantasy world in Disneyland, like the Magic Kingdom. It was just unbelievable.

THE DAY-TO-DAY

On a typical day, I would go to the staging area and put on a Tyvek suit, helmet, my boots, and a gas mask. I shouldn't call it a gas mask; it was actually a protective mask. I walked down West Street to the corner where I was assigned. We had air compressors in a paneled truck and on trailers.

When the attacks occurred, all communications to the whole area were wiped out. We sent down teams of cable splicers, and I was the only representative from Long Island who was trained on air compressors. We pump compressed air into the cables to keep them dry. Of course, the rooms normally occupied by the air dryers were completely disabled. The basements of all the buildings were flooded with ruptured diesel fuel tanks and water. So these teams of cable splicers created new cables above ground, and they ran them from point A to point B. They got communications up and running in no time. Then we had to tear out the old, destroyed stuff and replace it with new compressors. It was a long project.

My responsibility was to keep the machines [i.e., compressors] going. We pumped all the air into the basements and into the new cables. The system won't work without that because any moisture that gets in there would destroy it. So I was there on that corner. And I'd go back and forth to the Fire Department, which provided the gasoline for us and made sure that our fuel levels were right. I monitored the machines, made adjustments here and there, and replaced parts that blew out. All this was outside.

They had triage areas where you could go for things like underwear and socks and stuff like that. Whatever you needed. They had cots where you could lie down and relax for a little bit. They had nurses coming around and they had counselors you could speak to. They had people who represented different churches. It was comforting.

THE SPIRIT OF LIBERTY

For a main meal, I made my way down to the waterfront where they have the boat, the *Spirit,* that normally takes people around on cruises. But they anchored over there and they provided excellent catered food and everything. We went there just for the camaraderie and for the respite. And you could hear laughter. You'd take off your protective equipment. The Statue of Liberty was right there. Around the promenade on the way down to the waterfront, there was a railing. I started keeping a journal while I was down there, and I took some pictures, too. On that railing, as I went around the whole railing, I actually transcribed what was written on the railing. It was a poem by Walt Whitman called "City of Ships." It said, "City of the world, for all races are here. City of the sea, city of marvels. Tall façades of marble and iron. Proud and passionate city. Mettlesome, extravagant city."

I thought that was pretty ironic because it captured the spirit—I was born and raised in Manhattan, and so I was a New Yorker all my life and a city dweller until I was thirty-three. One time, I went down there, and I got back to my work area, and they were frantic. I said, "What's everyone so frantic about?" They said, "We were looking for you. Where were you?" I said, "Well, I went down to the *Spirit.*"

They were looking for me because all these little seismographic meters detected something. They were posted around all the buildings to warn of possible collapses. So they blew all the air horns and evacuated the area. But nothing collapsed. But they were looking for me. They said, "Holy mackerel, where is this guy? Could he possibly be in the area? If a building collapses, we're going to be out a man." So I got a little chastised for that.

I would leave the area around nine o'clock in the morning, and I'd go back to the hotel, and I'd just change all my clothing and leave everything outside the door because I didn't want to bring anything into the room with me. Then I would take a shower, go down and have a good meal, breakfast or whatever. And then I'd go back up to my room and sleep. Set my alarm clock to get up at like a quarter to three in the afternoon. So I would only sleep for like about five or six hours. I didn't look forward to going back, but I knew that I had a job to do down there.

It was ironic because I'd see all these tourists. They'd all be, "Oh, yeah, look! Look! You can see it! You can see it!" They were just looking at a crane. I mean, you couldn't see Ground Zero from there. But all these people were completely oblivious to the agony and the destruction down there. People were making it like a tourist thing. But I'm thinking to myself, "these tourists that came from other places, they really didn't know." I felt like a ghost going back down there to work. But I did reach a point. After fifteen days, I requested to go home. I'd had enough. I really had.

SOUL-SEARCHING

I did a lot of soul-searching while I was down there, looking for a reason, a purpose, why I was there. Of course, I was there to do a job. When it first happened, my wife and I donated blood because we wanted to do anything that we could. The worst thing was, when they were searching and there was so much agony, and nobody was found alive. That I was actually bearing witness, like I was bearing witness to a funeral pyre, that I was a sentinel for all these souls. Even though I was doing my essential work down there, I was watching as so many souls were being released from the agony below in a strange and unusual way. In an ironic sense, I felt blessed to be there for them. These were emotions I'd never felt before. I still feel, deep within myself, that it became a permanent part of the very essence of my heart and mind. That's just the way I felt.

Even to this day, I have apocalyptic nightmares, dreams. There were certain events that occurred after Ground Zero that contributed to me falling into a depression that I still have. I'm on medication now, and it's under control. But I had to be hospitalized for about six months. Because I just couldn't discern reality from apocalypse. And the fear.

I became fearful for everybody. I mean, look at the world the way it is today. So much has changed. I try to relate to the life I led as a kid, all the way up to Ground Zero. It seems like the world will never be the same again. It hasn't changed the way I think about government. I still have respect for authority. I have to commend quite a few people who were down there representing the government.

But there's a pre-9/11 Steve and a post-9/11 Steve. I feel that I went from being optimistic about everything to becoming a cautious optimist. Now I don't trust optimism anymore. You never know what's going to come day to day. My spirituality suffered quite a bit from it. I'm trying to regain it now. I realize that the only thing I can really trust is the man upstairs.

It's important to never forget what this country's about. I was always taught that we're borrowing this Earth from our children and from future generations. So we should give them this Earth the way we found it, the way it should be. But that's not happening. All I can say is just keep having faith, keep believing that good will overcome evil one way or another. The power of love will overcome the love of power. Jimi Hendrix said that.

Just pray. Just go on and educate yourself, and try to make good for your own families. And never forget. Try to never forget.

CHAPTER 16

COULDN'T PULL MYSELF AWAY

Ronald escaped extreme poverty in Guyana and came to the United States as an illegal immigrant, eventually gaining citizenship status. He offers a unique perspective on patriotism, and his strong sense of gratitude to this country drove him to volunteer at Ground Zero. He speaks to the sacrifice many made as they responded to the call of duty to serve their countrymen. Upon arriving on the Pile, he describes his visceral reaction and his deep sense of uncertainty. The residual trauma that first responders continue to experience is apparent in Ronald's story, but he saw the 9/11 disaster as a vehicle for repaying the country he loves.

I JUST HAD TO BE THERE

I HAD TO GO. I JUST HAD TO BE THERE. How could I just lay in bed and look at this on TV? I couldn't do it. I'm in America thirty-something years, and there's not one day that I haven't thanked God for the privilege and the opportunity. I was one of the recipients of the compassion of this country. I saw the compassion that they had for me in my time of need. So it's no way I was going to walk away. No way. I couldn't do it. Maybe without this country, I wouldn't have gotten a trade; maybe I wouldn't have learned anything. Because after my father died, we had nothing. Without the assistance of the U.S. we would not have survived. It was just cornmeal. It might seem like just cornmeal for a lot of people. But for me, that was a lifeline. You could've gotten cornmeal, you could've gotten milk. I could remember those packages clearly: "USA, not to be sold." I can see my mother going into the cupboard and taking that out. That was all we had. I'm not ashamed to say that. That was all we had.

So midnight, I just got up and I turned to my wife and she says, "I know." I left. I got down at Chelsea Piers about two o'clock in the morning. I stood in line and I went in. Then a cop came out and he says, "They need oxygen, they need acetylene." At the time I was working for New Roads. They had buildings and so that they were doing. I used to just report when the construction finished the job. So I called the owner of New Roads and I said, "Look, this is the situation here. We need oxygen, we need acetylene." And he says, "Not a problem."

When I went in, the first thing you got is the knots in the stomach. Then you got anger. Then you come to uncertainty. So it was so much going on. I went in with a temporary pass they gave me and it expired in about a month. When the month was expired, they say that we can't work anymore. I went back into the line and got another pass. I just couldn't pull myself away. I went down there on the 14th. I had an ID. Then I went back and I get another ID. But after that, they changed the badge again and it became…if you go and ask someone if they need help, you could've helped, but you had to be paid. I wasn't prepared to accept cash. That was one of the reasons that I had to leave. I left sometime in December.

When I got there first, there was a group of people working and then they gave us buckets. So I went straight in and I started helping. From Chelsea Piers, they gave us buckets and a hook that you can pull things up. I had gloves. Someone did give me a mask: the paper mask. The problem with the mask is that when you work and you become tired, you have to remove it to get a good set of air. If you're working at a slow pace, the mask is not a problem, but if you're working at a heavy pace, you have to take it, remove it after a while. It gets clogged up. There was a lot of dust. But they had said that the dust was okay, so you weren't thinking about wearing a mask. And officials was there without masks, so that you have nothing to worry about.

You see so much things there. I can remember one guy was staring into the ceiling, a firefighter. I turned. He's staring into the sky, and I turned to the guy, I said, "What's the matter with him?" He says, "He just lost his best friend." Man, it was so horrific. When the body bags started coming out, everyone would stand still and just look.

Many times, I would just come off and just walk to the waterside and sit down for a while, right where the *Spirit* was parked. There was a little park. I would go down there and sit down. There were other people [and we would talk]. We found out that one of the hijackers lived in the country for a while. How could he stay here and see the good that's here, and still carry out an act like that? It was beyond my comprehension. I couldn't put it together.

I WOULD DO IT ALL OVER AGAIN

I still feel anger sometimes. Still hard. I would go to work and then what I found, I started getting angry. Because once another supervisor told me something and I went into a rage. And I couldn't understand it. And I started looking into it a little deeper to see what's really going on. But it's such a horrific thing. It's such a—and seeing it on TV and being there, it's a different thing altogether. Because when you're seeing it on TV, you feel upset. But when you go and see the natural site, the knots in your stomach, it—phew. And the anger. And when you see body bags that's coming out, it's very, very upsetting. Very. I wouldn't wish that on my enemy. If someone don't believe that the devil exists, you just have to look at what happened there. You can never feel that another human being can do something like that. It still is hard for me to, so I just don't even think about it sometimes.

I can honestly tell you when it happened, and I don't want to sound any way bad towards anybody, but I was coming over the bridge and there were two Arab-looking guys. They were dancing and beating on that thing—and a little more, I couldn't take it. I was going to—I don't want to say. I couldn't take it, to see that this is going on. One day after, and this is how you are. I'm not saying that they were laughing at that. But all I was asking was just to show some respect.

But you know what? If God forbid something like that should happen again, there's no force on Earth that can stop me from being there. I would do it all over again. I have no regrets. None. The responders are a great bunch of people. The same guys who is maybe angry now, they would respond in a second. They're just angry now. They would respond in a second. They wouldn't change anything they did.

This country is still the greatest country on the planet. There is nowhere else I would've rather my kids to be raised or *any* other country. If there's another country, it's probably in a different galaxy, not on the Earth. What you have seen—that is what America is about. The strength of this country is not its military might; it's its people and its compassion. And I would've given my life for this country in a second. And I truly mean that.

There's some people who come here from another country and bad-talk this country. I always let them know that the guards at the airport is not to stop you from going, it's to make sure you have a safe trip. So who don't like it, can leave.

CHAPTER 17

THE ART OF CLEANUPS

From October of 2001 until April of 2002, Christopher, formerly of
Sayville, New York, was contracted to do cleanup at sites impacted by the
collapse of the World Trade Center. Christopher, who died in December
of 2010, was, at the time of 9/11, the general manager and part owner of
the company that he worked for. He had done fire, water, and hazardous-
material cleanups before, but tells us that nothing had prepared him
for what he came to witness. He explains that prior to his arrival with
his unionized workforce, building owners had hired day laborers to
clean Ground Zero sites without proper protection. In these buildings,
the silicate dust, which Christopher saw as "the most dangerous kind,"
could be an inch, or even two inches, thick. Christopher's narrative
is open and frank about how working on the cleanup devastated his
emotional and physical health. Sadly, he confides that he subsequently
was divorced, then stopped working. Before his death he claimed that he
felt as if he lived in the shadow of what he used to be.

I HAD DONE WORK AT THE TWIN TOWERS in the past—some consulting work and some actual asbestos-removal work. So I do know about the asbestos dangers in there. However, one of the Towers, to my knowledge, was built without any asbestos, because they were built '72, '73. The other one was probably half to three-quarters with asbestos on the fire proofing until it was outlawed. I knew there was going to be a danger of the asbestos, but people tend to forget other building materials that could be more dangerous.

I drove to my office immediately after watching the news segment because we did disaster cleanups. I was general manager and a part owner, and I went just to see what was going on.

I had some competitors that were down there the next morning soliciting work, but I just couldn't bring myself to do that. I might've missed out on a lot of work, but I just couldn't go in and take advantage of a situation.

Companies that were down there right afterwards got a lot of work, but I was really unsure of what work they were doing. They were doing cleanup work, but in my mind it might've been a bit premature, because in something like that you really have to have a plan. If they went in there the next day and started doing cleaning, it probably did no good.

I knew I was going to get called because we had a relationship with building owners and insurance companies, so I waited till we got a call. At the beginning of October, we were called in by an insurance company. Building owners were in dire need of cleanup to get things back. It just snowballed and we wound up doing a lot of work. We went in, set up plans, worked with building owners, insurance companies, and cleaned up as many buildings, as many places as we could. We did it progressively rather than haphazardly. It seemed to work out.

I was there for eighteen months. I lived in Manhattan, in a hotel, approximately six months. Then I was there, living in and out of Manhattan, for the next six months, working pretty much full time. Then the last six months, it was intermittent.

LIKE A GHOST TOWN

I didn't know what to expect at first, and it was a bit of a shock when I first went there. Went in on the Long Island Rail Road, got to Penn Station, and Penn Station was like a ghost town. There was hardly anybody there. Plastered all over the walls in Penn Station were fliers with people's pictures on them saying, "Have you seen...? If you've seen this person, please call this number." People are looking for their friends and family members. I mean, walls *totally* pasted, all over. All over. You walked into the street and there was hardly any traffic. I expected to go there and help and do a job, but I really didn't know... Now, I've done catastrophe cleanups before, but this was personal. These people may not be dead, but are missing because they couldn't get home. It was devastating. The emotion was like a lump in my throat. I wound up actually staying in Midtown after a few days because I wanted to get away from the downtown area. I stayed at the Marriott in Midtown. There were maybe six, seven rooms that were taken in the Marriott. They offered me a special rate to stay there because they had nobody else. There was nobody there. For three months, I didn't hear a taxi beep its horn. Not at all. It was just totally different than New York was.

We went down to the site, took the subway partway down. Then we got off and walked down. They had barricades up on Canal Street south. I had identification; I had to show I was called in by a building owner so we can get the police to let us through. When I got closer to the World Trade Center, it wasn't like normal the hustle-bustle. It was workers there. See, when I got there, your quote-unquote "first responders"—some of them were there. They were there initially. But what I saw mostly were the workers doing cleanups. Telephone company workers, Con-Ed, people trying to get the communications back in order. We saw the big piles and the smoke. I was totally shocked. All you saw was this gigantic pile of rubble. There were these humongous machines that were cleaning up, but if you stood on a rooftop three or four blocks away, compared to the Pile, they looked like Tonka Toys. It was just an amazing feat, what they did to get it all cleaned up.

So we did a building at 100 Church Street, which was six blocks from the New York City Law Department, Bank of New York, Merrill Lynch. There were condominium buildings that had gotten an estimate or a proposal from an out-of-state restoration company to come in and cleanup. So the general adjuster on that knew us and called us in just to check prices and, well, we wound up doing the work because we were local. Other companies would hire day laborers to come in and just do the cleanup without any protection, without any structure or setup or contained area to keep all the contaminants inside. It just went all over the place.

DANGEROUS DUST

We had our laborers that were from New York—our employees, union employees—and we'd supply them with protective gear, so we wound up doing the cleanups in the condominiums, two separate buildings of condominiums on Greenwich Street. I think these condos, apartments, were like eleven stories, and they were approximately three, four blocks away. The typical part in the beginning was getting testing done and relying on building owners to do testing of the hazardous materials. To identify where contaminants were was very difficult. An independent laboratory would come in and take dust samples, swipe samples of areas to test for contaminants. They tested mostly for asbestos when asbestos wasn't the big problem there. Of course, I found there were mistakes made because people went in too fast.

Depending on their exposure to the site, the south, where it was on Greenwich Street, the southwest buildings—the dust there could be an inch, two inches thick inside the buildings. From what I understand, it gets through cracks, it gets through everything, because what you had mostly there was silicate dust, which was the most dangerous. All the concrete and laboratory testing was done, but you can't test every area and every little piece. You may have contaminants here. Well, you may have contaminants on the 5th floor but none on the 6th. Maybe the windows were closed. There were so many buildings. It was so difficult.

On the streets, the ash flew for months. Every time one of those big cranes stuck its crane into the Pile, lifted it up, for three, four months, flames would shoot up because the core of it was so hot. We used to watch that. The EPA did testing on the streets, and they said everything was fine on the streets, but I can't believe that because the dust was just flying around. I remember being in a brownstone on a roof looking down, and it was about ten o'clock in the morning and there was a police officer standing down below, and the top of the hat he was wearing was covered in ash. This was the beginning of November, so he must've gotten there eight or nine o'clock. He didn't realize there was ash all on the top. So that's what everybody was breathing in. You couldn't hide from it. I guess the government couldn't shut down the business district. That would've been *totally* devastating. I mean, what happens when you really should shut down the New York Stock Exchange. You can't.

According to the New York City Department of Environmental Protection regulations and New York State regulations, the building owner has to hire the independent company to come in and monitor the air and do cleanups in accordance with the regulations from the DEP. That was done. However, because of the circumstances there and trying to get a cleanup, the DEP, New York City DEP, deregulated, to a certain extent, the cleanup procedures, because otherwise it would've been impossible. You would've had to put a containment area over all of downtown.

So one building I got called in to clean up the contaminants was a 57-story office building. They already had a cleaning company clean up the first four or five floors, but it turned out that there were contaminants on those first four or five floors. So all they did was go in, and the people that they hired were... dosed with contaminants. They had no barriers set up or anything, so the contaminants just spread elsewhere. These poor people, some of them were day laborers. Whether they were illegal aliens, immigrants or not, it doesn't matter; they still got dosed. We used to see every day five, six hundred people, day laborers, lined up. Contractors would go and say "I need forty guys," and forty guys would come out.

Union labor was really expensive. Naturally, it's like, okay, the insurance company's going to pay for it, so we come to an agreement with the insurance company. I mean, some of the people were like giving proposals that might've been ridiculous, but I just broke it down to time and material. How else could you do it? I told the insurance company, "This is what we pay for union labor. This is what our material costs are. We expect to make a profit, to keep the company going. These are our costs." But the unions, the different locals run under the Laborers Union, they set up a local for all of the New York City areas, one local, which was Local 78. Then they had an Insulators Local, 12A. They lowered their rates to try and get contractors to come in and set a scale. They'd raise it each year. But they did all the training. So it's like an electrician who was schooled by the Electricians Union. So rather than my company having to send people we hire to get their training, they got it from the union. And the union had a shop steward on the job who would ensure that things were being done safely. So it took not only pressure, but also liability off of me as a general manager. It's important. The way they were down there, it was, in my mind, absolutely impossible to protect yourself all the time.

Sometimes I'd work overnight, but if it was a day thing, I'd get up at like five o'clock in the morning and sometimes get back to the hotel at like twelve, one o'clock at night. It was do what you have to do to get the job done. In the beginning, you tend to spend a lot more time on the job, because sometimes the people wouldn't show up. There was such a demand for laborers there that people wouldn't show. If we'd have a crew of forty, maybe twenty wouldn't show up.

The work was physically demanding. I did what I had to do physically, but I was more in a supervisory position. There were no major injuries among my workers. There might've been a few nicks and cuts, but no major injuries. I definitely felt a sense of duty because you realize why that area was hit: because it's the business district downtown. You knew it was a terrorist attack. Patriotism was part of it. You want to get it back and get it going as quick as possible so the country is not devastated.

HEART-WRENCHING, DEVASTATING

I didn't communicate a lot with a lot of people. My brother was one of my business partners and he's fifteen years older than I am, so he expected me to be there all the time, so I was. My sisters knew I was there, but I don't really think they realized what the total devastation was. And I always thought, what about people in Utah? Do they really know what type of devastation was there?

You developed camaraderie with everybody working down there. No doubt about it. It started out like total camaraderie. No taxi horns for three months. Everybody was like one. It's an enemy of thine is an enemy of mine. Everybody grouped together. Then it slowly got back to competition between people. There were different heart-wrenching things. There were fire departments that came from different parts of the country to look with cadaver dogs. After a month or so I was there, there was a fire department rescue group from Chicago. It must've been ten, eleven o'clock at night, and they're leaving, walking by where we were working, leaving the site. There had to be like ten or twelve of them, totally exhausted, totally covered with soot. The cadaver dogs, they had boots on them so they wouldn't burn their feet. As they walked by, everybody clapped and cheered. And these firemen were from Chicago.

One time, [we found] a finger and body part on a roof, and it's devastating. Not just a physical body part, but on…rooftops that were strewn with memos and pictures of somebody's kids. Now, a person could've gotten out alive and been fine, but there's no way I would know…

I had a couple of friends that worked in the World Trade Center that were unscathed. One explained a story where they was getting into work, that a part of a plane came right over his head as he was running away. I have a friend that worked on the 102nd floor, I believe it is, in Tower 1 at the Boomer Esiason Foundation. He's a quarterback and…the [brokerage] company that…lost almost everybody…gave him space as a donation because his son has cystic fibrosis. His office doesn't open until ten o'clock. So they all missed it.

A woman that lives around the corner from me, her daughter was the catering manager at the Top of the World restaurant, and this is one of those horrible stories. She worked in another building and saw the whole building collapse, knowing her daughter was doing catering that morning. Sometimes you think you become hardened to stories like that, but you really don't. This poor woman and her husband, they're about my age, I guess. And where I live, there's like an island across the street, like in the middle of the road, and then the waters, a river, across from that. And the town gave her that island and she set up, like, a memorial to her daughter. I know it devastated her life. Her daughter was engaged, ready to get married.

I LIVE IN THE SHADOW

Initially, I didn't think the experience affected me that much. Then things seemed to start to fall apart a little bit in my life. I was having a lot of problems at work, having problems concentrating. I lost direction, couldn't keep my mind straight. I was tired all the time. I couldn't sleep at night. I just thought nothing of it. I thought this was me, wondered what was wrong. Then, all of a sudden, one day I started having a problem breathing. I went to a pulmonologist who sent me to Stony Brook to get the CAT scan that showed lymph nodes growing. So then Dr. Bilfinger took the lymph nodes out. They were benign, thank God. But [he] told me that he's seen a lot of this lately, asked me did I do any work down at the World Trade Center. "Oh, yeah, I was there about a year and a half." So it progressed from then, and as I read articles, I said, "My God; that's me."

I got divorced. I don't work anymore. I split up with my brother. I live by myself. I don't like to go out. I don't socialize anymore. I have the same health problems. I gained weight. I'm sedentary. I get out of breath right away. It completely changed my life. I feel like I live in the shadow of what I used to be.

I feel that as far as national defense, we should've been more prepared. From what I saw from the inside, everybody worked hard and I give everybody a lot of credit—everybody from the Red Cross to FEMA, the Police Department, the Fire Department. But I think we need more work, dry runs, training if something like that happened again. We should have step one, step two, step three, step four.

I think that the most positive thing I took away is the patriotism and camaraderie that everybody had, no matter what race, religion, color of skin. It didn't matter. You were down there, you were working. I mean, there could've been Muslim, Arabs, Chinese, whatever. Spanish, Caucasian, everybody was working together. And really, as long as you were there and working, there wasn't any animosity, even if somebody was Muslim. It really didn't matter. Because let's face it, New York City is a melting pot.

CHAPTER 18

THE DUMP

Michael is a homicide detective with the New York City Police Department. On the morning of 9/11, he and his team were searching for a suspect in Brooklyn. From the roof of a housing complex, they saw the Towers burning and immediately reported to the office for orders. It was from their office that they watched the Towers collapse. For the next three weeks, Michael worked at the Staten Island Landfill, sifting through debris, hoping to find remains, hoping to bring a sense of peace to the many families yearning for their lost loved ones. He also worked at the morgue, escorting the remains that came in. He was amazed at not only the self-sacrifice of the responders, but at the power and compassion of the national community. He feels that seeing the people, and the nation, come together that way was a life-changing experience that he will never forget.

NO COMMAND STRUCTURE

WE WERE ASSIGNED TO THE INTERSECTION of Flatbush and Atlantic. Our job was to take control of the intersection to allow for emergency vehicles that were responding there. If you're not familiar with Brooklyn, that's the hub of transportation. That artery leads to both bridges, the Brooklyn and the Manhattan. And the Long Island Rail Road is there and the subways are there.

I couldn't believe it at first.... The thoughts were of family members, people that you knew. It's funny how you become dependent on cell phones and when you couldn't contact anybody, you couldn't be in touch with anybody. You were out of touch. You saw so many guys that you knew who were going over there, and part of you felt like you needed to be going that way. Part of you felt you were here with your crew of people who had a job to do here.

It was crazy to see the people who walked over the bridge. They were covered in dust and dirt. Most of the people who were coming from Manhattan tried to get to, I guess, the place that would get them home, so that would be the Long Island Rail Road. There were thousands and thousands of people just streaming in a daze. I saw one guy I knew from my town, from my soccer club.

TO GROUND ZERO

We went back to the office later on that night. A bunch of us from the office then went into Ground Zero. At that point, being police, you had the full access to get in, so we parked and then we walked in. It was really amazing that there was nothing there.

People were in the Pile and just taking debris off. There were these horns that they were sounding; it sounded like buildings were getting ready to collapse and everybody would just run. People were just pitching in. There was no assignment. There was no communication. There was nothing. I've been to World Trade Center, I've been to the top. You didn't know how people could survive. It was just a mass hysteria of people.

You were just hoping that you could do something. I didn't think I was capable. I didn't think I had the tools. I had the physical will to be there and buckets, a stack of buckets. It was just a stack of buckets taking piles off people, just handing buckets down. It was not a job for the common man. Time stood still. We probably stayed into the next day. Maybe went home quick, because then we were going in twelve-hour tours, broken up by days and nights.

My brother-in-law and sister-in-law ended up on a ferry across to Jersey, but then you start to hear about the people that you know. [A] guy I worked with whose brother was on the impact floor, my next door neighbor two doors down, a fireman. You start to hear about all the people who had gone there. My partner Chris lost his brother. Matty Rogan from the Fire Department, a neighbor. Our kids are the same age.

Initially, it was hard to come home to the block because you were coming home and it's, like a guilty sign. You were home, but Matty still wasn't home. Chris still wasn't home. It was tough because you wanted to find them, to be the person to find them. I remember hugging my kids and just being home, and then gearing up to go back. It seemed like you had to go back. The twelve-hour tours were work tours assigned to the office, so you were doing your investigations as a detective assigned to the office, and guys would be rotating through going down to Ground Zero. Then after that you would go down on your own to the site to help. It was a twenty-hour day.

Then my duties changed. The site became a controlled environment where only certain people got in to do the work, so I ended up going more or less to the Staten Island Landfill. That was my next place. And I worked the morgue.

A VERY DISTURBING PLACE

To this day I still can't believe the Staten Island Landfill became the place for a lot of these people to go. I can remember going in on the first or second day it opened up. It was crazy because you drove your car there, you parked, you had your work boots and your dungarees, and you went there and big payloaders just dumped debris. You worked in little grids and the payloader would dump the debris and you would have a rake. You would just go through it. It was odd, these big trucks dumping this debris, and inside this debris was personal artifacts. It was the dump and you went to the top of the dump, raked through your stuff, and then gave the thumbs up. Then the guy would take it all away.

We were looking for bodies, body parts, personal items. At first it was credit cards, anything that you could identify someone with. If you found something, your hand went up. It was like being at the beach with a sand bucket. You walked around with it and if you thought something was interesting, you picked it up, put it in the bucket, and brought it to somebody else. That was a very, very disturbing place to be. That's my biggest memory of the whole thing, the landfill.

I was there the first week it opened up. I can remember people who had not found their own loved ones, who would camp there outside the gates of the landfill with pictures and signs like, "Please help us find Johnny." It was crazy. Every day there would be people there.

My father-in-law had thirty-five years in sanitation. The National Guard, I believe it was, had set up field mess tents for you to eat, and the night I was up there it poured. The ground bubbled from the gas underneath the ground and you ate in these tents among what was, maybe a week ago, the garbage pile. Some of those guys slept there. It was baffling. Twelve hours, fourteen hours at the landfill was a long time. I live out in Suffolk, so to go to Staten Island is about a two-hour ride. It was tough.

A BOND FOREVER

The first two or three weeks I was there a lot, and then it was a rotation through the office. So the guys who lived in Staten Island did a little bit more, so other guys didn't have to make that trip all the way out there. We covered the ME [Medical Examiner] office, so they wouldn't have to go there. Tours to the ME office were different. You were like a chaperone. There would be a group of you there and they would signal that they were bringing in remains, and you would be assigned to that person who came in.

It's almost like you're numb to it, but you're not. You're dying … not dying inside, but it's just there was nobody you could explain it to. Like, I could see my friend from the soccer club and share with him because he was there, but after that there is a bond forever in my life.

In our own community, we lost five or six. It was unbelievable how many people never recovered anything. The funerals were tough. It was absolutely a drain. We're extremely lucky that everyone came home, from myself to my brother-in-law and sister-in-law.

I was personally taken aback, positively, by all the people on West Street. There was a group of people who just seemed to be there all the time. Every time you went by they clapped. They were just there and with everything you needed. That was the most positive part of it. One thing that I remember from the landfill is singing "Happy Birthday" to someone whose birthday it was who had been missing. A whole tent full of guys, firemen. It was odd. His mom had baked a cake.

INNOCENT PEOPLE

The only thing that has affected me negatively is the downplay of the events of that day. You don't see them anywhere. You don't see them. They're not broadcast anywhere. You no longer see the planes, the impact of the planes hitting the building. You no longer see the pieces of destruction. You never hear about people who were in the landfill. You don't hear any of that, and it's almost like taboo to say. I don't want to see it played out on TV every day, but I want my children to understand that a lot of good people just went to work, average people who were not soldiers, not warriors, who were just innocent people.

It really is important to live in the moment that you're in. The moment you have with your kids, the moment to say goodbye to somebody. It's funny because you take for granted that everybody goes to work and they're going to come home at the end of the night. For all those who aren't in a job that has danger every day, those people got up and went to work on a beautiful day, and it's not supposed to be like that. It makes you appreciate every day.

And then all those responders, who just put the time and effort in every day. The self-sacrifice. It's just amazing. It was amazing to see people, and a nation, and a community come together.

It's funny how that brought everyone together for a common goal of just comforting each other. You don't see that too often. It was a life-changing experience.

CHAPTER 19

HOPE WAS ALL WE COULD GIVE

*Anthony was a New York City police detective when the Twin Towers were
attacked. His narrative is rather special for a number of reasons: It is the
most comprehensive description of a responder's personal journey, from the
moment he found out what had happened until he returned full-time back to
his unit. It is also well-articulated: He has a phenomenal memory for details,
and he is thoughtful and reflective. He covers many of the perspectives that
others did, but his story includes some observations that are uniquely his.*

*On the morning of September 11th, Anthony was on his way to a
training session at Chelsea Piers in Lower Manhattan.*

I CALLED MY OFFICE IMMEDIATELY, and my boss said do
what you can to get in here. My office at the time was working in the
police impersonation squad; [it] was in Long Island City right off the
L.I.E. It took me about forty minutes to get from where I was on the
L.I.E. to over there, which is normally a five- to ten-minute ride.

Everybody was stopped. There were people standing on the L.I.E.
looking at the burning towers. Nobody was going anywhere. I think at that
point, bridge and tunnel [the Port Authority] was starting to shut down
everything. People started making decisions in the city to not let anybody
in and not let anybody out.

DON'T GO DOWN THERE

We had a TV set up in the office. We're just watching the TV and waiting
for word from the higher-ups for what to do. In the building that I worked
in, there were several investigative units. The highest-ranking boss at the
time was a deputy inspector. So they put him in charge to get all of us over
there. He started rounding up all of our cars—and we all had unmarked
cars—to just fill them up with bodies and just get in there.

On the collapse of the second building, I was on the 59th Street Bridge
going in the oncoming traffic lanes. When I was a kid I had a book about

World War II from Time-Life, and it had pictures of these soldiers who were POWs and they all had this blank look on their faces—nothing going on, the lights were on, but nobody was home. We had seas of people walking over the 59th Street Bridge to get out of Manhattan, and as I'm darting my car towards them, they're just parting like the Red Sea. It was like, everybody had that same look. That's when it started for me. They're all going this way, and I'm going that way.

You didn't know what to expect. You say, "If they were this organized," I mean, "are they going to blow up this bridge as I'm driving over right now?" That's what we were really worried about, because if they did have ordnance throughout the city, that was the start of it, and let's see what else we can blow up—George Washington Bridge, 59th Street Bridge, things like that.

We finally got over, and we were directed to go to the Police Academy to rally up there to find out what we're going to do. By the time we got there, there were already first responders who went there and were coming back. A very good friend of mine—Steven, who was the commanding officer at the time of the K-9 unit—was my first real harsh recollection of what 9/11 was all about. [He] was standing in front of me covered in soot, dust, whatever you want to call it—and his dog was covered in dust, and he had that look on him.

I said, "What's going on down there?"

He said, "Just don't go." He goes, "Don't go there."

I said, "What do you mean, don't go there?"

He said, "Don't go down there." He said, "There's nothing to do right now. There's stuff falling all over the place." He said, "Guys are going to get hurt real bad if they go down there. I'm lucky to be here."

WAITING AT THE HOSPITALS

Since we were an investigative unit, they wanted us to find out from survivors and the injured, "What did you see? What do you know?" It was good calculated move to find out what we could, because we're under attack, we don't know what's going on. So they just started sending us in groups to area hospitals.

And we're waiting, all just sitting there waiting in the parking lots, right at the emergency room entrances—pads in hand, waiting for survivors and people who were injured to come in. We're waiting and waiting and there's no ambulances coming. "There's got to be some people hurt." We knew down there they almost immediately set up a triage. A lot of the injuries of course were going to be glass and cuts and bruises, things like that, so we knew they weren't going to just start flooding emergency rooms with people with "I hurt my arm." This was for people who were messed up. We're waiting. Nothing.

Finally a couple of ambulances do come in, and the one guy I interviewed was a fireman. He blew my mind. He was on the 14th floor, going up towards the 15th floor, and what they were doing was holding on to each other's coats as they were going up the stairs. He was a big Irish guy. He knew that the building collapsed, but he didn't know what happened. He said he got blown out "and the next thing I know I'm on Trinity Street, or Church, I can't remember where the hell I was." His head was messed up. He was in bad shape. I don't know what he saw, but I'm sure he was seeing things that I can't even fathom.

And at that moment he knew. He knew that he had survived and others didn't. He was very upset. All he wanted to do was get back down there and help his people, help his men out. I said, "You're not going anywhere." It's a very hard thing when you work with people that closely to be the guy that got out. You say, "Why me? Why not him?" You start thinking in your head immediately, "He's a better guy than me. I'm a good guy, he's a good guy, but he's got four kids. Why me?"

Survivor guilt is huge. I have no qualms in saying it—I suffer from PTSD from the events of 9/11 and the events thereafter with the cleanup effort and all the things I had to do in regards to it.

One of the very surreal moments for me during that time were the jets. You're standing out in that parking lot waiting for ambulances and an F-16 flies over your head at 500 miles a hour, and you think, "There is something really wrong here when you have F-16s flying over your head right now. This is war."

No information was coming in. Of course in NYPD—love all my guys—but we love to make our own little stories up about everything, especially the rumor mill. So one guy came over to you …"I heard the whole entire first precinct, they lost everybody." I'm thinking, "Oh my God, we just lost 200, 150 cops there. ESU went in and lost everybody." You're getting all this misinformation the entire day, and it just drains you.

I think I was there for the better part of the day. I remember leaving, going home at about 7:30, 8:00 that night. One day melted into another during that time. I went home at the time, my present wife, my girlfriend at the time— the look on her face was like, "What are you doing? You're not going back. You're not going in." What do you mean I'm not going in? It's what I do. I gotta go. I don't want to go. I'm not going to lie to you, I don't know when the next hit is going to be.

I was exhausted. I know I slept, I don't know how well I did. I just know I was so glad to be home. It was the sanctuary. I was away from the madness. The madness is over there, 40 miles to the west, and I was away from the madness, and I had to be back there in seven hours.

THE BEREAVEMENT CENTER

September 12th, I'm not going to lie to you, was a total blur to me. My next recollection is about the 13th, going into the 14th. Our unit was picked. We set up the bereavement center. We were first set up over at Bellevue, and then they moved us over to the armory.

You have lines of people, like they're getting on a roller coaster. That's what it looked like. Through media, we were telling people bring a hairbrush, bring a toothbrush, bring a picture, try and find out what they were wearing so we can start identifying people, bodies. Now our job is sit down, have an interview. What was sad was I got to know every single victim I had to intake, intimately. Asking very personal questions of people was very hard. Asking if the person was circumcised, things of that nature. Here's a father and a mother sitting there, "My son, he's twenty-three years old. He went to the Trade Center to go to work today. We haven't seen him, he hasn't called…" And I have to turn to the mother and say, "Was your son circumcised?" How is this comforting in any possible way? "Do you know what he was wearing? What watch, jewelry?"

Every person that I interviewed asked me, "Do you think that they're alive?" I held their hand and I said, "I hope they are." That's all I could do. But I knew. I knew after two or three days that their chances of survival are greatly diminished. You don't want to say, "Don't get your hopes up, but miracles do happen and hopefully it will happen to you." My problem was I was talking to hundreds of people a day. Hundreds of miracles don't get handed out very often. I knew what was going on.

We did that for a while. I don't know if this is the truth or not, but this is what I would like to believe—they saw it was starting to wear us out and we got pulled. I think they started realizing that we really need some professional help. They did bring in counselors. I remember talking to a priest a couple times while I was there, just to help.

Every day was packed. It also became the center for answers. So people we already took care of were coming back and just hanging around. I remember this one guy—he was a sweetheart of a guy. Very realistic, on the same page with me. His brother had passed away in the Trade Center and he was there with his parents—a very tight-knit family, you could tell. He was there every day. I would pass him and say, "How you doing? You hanging in there?" I would sit with the family for a few minutes and just talk to them. They would always be looking at me with these wide eyes, "Do you know something?" I said, "Believe me, the second I find out about anything…"

There were some good moments. We did have a couple. I remember information coming in on someone and it was like the family of Joe

Jones, "Are you here?" And people would be like, "That's us!" And they would whisk them down. I remember a couple moments like that, so that lightened up, for what we were doing.

A homicide detective or even a precinct detective that investigates homicides will only have to give, in their career, a tops of twenty notifications, that one detective. I'm talking about when we were having a thousand homicides a year. Nobody wants to do the notifications. To call somebody and say your loved one is dead. I was doing it on a scale that no one could believe. I wasn't ever really a homicide detective. I never really gave the bad news, as they say, to family, and here I am—do it.

They gave us a list of questions. That's what my job was. But my job turned out to be a lot more than just asking questions. There were a lot of people breaking down, and a lot of us were breaking down because not only are we dealing with your problems, I'm dealing with myself and my own problems. I'm dealing with your death, and one after the other after the other. It was overwhelming. But we got through.

GETTING THROUGH

It was my job. I felt it was a duty. If not me, then who? I'm doing it for the men. There is that there in your heart. But it's what you do and you can't run away. You can't just say "no," so you go and that's it. I'm not going to lie, I didn't want to. Some of the reasons why I went through PTSD was the way I felt I responded to responding. I didn't do enough. I wasn't there enough. How could I have a feeling of *I don't want to go*?

I've seen dead people many times in my career. Kids would shoot each other over a bandana or over five vials of crack. Things of just utter evil that you can't understand, like a father who hacks his whole family up. That's stuff that's going to mess you up. This, the World Trade Center getting dropped by two planes, that wasn't in the sheet. You're not prepared for this. When I signed up to be a cop I was going to chase bad guys and I was going to help people and respond to accident scenes. Yes, there was going to be some gore and stuff like that, but not this. This is a war zone.

I was talking with my parents a lot at the time. They were both still alive. My father was very insightful and just, "Be strong." The other detectives and I talked a little bit, but it's a very tough world like that. You really don't want to show too much of your true colors when you're in a working environment. Some people were wearing their hearts on their sleeves. I remember one of the girls I worked with was a very emotional person. Her heart is gold. Every time she did an interview, she needed a hug because she was devastated. Then there were other guys that seemed like these pillars of strength, and you look at them and say, "How are you dealing with this?" Then ten minutes later you're in the bathroom and you hear sobbing. They dealt with it on their own. I guess we all deal with it in our own way. As long as there was help for us. That was the biggest thing.

THE LANDFILL

We were then assigned to start working at the landfill in a rotation. I wasn't there every day. I would go once or twice a week, depending on how much was going on. Because as time started getting away from September 11th, we also had to realize there was still a lot of police work that had to be done. So you have to start working your cases. Then from there you go dig for bodies over in the landfill; go look for evidence, they would call it. It was the funniest thing I ever heard. Now dig for the people you just talked about for two weeks.

I gotta say: I look back, it's numbing. My brain was just on autopilot. Through therapy that I had to go through, which we'll get into later, but you learn that you're just going, you're just doing what you have to do and your brain is shutting off. But all this stuff is still being filed in a lot of wrong places. And comes up in the worst possible time to remember something. That's what trauma is all about.

The landfill for me was another—you've got to be kidding me. I've driven through Staten Island a hundred times in my life and you look at the landfill and say, "Wow, it's a big hill garbage is dumped on." To start saying we're going to go dig for body parts and whatever we can find on a garbage dump left a bad taste in my mouth. This is stupid, I was going to say, "We should have used Central Park because it's such a beautiful place, and what better place for people to be their final resting place." But …why ruin Central Park? I mean, you could understand my mindset. We have to use the biggest landfill in the world to do this? Then again, maybe it actually worked out to be one of the best ways to deal with what we had to do. I understand the decision-making; it's just personal feeling that just a lot of the debris and things that we had to go through were the remains of humans, were the remains of the people who died there, and basically it's dust and dirt now. It's not going anywhere from here. This is where it's going to end. This is their final resting place.

I think it bothered a lot of people, but then again I would love to see at this point that become a hallowed ground. Let's get away from calling it the Staten Island Landfill and let's call it something else. The final resting place of many people—it's not their entire body. People were turned to dust and they now lay there amongst the dirt and debris that was brought. I think we should do something about that in the future.

At first it was just like anything, because nobody ever dealt with anything of this nature. But when I first got there, one of the first two days we didn't have much. They gave me a mask. I'm sitting there like I am today—very comfortable clothes, sweatpants and a T-shirt and a little jacket—and they basically told us, what you're wearing today is going to go in that bag, and they gave us this big plastic bag and said do not take it into your house. The workboots and everything I had on—everything basically stayed in that bag, I tied it with a zip tie and I left it in the back of my car. I don't even know if that was the safest thing either, with all the stuff that I had on.

So the first couple times I went there, all they gave us was a respirator and goggles. Then they started giving us the Tyvek suits and the rubber gloves with the duct tape. And they really started treating this as a biohazard scene now—and other kinds of hazards, as well asbestos and things of that nature.

The first time I pulled up there, I remember they gave me a respirator and it only had one filter on one side. They ran out of filters for the other side, so the guy said, "We'll just duct tape that one." It was like, don't bitch about it. At least you got a respirator. They didn't know. They had no idea. Nobody knew.

They knew that if we didn't start digging this thing out and looking through this debris, we wouldn't know if there were any survivors. That's why they were really rushing. You had ironworkers and firemen and cops and all kinds of people just descending upon the Pile as we called it, decimating huge pieces of debris and making it manageable to get shipped across to Staten Island—trucked in—and we would sift through to try to find things.

What they did was they gave us garden tools. Rakes, hoes, and things of that nature. A truck would bring in a full load of debris. There was a shaker, so they would dump the dirt onto the shaker and that would separate any large pieces of debris off, and then you would have finer debris underneath the shaker so the larger pieces would go to the side. Half a body, piece of body come down. Things like that. So you had to stay by the shaker. After that they would come by and scoop up the dirt that went through the shaker that was finer, and he would bring his bucket way up into the air and finally sift this dirt across the field, and we would get out of the way and put the dirt down and a whole bunch of us would descend upon it and start picking through it.

Whatever things we found that we thought were personal effects or important to an investigation, we'd pull out. We'd have five-gallon buckets, put it in there, and we'd take our five-gallon buckets and bring them to a central place and go back.

As time went on for us to do this task, I remember it getting more and more equipment. Big tents so we can eat. The first week I was there they were having sandwiches, and they were donated by some wonderful deli that was in the area.

I have a lot of memories that stick with you for the rest of your life. There were people who stand out there every day with signs thanking us. Thank me? You're taking your time to say that I'm doing something great here?

They would have us washed basically before we would go into the mess tent and eat. They were all volunteers. I remember this kid from Alabama was scrubbing my boots. And I said, "What are you doing up here from Alabama?" He goes, "I got nothing better to do, so I thought I'd volunteer and help you guys out."

I looked at him and said, "You're doing this and you're not getting paid for it?" I just sat there and rolled my eyes... Now I'm going in and sitting and eating a meal that somebody else prepared for me and feeling a little self-loathing that here I was bitching that it took me two hours to get to a landfill today on the Staten Island Expressway—and this guy came all the way up from Alabama to scrub my boots because he wanted to help. I just sat there and shook my head.

He respects me and I'm looking at him like: no, dude, you're the guy. I'm just doing my job. You're the guy. And that's the way I felt about it. The people who sat out there and waved flags as I drove in from my house in Long Island—those were my heroes. Those were the people that made me feel like I wasn't even worthy to be there.

It's unbelievable the things that you learn. The Red Cross was always there for us. A lot of volunteers—and they're enamored with me. I get a paycheck every two weeks to come here. I still get a paycheck. Not that I was doing this only for money, but you understand what I'm saying? I'm still getting paid—and paid very well with the overtime—and you're coming up here on your own time to scrub my freaking boots? Are you kidding?

PTSD

I relied on my girlfriend tremendously. She was there for me every step of the way. But I have to say that I wasn't there. It was a one-way street. I wasn't producing at the time or being a good mate because I was dealing with what I was dealing with.

Thank God I never really drank heavily, but I was drinking. It was a little bit of an escape on the weekends just to get away, but it never became, thank God, a problem. But I know that there were times when I said, "I know why I'm doing this." It never became a daily thing, but it became a part of how to deal with it. You learn that's not the right course either... It's okay to unwind, but let's not go too far.

I was a very lucky person. Some people aren't as fortunate as me. I'm sure they're still out there hurting deeply. All I can say is: Go find somebody to help you. It's out there, we're out there. If you're a cop, call POPPA; they saved my life. They saved me from utter destruction, because I could definitely see if I didn't take the path of going to really bad places. I do suffer from PTSD. It took me five years of intensive therapy and drugs to get through that. About 2004, I had a massive panic attack that I thought was a heart attack. And in 2004, I was thirty-five years old. I went to the emergency room, the whole nine yards. The doctor said you're as fit as a fiddle. You're a little overweight, but your heart is fine. He looked at me and said, "Is something bothering you?" I just broke down. I couldn't believe it.

I didn't know what was going on. Thankfully I got into a program through the New York City Police Department, POPPA, and they found me a therapist I had actually seen before 2001 September 11th. I was going through a divorce. I could never say I'm cured. Two nights ago, I'm watching TV with my wife. They had a special on K-9s. It was a National Geographic Channel show about the working dogs, and they were doing the New York City Police Department's bomb dogs. They panned on the garage that I was talking about earlier, when I saw Steve and his dog and all the guys from ESU covered in the ashes and stuff. I'm getting chills just talking about it right now. I looked at my wife and said, "Some memories just never go away." It brought me right back to that day and I started to cry.

I'll always have those memories. It's just indelible in my mind, and thank God for the therapy I did go through. I don't know, maybe this will help— it was called EMDR [eye movement desensitization and reprocessing therapy]. It was using your eye movements to recollect. Trauma is taking a tomato and throwing it against the wall and it splatters and goes in all different directions. All those little pieces have to come back and be put in the proper filing. Most of that's done while you're sleeping, while you have rapid eye movement, REM stage. They take this little machine with LED lights and I'm going back and forth and just follow it with your eyes. Then you talk about the events that bothered you. It's like peeling back layer after layer, and what's amazing is I started with September 16th, 2001, one of the events I was going through, and it brings me back to when I'm seven years old by the time we're done. I won't get into it tremendously, but it's amazing how your mind connects things from your past to something traumatic and to where you are right now—and how all of those things interlink. And then next thing, you can actually put it all in a neat little package and understand it better. You never healed from it, but you have now learned to deal with it.

For the last three years I haven't been on any psychotropic drugs, and

I haven't had a panic attack. I've had little flutters here and there, you always get them, but I haven't had a real full-blown panic attack in three years. I'm pretty happy 'bout that because they suck, bad.

PEOPLE HAVE TO REMEMBER

A lot of people seem to want to forget it and put it in the past. That's understandable. I do too. I don't want to sit there and relive it. There are days where, like National Geographic has the conspiracy theory on, and then 9/11 minute by minute. I don't even watch them.

I get it. 9/11 was a big thing, but it's got its time and place. We can remember on 9/11, and we just have to not forget what brought us to 9/11—what it was all about, what happened that day. But we don't have to sit there every single day and think about 9/11. We all have lives too. But when certain things come up, we have to remember why it happened, what happened, and who did it.

Lately with the people with the body scan, it's become the big thing, such an intrusion. Tell that to the 200 some-odd people whose plane went flying into a building that day. I guarantee you every one of them would be here sitting here saying, "Oh yeah. I'll strip down naked and do the herky-jerky so that someone doesn't fly a plane into a building again." You won't be able to travel, you won't be able to do what you do now if we don't do what we do to keep ourselves free. You have to take away freedom to get freedom. It sounds mind-boggling, but that's the truth.

I get very angry. I don't want to get political, [but] the whole mosque thing gets me very upset. People forget that the reason that building wasn't used for ten years, if you're watching this, was because a piece of the engine was in the building. That's why they condemned it for ten years, and now we want to make it a mosque? I'm sorry. Find another spot.

I remember September 12th and on, people almost having fistfights in the middle of Walmart to get a flag. July 4th I looked down my block, I'm the only guy with a flag out. September 11th, I put my flag at half-mast. I'm the only guy with a flag on my block. What happened? 'Cause September 12th, I remember everybody driving around with flags hanging off their cars almost causing accidents and stuff like that, but people were damned [proud] to show their patriotism. Not any more.

I would love to go back, if I could, in a time machine, and pull a guy over who stapled or taped a flag to the front of his car, and see if he has that flag flying in front of his house—a flag, any flag, I don't care—and then take him with me. Remember that guy? Hey that's me. Yeah, that was you ten years ago. What happened? You were a patriot then; what happened today?

People were happy. People loved each other in a brotherly love sense. We're back to where we were September 10th, 2001. Everybody's got blinders on. I think that's the biggest message, if I could ever get to people, is don't forget how you felt on 9/12. Don't forget that. You don't want to think about the bodies and the people jumping out. I want to forget all of that, believe me. Those things haunt me, and I don't want to remember them.

That guy from Alabama I spoke of earlier, he just came up to hang and help out another American who was going through a tough time. I look at Katrina, during any kind of... it doesn't matter what it is. There are hundreds and thousands of people who will flock on their own time and not ask for anything in compensation. Maybe, just can you house me and maybe give me a meal while I'm down here to help people. It's utterly amazing, and if we all keep that in our head I think the future of this country will always be that way. That there are people who will put themselves in harm's way just so that the other guy can prosper. It's an amazing thing to see. I witnessed it firsthand, not only as a first responder.

I'm still quite scared that I'm going to come here one day and I'm going to take a video of my chest and [they'll] say, "Oops, we found something." Every time I come here and they tell me I got a clean bill of health, I do a double-heel click when I walk out the door, because nobody wants to go out that way. So God willing, things will be that way for me. Some of the other ones weren't as fortunate as me, Jimmy Zadroga—thank God the bill just passed—but you think of a man like him. Every single day down on that heap, and then he gets sick, and then politicians start playing a little game—it's disgusting.

I guess my only last thing I would say is that even if you weren't there and you weren't affected, speak out about it. If it hurts you or pains you to see people like me that were in pain over this, not get certain things that they should get, pick up a phone, call your congressman, and bitch. Don't just sit there, look at the TV, and say that's a shame. Do something about it.

CHAPTER 20

BURN-OUT

William is currently retired from the police force, but works part-time as a park ranger. He was a New York City police officer in 2001. He comes from police officer's stock. "My whole family is cops," he says proudly. "We go back over one hundred years." He served for sixteen years in emergency services, including intelligence and counterterrorism. Over his career William had been involved in rescue operations of plane crashes, train derailments, hundreds of car accidents with fatalities, shootings, homicides, body recoveries—yet nothing prepared him for what he went through on 9/11. It had changed him forever. William tells his story from the perspective of a tough and seasoned law enforcement professional, but when we read his testimony, we realize that despite all his experience, he was affected just as much as all the others. Through his candid story, we learn about his incredible courage and his humility.

I RETIRED AT THE END OF '06 FROM THE NYPD. I have about sixteen years in emergency service. I did some intel stuff, some counterterrorism stuff, but most of my sixteen years was in Emergency Service Unit. It's a SWAT team, but also a rescue unit.

I actually retired in '04 when my twenty years were up. I got asked to go back to the job, and I stayed until '06. I earned my detective shield, but it was different after 9/11. A lot of my friends were gone by the time I came back. A lot had retired. I was only out for seven months before I came back again, and I came back not so much because I was asked, but because I felt stuck. I didn't feel like I fit outside.

I was scheduled to do a 4 to 12 [on September 11th]. I got woken up to the news coverage that a plane had hit the Tower. And even at that point, even before anybody realized it was a terrorist attack, I knew what my unit had to do. There are only 200 of us for the whole city of 30,000 cops. I started getting my stuff together. I called the office and they said, "Yeah, you have to get in."

I remember myself and a couple of other guys—one guy I remember, Jack—we had to get a bunch of generators and tools we thought we were going to need. We commandeered a city bus. We threw everybody off the bus and told the driver he's going through the Battery Tunnel.

You might be based in Brooklyn, but you work with guys from every other borough—Queens or Bronx—Emergency Services is a very interchangeable unit. We just hook up with guys from other trucks. We felt bad for the bus driver. We got there and he said, "What do I do now?" We said, "I don't know what to tell you; you can try to turn around." We just got through the tunnel, unloaded all our stuff, and the people who got off the bus were saying, "Don't worry about it, man. Just be careful."

It starts to hit because we're at a pile that was still on fire at the time, and we're trying to recover bodies, and there was such chaos because we lost thirteen guys from our unit—friends of mine, guys that I had played on the football, lacrosse teams with. They were in emergency services and later we found out they didn't make it.

I remember the first night working till—I think they pulled us off at like 3:30 in the morning. I was in a little hole with another fireman digging out the Port Authority guy that was buried for so long, and waiting for another team to rotate in as we came out. And then had to be back at work at seven in the morning.

I felt like I needed to just touch base with a sense of reality, and shower and wash my clothes and then go back. I remember my hair was so thick with this stuff. I tried to wash it four or five times, but my hair was so matted with this crap—in my ears, in my eyes, in my nostrils, everywhere. My clothes wouldn't come clean. That first night, no one really had masks; we had those paper things.

THE MCLOUGHLIN RESCUE

As I was getting to the Pile there was his partner—I forget who it was, a Spanish guy. And we just waited to rotate in, because the hole was only big enough for two people. The hole was so small that we had to crawl, almost snake. You had an entrance and you had to lay on your belly and snake around. It was dark. There was fire—you could see the flames burning underneath. It was right next to an elevator shaft.

I remember because I was leaning on it and a guy said, "That's an elevator shaft." And you could see down. You thought you were on the ground because there was a pile, but we were like six, seven stories up.

He was buried, and the hole was so small we had to take our packs off to be able to get in that way. That's how tight it was. We were scraping, trying to scoop up dirt. We would push it back, and then you put it in stuff, and you try to push it back out of the hole and eventually …

What I remember most was they put a line around our waist. And the first thing I was thinking was, "Well, I'm going in this way. I'm snaking around on my belly—there's no way you could pull me out." And the guy just looked at me, he was a fireman actually, he looked at me and… It was just so that if it collapsed on us they would just know where to look later on. We would be on the end of the rope. It wasn't to pull us out, it was just to find us if we died.

I didn't really think about it. I was scared, but it's what it is. I was in there with a fireman, his first name was Liam, he was from a rescue unit. We were talking later on in the cafeteria, a day or two later. It was fucked up being in there. But thank God McLoughlin came out, and he's as okay as he can be.

They didn't get him out until seven in the morning. I was just one of the teams that rotated through. There were teams after and before me.

IT DIDN'T LOOK REAL

It didn't look real. You're almost numb walking in. Being in a unit where we saw so much, and so much death—we did building collapses, we'd done plane crashes—but there was building after building. It wasn't just *that* building, but it was buildings around the outside that were falling as we were working, and they were on fire.

During the early part of the day, guys were very jumpy because they had fighter planes that were circling Manhattan. I guess they were going to shoot down whatever was inbound instead of waiting for it to hit. And we were all double-checking: Is this a plane coming in?

FILTHY

We team up in the morning, you get the equipment that you needed for the day. You get a grid to go search, you muster up with your team, they load you on the back of a truck. Then they take you onto the Pile, drop you off. They leave and pick you up maybe four or five hours later when you had your break.

On break [you] just eat, [make] a lot of phone calls. Guys were on the phone a lot. Getting their eyes washed out, trying to switch their masks because they were filled, they were so heavy. You were out there a couple of hours and you couldn't breathe through it anymore. It got so loaded with particles, it was either so heavy it would fall off your face or you just couldn't get air through it anymore. So guys would just get rid of them, or you just hung it off your belt until you could change your canisters.

For the first couple of weeks we were eating under a Red Cross tent in the open air. [After] a couple of days, a guy said, "I don't know how safe this shit is." Because before you had your sandwich, you had to wipe the dust off it. You were getting juice and stuff like that, so whatever you were eating the shit was all over. We were eating this stuff for weeks.

The thing that stuck in my mind that I thought was funny was that we're sitting and eating in this stuff and breathing it all day, but there was no decontamination when we left the site, but when we left, they would have a checkpoint and they would wash our cars off so we wouldn't contaminate the rest of the city. We're caked in this shit, and we're driving home and back to our headquarters or back to our command with this stuff in our hair, our nostrils and everything else. But they want to wash our car off to make sure we don't contaminate anybody on the way out.

You were so burnt out, honestly, you didn't give a shit anymore. And then you hear Christine Todd Whitman: Oh, she took readings—the air is fine. What do you mean the air is fine? Come stand with me in the Pile, okay, with this paper mask, and you stay here with me until we're done here, and you tell me the air is fine. Go have a sandwich, a cup of juice. It's fine, you won't have any problems. Really?

Nobody had any regrets about going in there—even as sick as the guys are and all the things we've come down with healthwise. I don't think there is anybody that still wouldn't want to be there and be able to contribute and be able to look for their friends and do their part and serve their country.

It's who I am. It's who we all were. It's why we choose it as a profession. Not just the cops—the firemen, the EMTs, everyone [who] was down there, the Red Cross, everybody. It's why we chose that profession. It wasn't to get rich. It's what you felt in your heart. I would do it again. It would suck, but I would do it again.

THE CITY DIDN'T CALL A TIME OUT

My memories are just how difficult everything was—everything—home life, getting along with people at work. Healthwise, just I remember the tiredness and fatigue that kept at me for months. It just sucked.

And the thing was done. They're already trying to scrape out a foundation at this point. All the ceremonies were done…But there are these two Port Authority guys, and they're still down there. I gues s they had to detail. They're like looking for stuff. I walked there and said, "What are you guys up to?"

And they said, "We got the detail today."

I'm like, "This thing is ending tomorrow, right? They're starting construction." They just looked at me. I said, "Dude, it's over."

They looked at each other like … there is nothing else to look for. I think it just hit them. It was fucked up. I felt bad. We're done. You were like machines, you were programmed.

They had the plane crash in the Rockaways right after 9/11, and I was involved in that too. That was my third plane crash that I pulled bodies out of. I did Flight 50 in 1989. I did the other one after that in 1991 in LaGuardia also, where they had ice on the wings and it flipped. And this is the third one. We had everybody cut out of the plane and bagged by 6:00 at night. The FBI couldn't believe that we did it this fast, because we were like machines. We've been at the Pile doing this. It wasn't anything. It was almost like you were just collecting things. It wasn't even people. It was fucked up.

I remember everyone was burnt and there were body parts. This guy … we get him on the thing, and I'm looking around, and I remember he had a blue sweater or blue shirt. They're ready to take him and put him in the thing and I said, "I saw an arm with a sleeve that matches that. Just give me a minute." I'm walking around looking through the Pile, and I found the arm. I said, "Hang on a second," I threw it in. It's like, "You forgot a shoe; don't go outside." It wasn't like it was this gross thing. I just felt like the guy should have the other arm. But you're that desensitized from years of being in emergency service, and the coup de grâce was 9/11.

You had regular things. All of the other stuff never went away in emergency service. You still had your cycles. You still had your car accidents, you still had your perp jobs, and all the other crazy stuff that you did, it didn't go away. The city didn't call a time out on all the other lunatics. Here we are with 260 dead people from a Dominican airline jet, and we're cutting people loose because we're too busy. How insane. We didn't catch a break. It was just one thing after another.

YOU NUMB OUT

After a while, we were so burnt and calloused and fried, we didn't give a fuck. I remember that they would have these psychologists that would go down to the site. They would come around and ask, "How are you feeling today?" And I said, "I feel like I'm going to be a real danger to myself and others. We were all having thoughts." And they ran over to their supervisor, and we would just laugh because we just didn't give a fuck no more. We were just having fun at this point.

Nobody was really themselves after all that. I was [at the World Trade Center] the first day. I was there till middle of January, I think. You'd go in two days a week, or whatever, you were at the Pile. The other three days you were on patrol doing the warrants and all that other stuff.

The neighbors were great. They were making meals. I was coaching a football team. One of my sons was on the team, and I remember I was gone for a couple of weeks because it was so nuts. But I showed up one night to practice to coach, and they saw me coming across the field, and the team just came up to me and started hugging me and shit. It felt good. A bunch of 10-year-olds.

Both of [my sons] joined the service because of [9/11]. My older one was in Iraq during the surge. My younger one is in now. He was in BUD/S [Basic Underwater Demolition/SEAL Training] for a thing called SWCC [Special Warfare Combatant-craft Crewmen]. It was a Special Warfare for the Navy. He busted his ankle, but he's on an aircraft carrier right now.

I feel like I'll never get back to the way it used to be. I was a lot lighter. I was a lot funnier. I feel it's really hard to be truly happy now... I'm proud of my sons and I love my sons and I'm grateful for all of that, but [not happy in a sense where] I feel like a real laugh, a goof-around laugh. A certain amount of stuff happens to you; it took that away from me.

The whole thing was unfortunate. To tell you the truth, there was nothing good about it. There was nothing inspiring other than the camaraderie that we had as a group—the cops, the firemen, the ironworkers, EMTs. Everybody who got together, we said it all sucks, but it all sucks for all of us. We all help each other out. No one will understand what our group went through. I hope no one does. I wouldn't wish that shit on anyone. That was horrible.

I don't even know how many guys died because of 9/11 illnesses, but there is a lot, and I don't think people realize that. I just hope people don't forget—especially the real heroes. They aren't here talking about how they felt about that day. The rest of us were just doing cleanup and body recoveries. The heroes are the guys that we were looking around for their gun belt or their shield so we could bury them, because that's all that was left. There was no body. I just hope that people don't forget what everybody did there and how shitty it was.

I'm proud as hell to be an American. Bet your ass on that.

YOU'RE NOT CONTROLLING ANYTHING

I watched this shit at 9/11. Every year they have all this crap. I disappear for two days. I don't want to know shit. I don't want to see any more building collapses. I don't want to see anything. I don't want to see footage of it anymore. I don't want to go anywhere near it. I don't want to know about it.

It was the people who weren't there who want the experience. And trust me, you did not want that experience. Be thankful that you're watching on TV, that you weren't there. Just be thankful because it sucked. Everything about it sucked.

[We lost thirteen guys.] Out of a population of 200, thirteen guys is a lot. And they were just good, solid guys. I played lacrosse with two of them—Vigiano and Kloepher. It sucks to look at their empty lockers. I think the hardest part was just going to all the funerals. It never goes away.

I think everyone was just shocked emotionally. I think there are a lot of guys who were depressed. A lot of guys had problems at home. A lot of guys got divorced and separated. I ended up getting separated for four years. It's just tough.

So try to be as good a person as you can now, because a lot of times people don't have the chance, and it's too late. But if you see enough death and you're involved in enough situations that you could have gotten killed, you really realize that. And so as far as being spiritual … yeah, I don't believe anybody is really in control of their own destiny. I always believed that you may think you're driving the car, but God is having a good laugh. You're not controlling anything, so just try to be as good a person as you can while you're here.

FROM GUEST TO PEST

I remember we would go down there, we were leaving the site. The people from the city were out clapping and cheering us on as we pulled into the Pile and pulled out. And it felt great.

Now we're at the point where we have to wait for the Senate to vote on whether they want to compensate the guys there for medical coverage—compensate us monetarily for the stuff we did down there.

It's funny. When you're here you're a guest, when you're gone you're a pest. And now all of a sudden, it's… "Who are these guys? We really have to do that? Why should I lay that money out? That wasn't my state." *Really?* But if it was, how would you feel? They don't realize a lot of these guys are too ill to get the job that they wanted after they retired. They're too sick or mentally not able. We didn't go away, and more of us are dying, and more of us are getting sicker. Now they don't know if they want to take care of us.

It's a shame. I wonder how they would feel if they were with us every morning getting on that truck and breathing that crap in and pulling up bloody shirts and fingers and arms and everything else until January. Guys aren't asking for anything they don't deserve. They're not being greedy. Take care of us.

We didn't ask any questions: "Wait a minute. Before we go into the Pile, we have a checklist of everything we want when we're done." We just went because that's what we were supposed to do.

Stop with all your bull, and do what you're supposed to do—like we did. The guys are feeling very betrayed. All of us. I hope this thing called the Zadroga bill goes through, because I will commend [Congressman Anthony] Weiner for standing up for us.

Just don't forget the people who didn't make it, or the people who are going to die as a result of it. So when you read about these guys that got killed down there and all these people, [realize] how truly heroic they were and the sacrifice they made. Just don't skim through it in your history book. Read it, because I lived it, a lot of people lived it, and it was horrible.

CHAPTER 21

WE HID AND CRIED

Christine, a longtime resident of Bay Shore, Long Island, was an officer with the New York City Police Department for twenty years. She had spent most of her years of service patrolling the streets of South Jamaica, Queens. Christine has a special style of describing her experience from a female police officer's perspective. Her account of those first hours, and the days that follow, is not so much a story as it is a collection of impressions that are carved into her brain; she brings them up and shoots them at you in a staccato style.

AS I SAW IT, I STARTED PACKING A BAG because I knew it was bad. The first plane had only hit, and I knew it wasn't a joke, I knew it wasn't an accident. I call my parents in Florida right away. My parents are World War II heroes. My mom was a nurse; my dad drove the landing craft on the beaches. I said, "Put on the TV. Something is going on in New York City. I'm gonna go back to work; they haven't called me yet, but I know they will." I said, "I packed a bag. I'm going back to work. I love you." I hung up, got back in my car, and then drove from Long Island.

Christine made it to her precinct planning to load up emergency supplies and take them down to the Trade Center.

I was ready to load up my truck and it was organized already. They said, "You, you, and you: Suit up. You're getting on a war bus." I said, "What is a war bus?" They said [to] suit up and they put twenty-five of us on the city bus. They had body bags and MREs [Meals, Ready to Eat]. Some food. They told us to just keep driving around. And I guess they were waiting for another attack. We couldn't understand what we were doing at first; we were listening to Citywide and we were listening to the chaos, and we were like horses in the gate. Let us go down there. I think they just didn't want us all to run down there and then have something else happen and then have no cops. They definitely had a plan in place. And some of them were thinking enough to not have us all run down there and get killed. It's actually brilliant. Pissed us off, but in the long run, brilliant.

There was a couple war buses floating around from every command. We [were] just driving around, waiting for someone to tell us, "Alright, they hit us over here. Go over there." We were angry—almost wanted to take the bus and just drive it, throw the bus driver out. Then they brought us back into the precinct and they starting setting us up in long, like, different charts and different squads. 'Cause they knew we were going into twelve-hour tours, no days off—how it was gonna go down. It was late, it was dark, and they said to me, "Four a.m. tomorrow you're going down to the Trade Center." I went home, took a shower, took a nap, watched the news. You couldn't sleep. It was just chaos. I don't know what I expected to find. I was definitely frightened.

When I went back to work, there were more buses in front of the precinct. At four o'clock, we all got on the buses to go down to the Trade Center. I'll never forget riding over that bridge. We were the only bus on the road. Just seeing the smoke and you could hear a pin drop. You got forty, fifty cops on a bus, and you can hear everybody breathing. We got off the bus and we were going to do, like, an inner perimeter. So like in the dust area, they still had no equipment for us at all. Nothing. As we were walking in, we could see firemen and other cops walking out. I'll never forget the looks on their faces. It was like hollow souls. We're walking in all clean and shiny and they're coming out just looking like hell.

We knew where we were supposed to be, but everybody went over to help. And the minute me and another fellow cop from 113 walked into the site itself—the hole like the canyon—guys were yelling, "Help us over here! Help us over here!" And they were pulling out a Port Authority cop who was deceased. We were helping them with the stretcher; we were trying to get the shield off and the gun off. Everything was burned. It was just horrendous.

Out of nowhere, an ambulance just backed in. Out of nowhere, a flag was handed to one of the guys. We did, on our knees, a little makeshift memorial quickly, 'cause we heard all the guys yelling for help. Actually, I think I even heard some gunshots down there. I think that was when they rescued one of the last cops. We got that guy into the bus, [and] we pulled out another Port Authority guy right away.

After that, somebody grabbed us. I think they were with the Fire Department. They asked, "Can you guys help right in this area with finding any body parts, any IDs, things like that?" We were like, "Absolutely." They gave us bags, tags, and all kinds of stuff. You were looking at stuff down there and you couldn't make out what it was. The first thing I found was an entire body, burned to the rebar. But you had to look a couple times. We needed a wheelbarrow. You couldn't just bag this, tag this, and carry it out. I thought I saw a driver's license. It turned out to be a business card. I saw a women's pocketbook. I picked it up [and] it was the top of someone's skull and it was burnt, the hair was burnt. But the majority, it was so unexplainable—the rubble down there. There was not a desk, there was not a chair, there was not a computer, there was not a briefcase; there was nothing but dust, concrete, rebar, and papers flying around. It was an unbelievable mess.

That day there was no food available to us. So we met our sarge back at the original post we were supposed to be on. Everybody was so crazy down there. I just said, "I'm going on a reconnaissance mission to try to find some food for us," 'cause now we're down there probably sixteen, seventeen hours and we are starving. So I took this little rook with me and we went looking around. We find a case of water abandoned. I guess people were dumping off stuff. We find a case of juice. Somebody from the Red Cross waved us down and had some wrapped sandwiches. And then I found this seat from a police van, so we stacked everything on the seat from the police van and we carried it back. When we walked back our sergeant was with a chief, and normally you don't come walking up to a chief. I didn't care. We walked up with food and the chief was like, "Keeping this girl! She found the food!" It was no rank, and it was, like, together.

WE NEEDED HELP

I've been on NYPD long enough to know we never need help doing nothing. But we needed help. Then the help started arriving. It was incredible. Guys just started rolling in their personal cars—buses of guys coming in from Virginia, Pennsylvania, and then from the Carolinas, and Florida. The feds started showing up like crazy. The soldiers started showing up. It was incredible. It was absolutely incredible how everybody came to help.

We had no equipment; it was not a pretty sight. You're throwing up. Your nose is bleeding and stuff is falling. I was down there for months, and when you are working on this rubble heap, they blow a whistle. That meant [you should] run off the heap really fast because glass shards are coming down. A guy not too far from me—his arm just got cut off by a giant glass shard. So they were trying to get us off as quickly as possible. A few days into it I was down there working on a rubble heap when they blew the whistle, and they just started yelling, "Run! Run! Run!" There was cranes lifting things above your head. One time, they dropped a steel bar on the steel rut we're standing on. We all went flying. The guy next to me: compound fracture. I had a bruise from here to here. Thank God no one got killed. But everybody was trying like crazy to still find people. You'd be digging out a fire truck for twenty hours. Then you pull it out and it's completely crushed—there's nobody in it. They cut it open at Staten Island—six guys in it. We didn't even see them; we didn't figure that they were in there because it was just impossible for someone to be in there.

Overwhelmed—just overwhelmed. I think once we realized that nobody was alive, that was when it really set in—like, "Oh, man."

The first day we were down there like twenty-seven hours. Then we went into twelve-hour shifts of patrol, and then sixteen [hours] down at the Tower, which sometimes turned into twenty-four because when they needed you down there, they needed you down there. So every third day, for like twenty hours we were down there, running out of clothes, not eating anything normal. I mean, thank God for the ladies in South Jamaica that brought us food and boxes of socks and underwear. And the stuff that came in from all over the country—it was incredible. Sometimes I went home, but what could you really do? I cried, I would try and call one of my sisters. And then I watched the news, which we started calling crack TV 'cause you couldn't stop watching it. You would cry yourself to sleep and just take a shower. You really didn't have time to do laundry or anything like that 'cause it was such a quick turnaround.

About two weeks into it, we definitely had all the gear, but the gear didn't matter because it was such a stench of, like, a crematorium—just bodies burning. You couldn't get away from it, you had to just rub Vicks all underneath the masks and pray to God. Then you would still go throw up. It was just terrible.

About two weeks into it, though, a wonderful little funny thing happened. The dogs were the ones getting hurt down there—they were the little unsung heroes—dogs were getting depressed 'cause they weren't finding survivors. So I had been down there with a guy from the 113, and they had asked for volunteers to hide in the rubble. They pulled everybody off the rubble and they hid a bunch of us up there and told us to lie down like we were hurt. They sent all the dogs in, and the dogs started barking. Everybody was clapping. Life came back to the place and we pretended like they found us. That was something unbelievably moving.

Cops—we tell jokes about everything. There was not a joke told probably six, seven months. I can remember one of my old partners standing in the precinct going, "Is it ever going to be alright for us to joke around again or to tell a joke?" It was just total silence. It took the wind out of our sails. We loved watching the military guys when the war started. There was a TV on in the muster. When they were painting NYPD and NYFD on those missiles they were launching over, there was not a dry eye in the entire precinct.

When we pick up a piece of something, they would yell, "Hot! "Sharp!" or "Heavy!" We would pass it to the next person, but it would be an NYPD guy passing it to a Fort Lauderdale cop passing it to a federal agent from Washington passing it to a Virginia cop passing it to a fireman from Daytona Beach. FEMA came. They came—the shiny uniforms—they pulled up in three huge buses. They marched out and I watched them. They marched right up to the edge of the barricades and you saw them do this: "Oh my God." Guys, you can suit up, but you cannot fix this thing. I think they come [thinking], "We're gonna fix this thing." You ain't gonna fix this thing. We need all of you to keep coming. When you look over your shoulder and the guys kept coming: from California and Oregon. We had border patrol guys from San Diego, California, staying in a hotel on our precinct.

The camaraderie—that is one thing. Let me tell you something: We are a force to be reckoned with and people, we're gonna always just stick with each other. The thing I carry away from this that is so sad—that I never want to see again—is that I work with a ton of big guys. Whether they're firemen or cops, I'm a little scrapper. When I need help, I need six guys and they know it. I never want to see a bunch of huge guys hiding in corners and down on their knees bawling like kids. You weren't allowed to cry down there, so we would hide. We built barricades—built little secret rooms where we could all go. I never want to see big giant groups of men like that crying. It was so overwhelmingly sad that we just had to keep standing each other up. Now you help me and I'll help you and then we'll help that guy.

A friend of mine drove the mass trauma bus down there. Her partner was killed instantly by a body. She ran and said the last thing she thought of was "God forgive me, but I hope to God that these buildings fall, because America will never understand all these people leaping out holding hands together, smashing down on the pavement." As quiet as it was kept, they never really showed you what happened down there. And the guys who saw that—I don't know if there's any way you can correct that.

I'm actually so blessed. A little guardian angel said go to the precinct 'cause I know I would have been down there running in like an idiot.

If it happened again, sick or not, I would go back again. I was a New York City cop. That was my city, my watch. You almost feel a little guilty. How the hell did we let this happen? In all the think tanks in the world, would you ever think that they would take a plane with innocent people and do that? That's pure evil.

I never was a crier. I think a bunch of us are criers now. We're more jumpy. A little more prepared, like I always have an NYPD Go Bag. I have a little cabin up in the mountains. It's stocked up, if Armageddon comes. It's like that weird.

We had stuff in the girls' locker room in our precinct. We had wipes, hand soap, and it would say on it, "We love you!" We wanted to write thank you. And the kids' things all over the precinct. "I love you" notes covered the walls. It was incredible. That is so motivating. The ladies in our precinct cooked for us every day. When they came in with the first spread of food after about a week... We just kissed them. We loved them. We were like, "Chicken—fried chicken. The thoughtfulness."

When we came back after the first day we went down for twenty hours, the bus stopped in front of the precinct across the street. The minute two to three got out of the bus—they were covered in dust—the cars on a big boulevard stopped going both ways. People got out of their cars and started applauding. It was amazing. I was like, "What happened? Where are we?" This a precinct where they kicked on you. Cops were not the highest on everybody's "I love" list back in those days. Being a cop was suddenly alright.

I think 9/11 has made us more prepared because we probably should have thought ahead that this might have happened. I know so many friends who have died from being sick after 9/11. I heard they finally put eleven guys on the police roll at 1 Police Plaza line-of-duty deaths from getting sick from being down there working without gear. Before 9/11 we didn't carry anything. The guys on the job now carry some good stuff. Now we carry very sophisticated masks. You'll see guys on foot in the city. They always have it on them. We always have it in radio cars, response autos. We have a giant suit—the big "weapons of mass destruction" suit. We can tape up, put a high-level mask on, go into pretty dangerous situations, and maybe try to get as many people out as we can. The training we got after 9/11 was incredible. It was very, very, very extensive training.

I think pictures don't do the devastation at the World Trade Center justice. You will never get it unless you were right in it. I don't think that you'll get that it took five hours to walk around the perimeter, that there were stations to feed dogs, dog triage, eye triage—because your corneas were constantly getting burned. I just hope that enough people recorded and wrote down enough things that you know it was really bad. The biggest, most important city in the world... We can never let this happen again. Absolutely not.

PART FOUR

THE RESPONDERS NEED HELP

In many ways, America was unprepared for the level of destruction and loss of human life caused by the World Trade Center disaster. However, there was a unifying sentiment across the country that New York City needed help. People came. They came from all over the country to assist New York City, to support their fellow Americans, to grieve, to hope, and to survive. In this next section, you will read the stories of people who may not first come to mind when we think about World Trade Center responders. They were the people who gave emotional support to the responders who worked the Pile, who mended wounds, wrapped sprained ankles, massaged away pain, and advocated for them for years after the cleanup was over. Their stories are about the interdependence of human beings in times of devastation, and renewal of the human spirit.

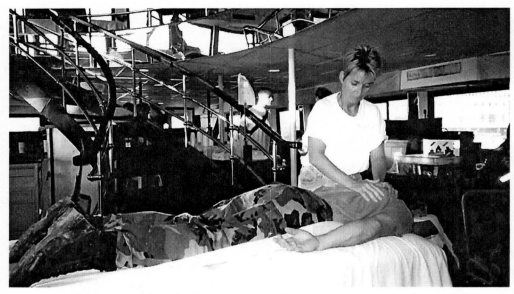

▲ **Licensed massage therapist Terese,** who shares her story as a volunteer at Ground Zero in Chapter 22, relieves a responder's aches and pains with a medical massage. *Photographer unknown.*

▲ **Responders' eyes are soothed and cleared** of ash and grit by volunteer medical personnel. *Photo by Roy and Lois Gross.*

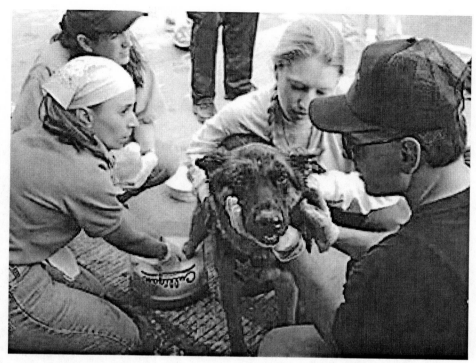

▲ **Veterinary volunteers examine and scrub down** a search and rescue dog to remove potentially toxic ash after a shift on the Pile. *Photo by Roy and Lois Gross.*

▲ **A responder is treated** at the site for a minor leg wound by a volunteer doctor. *Photo by Roy and Lois Gross.*

▲ **Responders document and declare their commitment to the recovery and cleanup** by writing in the dust on the columns of a blown-out, debris-strewn shell of a building near the World Trade Center site. *Photo by Roy and Lois Gross.*

CHAPTER 22

THE HANDS THAT HEAL

Terese, a licensed massage therapist, spent two months working around the clock at Ground Zero, coordinating efforts to provide medical massages to emergency and rescue personnel. What sustained her was the camaraderie of the rescue workers. She thinks that, in society, everybody really pitches in when they need to. The common wisdom is that New Yorkers are tough, and they all pitched in together that day and did whatever needed to be done in order to get through it.

Terese gives us a new perspective—that of a close, yet outside observer. Though she herself did not work on the Pile, she worked on the sidelines, providing a desperately needed health service to the workers. She took it upon herself to help the responders—in a way, to rescue the rescuers. The experience had a profound effect on her, and while she admits she will never be the same, she would do it all over again if she had to.

GIVING RELIEF

I WAS WATCHING IT ON TV, actually seeing it happen, in disbelief, shock, and feeling helpless and wanting to help. I didn't know how. I had two brothers. One was FDNY, and the other one is a New York electrician who witnessed it and was down there helping since Day One. I just felt like I had to do something. Coming from a family of firefighters—my father was a retired battalion chief—and knowing that what I do for a living can help these people. My brothers inspired me so much that they got me off the couch. I just packed up my massage table with a few supplies and went down to the site.

I was very welcomed, because the guys knew that massage was needed. The guy who greeted me at the site was a retired FDNY for twelve years—he ended up knowing my father. He brought me over to where the other chiropractors and massage therapists were, just around the corner. They became my new family, my new team, and we got right to work, helping the rescue workers.

I just remember, it was pure devastation. My senses were heightened.

The smell. The smoke coming out of the buildings. Half the buildings were down, buildings were collapsed. At the same time, seeing all these men and women just going through the Pile, organizing, moving things. Everyone was pitching in, doing something.

There were not enough therapists. The lines were growing. They were getting such relief from our treatment. I just felt like I needed to do more. I taught massage as a faculty member at one of the colleges in the city, and all my friends at the time were massage therapists and they also wanted to help, but no one knew how they *could* help because everything at Ground Zero was secured. So then I called my colleagues—licensed massage therapists and chiropractors—to come down and help out maybe a couple hours a day, maybe a whole week. Then we started making a list of names of volunteers. Then the Red Cross got involved, and I became the coordinator with the Red Cross to lead the relief effort, which involved getting over 400 massage therapists, physical therapists, and chiropractors united and official, so now we could get credentialed and start work.

The types of massages we gave were fifteen-minute medical massages. They weren't the typical massage that most people think of, where it's an hour massage and they're relaxed. We just had to relieve the rescue workers' aches and pains. They were so happy to see us. By the third week or the fourth week, they were now dealing with upper respiratory distress, sinus congestion, and fatigue. So now the rescue workers are getting on our tables saying, oh, that they're missing their wife and kids, that they've been away from their home for so long. I ended up working there eighteen hours a day, seven days a week, until November, when they stopped the massage efforts.

A few weeks into the effort I remember the workers would get off our massage tables and say that they felt like a million bucks, that they could go for another three days to try and find someone. But we knew that they couldn't find anyone; that at this point, they were just trying to find body parts. Or anything. Clothing. They would come to us with such hurt in their faces that even before we got to introduce ourselves, they would be face down on the table, they were just hurting so much. Or the happy faces. Like, oh, I'm finally going to get relief from standing on my feet for twenty-four hours, or sitting in the morgue for eighteen hours, or just being on the Pit for three days straight. Those were like relief faces.

Then we would get people who had such sadness in their faces and devastation. Those were the guys who lost their whole battalions or lost their whole units. We couldn't break down. We had to be there for them. We had to tell them that they were doing a good job. We couldn't bring any emotions into it; we just had to support them. We got the thankful faces, who were so thankful that we were there and knowing that we really helped them get through it. And at the same time, with these rescue workers coming across our tables, not only were they experiencing the emotional aspects—the sadness, the hurt, the relief, the aches, the pains, the respiratory. These people were also…they're just like you and me. Normal people doing their job.

But on top of being on the Pit—seeing, feeling, and finding what they were finding on the Pit—they also had to attend memorials, wakes, and funerals to support their fellow firefighters and police officers. On top of that, they had families. I don't know how they did it. These rescue workers were so dedicated, so determined and committed to finding a fellow brother in the beginning. They would attend these memorials because they couldn't find a body part or a body. They didn't just go to one; they went to as many as they could because they knew everyone else was in the Pit and they had to be there for their fellow firefighter or partner. They were still dedicated and determined and committed, even after attending all the wakes, all the funerals, all the memorials. They still came back! They would probably go home, say a quick hello to their wife and kids—because they would say they missed their wife and kids. They would go home to hug their kids. They would wake their kids up as soon as they got home and hug them, and they'd just go right back on the Pit to try and find something to give their partners or their fellow firefighters some closure. Whatever they could find. I don't know how they did it. I really don't think they got enough recognition for what they did.

INSTANT BOND

We had an instant bond with one another. We were experiencing the same emotions. Even though we were strangers, we were family because we were down there. For example, I remember hearing that one firehouse lost all its guys. I remember this one firefighter—he must've been a guy from that house. He was in a daze. When you're a professional in New York and you're licensed, you have a boundary that you can't cross. I remember this guy in a crowd of people who just looked so lost. Like, he had nothing in his eyes. His eyes were so red from crying. He reached out to me and just grabbed and hugged me. He said, "I need help. I need to talk to someone. Can you help me find someone? I need to talk. I gotta find my guys." I didn't know what to do. There were people with yellow vests, therapists who were helping, and they were like eight to ten feet away. Just as I tapped someone on the shoulder to get help, another guy came over and they started hugging. They recognized each other. They were both sobbing. They lost everybody in their firehouse.

There were times that someone reached out and got you through the day, because they knew what you were going through. You probably wouldn't share that with a normal family member. A family within a family, a city within a city.

I had no clue what I did or saw down there would last, ten years later. I think my life stopped a little bit after that. I don't think I am the same person. I didn't lose anybody. I can't imagine what it's like for family members who lost people.

When I first came out, it was a challenge to go back to my work as a massage therapist. I couldn't be in a massage room, which is usually a ten-by-ten or a twelve-by-twelve room, with the door closed. I just felt like I had to get out. Plus, I had a constant cough, and then I had trouble breathing. So for a while, I had a hard time going back to work because of some of the conditions that I was experiencing when I first got out. Just putting hands on people was a challenge, because as a massage therapist or a chiropractor or a physical therapist, you're a caregiver.

I'd do it all again. I met a lot of nice people. I realize that no volunteer job is too small, because even just getting onto the boat or the respite center, we had to go through a process. We had to wash our boots, wash our hands. Even the people who were handing out paper towels made that job so much easier. So realizing that no volunteer job is too small.

I got awards for doing what I did. My own organization, the American Massage Therapy Association, had given me an award. I got letters from the Firefighters Association for my relief efforts, the Red Cross—everyone got a certificate, an award. But that's not why I was down there. We were just doing our job to help. I don't think anyone felt like a hero down there. We were just normal, everyday people doing our jobs, doing what we could to pitch in. We felt a sense of unity.

CHAPTER 23

THE CHURCH OF REFUGE

Arthur is a podiatrist who has worked out of Queens for the last fifty years. On the morning of 9/11, Arthur sat in his office's waiting room, along with his patients, watching as the Towers came crashing down. About a week later, unable to simply sit and watch, he went down to Ground Zero and volunteered at St. Paul's Chapel.

Though the tragedy greatly affected Arthur's health, he chooses to look at the experience in a positive light. In a horrible situation, people were able to come together from all across the country, united under a common cause, and work side by side as equals. Arthur takes comfort in this, in knowing that no matter what happens and no matter where it happens, the people of this country will rush to help in whatever way they can.

I GUESS IT ALL STARTED WITH THE TRAGEDY ITSELF, which happened to be on a morning when there was a primary vote going on. I had a hospital meeting first, and then I remember driving. I drove from the hospital to put in my vote, and as I was parking, I heard that a plane had gone into the World Trade Center. I'm thinking to myself as I leave the car, "Oh, it must be one of these little planes that just didn't know where he was going, or whatever."

So I went in, put in my vote, came back, and as I was driving to the office, I heard that the second plane had gone into the building, and I said, "No, something is going on here." I got to my office, which wasn't too far away, and my patients that were waiting for me were all looking at the TV, so I stopped in the waiting room and started watching with them. Everybody knows what occurred from there. It was just a terrible thing. We couldn't work that day. Everybody was just mesmerized.

It's like when you have some sort of major event happen and you know exactly what you were doing at that time. I remember, of course, when JFK was assassinated. It's the same thing with this.

WHAT CAN I DO TO HELP?

I thought, "I'm a medical professional. Let's see what I can do to help." I called our podiatry association to see if there was anything going on in the emergency rooms.

They said they would be setting something up to try to help out as time went on. Within a couple of weeks, the College of Podiatry actually established a little treatment center in St. Paul's Chapel, which was directly across the street from Ground Zero. I decided that I would do what I could, and became the Coordinator for the New York State Podiatric Medical Association. I got lists of podiatrists all over the country, through email accounts, to see if I could muster up a bunch of volunteers to come down and help out.

Everybody wanted to do something. This was not just in New York; this was actually around the country. The setup at St. Paul's Chapel worked out very well for us. There was an actual pew that was George Washington's pew, his private pew where he was inaugurated and prayed. It was a blocked-off area at the side of the chapel, and we actually converted that into a podiatry office. We put in treatment chairs and had a big shelf around with all kinds of medications, injectables, and anything else that was needed.

Everything that we used was actually donated by the college and by medical supply houses. Shoe companies were sending in boots and socks. For anything we needed, we could send out an inquiry and people were just willing to donate anything. I set up a coordinated effort where we put in six- to eight-hour sessions at the chapel. On a personal basis, I was there two to three times a week in six- to eight-hour shifts for eight months after 9/11. This was 24/7. They were working in the Pit 24/7, and we were there for them. Especially in the first two or three months, we had loads of people coming in because it was very uneven turf they were working on. They were spraining ankles, getting blisters, cuts and bruises, strains—just a lot of treatment of the foot and the ankle that we were able to take care of.

AN EMOTIONAL PLACE

A lot of times they would come in, we would treat them and tell them, "You have to rest this out. It's a sprain. You have to get off the foot for a while." They wouldn't listen to us at all and said, "No, we're going back out." It was do whatever you can for us; we're going back out there. That was the general attitude. They slept on the pews in St. Paul's Chapel. They would sleep for a few hours and then go back out.

Our wall was actually the medical wall. There was our podiatry section and, to one side of us, there was a chiropractic section because there were a lot of back injuries and strains. To the other side of us were the massage therapists. So we actually had a full medical wall on one side of the chapel. There were also people who volunteered for food. There were restaurants that were donating food. There were people who were serving all day and all night long. There were all kinds of supplies people could get: first-aid supplies, medical supplies, clothing supplies. Everything that was there was donated, and the people there were all volunteers. Church groups came in, temples came in, all with busloads of people. Everyone had set times to work at the chapel. It was an amazing place.

In the chapel itself, the atmosphere was emotional but uplifting. It was just something where you became a family. There were banners. Kids' schools were sending in banners; every inch of that chapel had banners, posters, letters written by the kids to the firefighters and the people who were helping. It was a refuge for the responders, the people who were actually working in the Pit itself. They had a place that they could come in. There were cots set up all around the periphery of the chapel; they could rest for as long as it was necessary, then they would get up and go back out again. There was an upstairs balcony area, which we used for all the supplies that were being donated. There were musicians that came in and set up on the other side of the chapel. They played soothing music constantly, pretty much all day long. There were also volunteers from Lincoln Center and other private groups.

There were three or four coordinators down there that actually coordinated all the volunteers. I did the podiatry, but I was sort of answering to the main coordinator, as to when people would come in. We had to have ID, of course, and sign in and sign out when we came in and out, which most of the time got slipped by anyway, but that was part of it.

PART OF THE FAMILY

I don't know if he was a priest—it's an Episcopal chapel—but the one who ran the chapel himself was always there also, and he helped with a lot of the coordination. They would run services and memorials and things like that during that time. The mayor, at that time it was Giuliani, came down a number of times and spoke to everybody down there. He was there to encourage and thank everybody that was responding. Afterwards, it got a little political, but during that time everybody was just into what was being done. Anybody who came down was considered part of the family. We actually still meet to this day; we have reunions and meet together, the entire St. Paul's family.

As far as the volunteers go, I would say over the eight-month period there were probably thousands. They came from all over the country. I had podiatrists that volunteered coming in from California, from states out West. They would pay their own way, fly in, take hotels or stay with people, but everything was on their own. Everything was totally voluntary, people taking time out of their own offices and practices.

The best overall feeling was that it was sort of a camaraderie that we all had. Not only just the podiatrists; I'm saying everybody. There was a commonality—we all had the same feeling of tragedy, but we were there to do whatever we could to get past it and make it an uplifting experience, to just do what we could to help the situation. I think everybody had a close-knit feeling because of that. To this day we still stay in contact. I have an email list of probably a couple hundred people, and we still have constant emails going back and forth. When things come up, such as this Zadroga bill for the health care, we're all involved in that.

WE DIDN'T WORRY ABOUT IT, BUT WE SHOULD HAVE

I've actually gone down to Washington with the John Feal organization and lobbied the congressmen up and down the halls. Telling them they're out of their minds not to get this thing passed. It seems to be a time that they'll probably pass that and give the medical help that a lot of these people— including myself—ended up needing because of the time spent down there. The health was sort of left by the wayside. Nobody seemed to care about themselves while we were down there and, of course, the EPA people— Christie Whitman, etc.—down there at the time said that the quality is good, don't worry about it. So we didn't, but we should have.

In the chapel, I don't remember anybody ever wearing masks, even out in the Pit, where they should have. For the first three months, just going into the whole area there, the odor was horrific. As soon as you walked in, you got this heavy musty odor where you knew that it involved all these toxins from the World Trade Center, biological toxins from, unfortunately, the remains, and you were just breathing all this stuff in constantly. The first three months it just lingered there. The smell never really dissipated, and then finally, slowly, it did. The people down in the Pit didn't wear anything for the most part. From what I recall, they sometimes used paper masks, which really didn't accomplish much. They should have had respirators, but they didn't.

There was dust all over the place, even in the chapel. You could take a shelf and run your finger along it and you'd see a big line. Eventually that started getting cleaned up. Also, they actually did close the chapel for a period of time. It was after a few months, but they did close the chapel and had a massive cleanup; the environmental people came in and did a cleanup.

AT LEAST I'M HERE

We were actually given tours the first few days we were there by some of the police officers that were down there. They took us, myself and some of the other podiatrists that were down there, to the site itself, which was basically across the street. We were able to walk in and around, and go down a bit to see what was going on. We cried. It was very emotional. Just knowing what had happened, and then, of course, seeing all the TV coverage afterwards of the actual building, the people jumping.

There was a feeling of satisfaction, too, though. Feeling that, "At least I'm here and I'm able to do whatever it is possible for me to do on an individual basis." And getting people to feel the same way, and then, of course, as time went on, just becoming part of this whole family of volunteers down there.

Occasionally, we'd find it a little difficult getting some of the supplies that we wanted. I would be making calls to some of the medical supply houses and just trying to get them to voluntarily give up a lot of supplies and medications that we needed. We did have a company that was supplying boots, and that was interesting. They would supply these construction boots for the responders that were working in the Pit. The first couple of weeks especially, it was all wet down there with puddles because of all the water that had been used to turn down the fires. Smoke was coming up for the first four to six weeks; you could still see areas of smoke coming up from the Pit. So it was a mess, all wet and moist. They would come in with the boots, and the boots were really disheveled. They were wet; they were messy. So we would take their boots and their socks, replace them with boots and socks that were sent in by volunteer companies, and then we would send the dirty boots out to these companies that would then clean them up and refurbish them. The socks were sent to laundries and they would clean them up and send them back and then they would just be recycled. So at least they [the responders] could go out with dry socks and dry boots all the time. That was part of that whole volunteer situation, too, because all that work was voluntary.

The emotions hit once you were down there and saw and were part of what was happening. To some extent, it stays with you, but I felt I was able to handle it and most everybody that I dealt with did, too. Some of the volunteers that I know, who were also down there for long periods of time, did have some of the post-traumatic stress syndrome and had to get themselves taken care of for that. We all were asked to get ourselves evaluated, which I did also. They said I was okay.

HONORED

The health part of it is quite an impact, though. At this point, I have to go down to Mt. Sinai Hospital three times a month for treatment, so it definitely had that impact. But even with that, it's something that I know I would have done in any case. Knowing what I know now, the only difference might have been that I would have been a little more careful maybe with asking for respirators or whatever, but nobody did that.

I felt honored to do what I did. My podiatry association, both my state association and my national organization, actually gave me very nice honorary awards for having put the thing together and working at it along with one of the coordinators from the podiatry college. A lot of people in the profession are aware of what was done, which is a nice feeling, knowing that at least it was recognized. Patients do, too, because I have a wall in my office that I dedicated to the plaques and the artwork and other things that were involved.

THEY'RE AMERICANS

I'm not overly spiritual, but as far as people getting together and being able to tolerate one another, I think that showed that it can be done. Even this whole thing with the Muslim situation; I think it's terrible that it had to become such a political thing. People want to worship the way they want to worship, and they're a peaceful people. They're not terrorists, they're people.

One of my office assistants is a young Muslim girl, and her family is the loveliest family. They're nice people. They're Americans. Let them do what they want to do. That's into the politics of it, I guess. There's always going to be a lot of emotional baggage and, of course, I don't blame the families that had people killed; that's strictly an emotional reaction. I can't blame them; it's just sad that it had to come to that particular thing.

The positives, though, are the basic good I was able to see in everybody that was there. They came from all walks of life: professional to nonprofessional, blue collar to white collar. Everybody was there, exactly the same, and doing exactly the same thing. It was sort of inspiring to see that everybody could just work on that same level and think, "I'm not better than you and you're not better than me. We're all doing the same thing for the same reason." That's something nice to have come out of it.

As far as the disaster goes, people have to realize that this happened in New York. It can happen pretty much in any city of the country. No matter where something like this happens, the entire country feels that it's been done to them, and they're going to want to help out and respond in any way they can. It's not just a New York incident. It's an incident that involved the entire country. People came in and wanted to help from all over the country, and I think that will happen any place this will ever happen. And it doesn't have to be an act of terrorism. It could be New Orleans. People just have that feeling in this country that they want to help, no matter where it is.

CHAPTER 24

FAITH RENEWED

Detective Michael arrived at Ground Zero after a frantic sprint from Long Island into Lower Manhattan. A second-generation NYPD officer assigned to undercover work, Michael spent several months at the disaster site. Three years later, illness forced Michael into retirement as he gradually became more disabled. Many of the colleagues who had worked alongside him at the World Trade Center site also began falling ill. He founded the 9/11 Police Aid Foundation to provide financial support to sick officers and their families as well as to educate elected officials, law-enforcement agencies, and the public about the relationship between environmental conditions at Ground Zero and the various cancers, respiratory illnesses, and other conditions that plague the first-responder population years after the event.

COMING IN FROM HOME

ON OUR WAY INTO THE CITY, YOU COULD SEE there was no traffic whatsoever, and everybody was off to the side of the road. You could see all these civil servants running in with their plaques in their windshields—it's almost like a caravan of first responders going into a city. They were coming in from home.

Firemen, you could see their franticness, trying so bad to get into the city that they were actually crashing their vehicles into signs. There were many accidents, and we couldn't stop. We knew they were okay, and we just kept on going.

As soon as we picked up a police car, we went right in through the Williamsburg Bridge, and we pulled up to my precinct and I couldn't believe my eyes. Grown men on their knees, crying.

When I got out of the car, I saw this lady. She was covered in blood and looked gray, like a gray human being, and she was walking around, mindless. She was in shock, and there was nothing I could do for her. I asked her, "Can I take you upstairs, clean you up, and I'll bring you home." She said, "I just want to go over the bridge and walk home."

The fire unit was right in our precinct. We were always very close. When I got there, I saw one of the guys on his knees, just crying. He was inconsolable. He had lost his son's godfather. He just kept on saying, "I lost my brother, I lost my brother." I knew it wasn't his brother *per se*, but it was a brother, like a brother firefighter, brother police officer.

When I got upstairs, we had another detective. His father happened to be one of the chiefs at the time, and he couldn't get hold of him, and he [the detective] was probably ten years younger than I was, a young detective. He definitely thought his father had died, and we couldn't really relate to him in what he was going through. We tried to console him, and he went down with us to the Pile, but he just stayed in the car and he was just inconsolable for the whole day. Later that night, we found his father. He happened to be alive, thank God. That was beautiful that we saw that.

We went upstairs, and our Lieutenant Goodbody, great man, had us suit up. He said for us to leave jeans on, that we're going in like we're going to raid. So we got our raid jackets on, and we left all our gear except for our guns, and we took plastic gloves and we went right to the site on the West Side Highway.

WORKING LIKE A MACHINE

I had no feelings at that time; I was a machine. I looked at all this carnage, and I just couldn't believe it.

Going on the Pile and hearing all the firemen's locator beacons going off. That bothered me the most. When I was there on the Pile that first day with my lieutenant, we just couldn't do anything. There was just too much. You didn't know what to do and where to go. It was chaos. It wasn't even organized chaos—it was lieutenants, captains walking around in a daze, firemen crying, police officers crying—it was horrible. I never thought I would experience anything that bad in my life.

Once we got to the site, we walked the Pile, we tried to locate other people that were inside the Pile. Our attention was brought over to Number 7, right off Church Street, the federal building. There were fires going on inside Number 7, and they were saying the building was going to collapse. You could see the motion of the building how it was undermined by the North Tower. By 5:30 [p.m.], the building came down, and we were right there. That day, we were covered in dust, debris.

You're trained to react in certain ways as a police officer, but the humanity of yourself is basically gone. You're working like a machine. You don't really look and reflect right there and then; you just do. That night we reflected a lot, though, once we got off the Pile, and we slept in our cars that night to the next morning. I think the scariest part was knowing there was going to be another attack. The radios were going off after Number 7 fell. We had our [short]wave radio. We have different bands, so one of us would stay on Aviation, one of us would stay on our Detective frequency, another one would be on Patrol frequency so we could get a general mind's-eye picture of what was going on in Lower Manhattan.

You could hear the hysterics on the air with the police officers up in the north by the George Washington Bridge. A distress call came over the radio and said here was a man with a bomb, and it was just a mental patient. But you could hear the police officers over the air say, "Shoot him! Just shoot him! Don't take no chances! Just shoot him!" These were guys who had just witnessed the worst tragedy in our nation's history, and we're getting all these calls. That was our first day.

I still have the nightmare of the locator beacons going off. That says a lot. That's a human body below you and you're walking on top of it. There's nothing you can do. You can't move these ten-ton beams. The helplessness was horrible.

OUR DETAIL

We all have our beards, we all have our cases going on; we're undercover, and we look like it. The only thing that says we're police officers is the shield around our neck and our raid jackets that in the back says NYPD.

I was doing organized crime, which entailed prostitution, illegal gambling, drugs, that sort of stuff. The first week, the department put its detective resources down there because they couldn't take their uniformed services and put it on the Pile to do rescue and recovery. At the time we had 8,000 detectives and the NYPD probably had 28,000 uniformed police officers. You'll see a disproportionate share of illnesses with detectives compared to the silver shields, the patrolmen.

They put us down there to make it a controlled-type of environment because they consider that a crime scene. Many of us were put to recover body parts on rooftops, knock down doors, make sure there weren't dead bodies in other buildings across the way. Go into offices, escort many civilians to their homes. For the next few weeks we did that.

The perimeter was I think nine square acres, something like that. It was huge, almost up to Canal Street, and as far down as Battery Park. There was no power down as far as Canal and even some parts of Houston. That was strange, also, because you'd see nothing, just black—it was completely dark. We did a lot of midnight tours; we're a midnight unit. We did caravans of bringing supplies for the construction people. We had people coming in from all over the United States with machinery to help. We guided other departments that really didn't belong there but came to help: Louisiana police, Florida, North Carolina, Chicago, California. We were escorting these people around and showing them where they were supposed to go, where they were staying.

It was probably one of the coldest winters we had on record. I think it was a Tennessee or Kentucky state trooper—he came over and threw a garbage can in the middle of the road and just said, "Come on guys, we're going to start a fire." And on almost every single corner, that's how we got warm. We were lighting fires to keep warm.

We all did our time on the Bucket Brigade; we all did our time in Freshkills. They gave preference a lot to the guys that came [from] out of state that wanted to help, so a lot of people from out of state came to do the Bucket Brigade.

This thing of everybody wearing a mask—that's another thing. By the time we got down there, all the supplies were gone. The day tours and 4 to 12s [shifts] took everything. If you got down there, you'd find a filter for the mask, or you'd find no mask. There wouldn't be anything, or there'd just be paper filters or a little canister filter, but there would be no masks.

By the second or third week, we were raiding Home Depot in Brooklyn trying to get masks out of there. My wife had bought a pile of bandanas for the guys in the unit, and they all had the American flags, so that's what we wore. We'd wear them up, we'd clean them, and we'd put them over our faces, and we'd go like that for two, three hours, and then we'd go, clean them again, put some water on them, and go back on the Pile.

We basically became part of an investigation unit. By the second week I'm going, There's nobody alive. There's nobody you're going to get out of there. And then doing the Bucket Brigades after that, we're not getting anything. We're just getting pulverized body parts.

A CONNECTION?

I didn't feel proud to do what I did. I just felt it was something I had to do. Would I do it again the same exact way? Absolutely. The only thing I have a problem with is that I don't think our lives were worth being on that Pile after the second and third week. In the morning, when the sun would come in, you'd see glass particulate in the air, and we knew that stuff's not good for you. Christine Todd Whitman said the air was fine. In your heart you knew it was bad, but the first two weeks, I don't care. I'm a police officer. I put my life on the line anyway. But [after the two weeks] they didn't give me the option to say, "I don't want to do this." They didn't give nobody that option. OSHA was basically removed from the site and the city took over.

In Washington, the Pentagon, OSHA put their men in bunny suits [hazmat suits] to recover what they did there. If you look at the amount of people sick from the Pentagon, there's nobody sick from the Pentagon recovery because they took the right actions. In New York City, they didn't. I think there are many factors in that obviously Wall Street needed to be put back in place and everybody was trying to get everybody back into some sort of relative mode of going back to your lives. I don't think anybody went back to their lives after that. You lost whatever you had.

The food we had was clean, it was great. They set up camp on the West Side Highway or they set up by the East River underneath the FDR Drive. It was just that you're eating in a contaminated environment. You're actually walking in dust to eat something, and then you go back into a car that was covered in dust; you had the windows open, so the car inside is full of dust. So now you're eating all this stuff. In hindsight, you didn't think about it, you're hungry and you need to eat, but thinking back now and looking at the illnesses that are going on—not that I'm medically educated—but you could see the connection as far as the GI [gastro-intestinal] problems everybody is having, and those issues.

Cancers are up, and our unit in particular because our unit worked a specific part of the site when we did the bucket detail. In my unit, five of us wound up getting Hodgkin's lymphoma. Two of them were B-cell type lymphomas, which are rare. I think it's one in 500,000 people get that. The cancer started in 2004, 2003. In our office, we didn't put two and two together or nothing. We just started seeing all these guys drop. You would see them—where's Mike, where's Ernie? Where's this guy? Where's this guy? Oh, he's out sick. This guy's got cancer. And then you had guys in ESU. We had guys that worked where the Pile was smoking, and it was like a crucible for months. It was a cauldron of the strangest colors coming out of this fire—greens and blues—and it was burning and burning. That's another spot that we stayed at. Those guys that worked that end of the Pile wound up getting leukemia. That's where the fuel from the jets was burning.

I always ask my guys, what part of the Pile were you working on? Where'd you work? Right now, we've lost 179 police officers in law enforcement and forty-nine suicides since that day. Yeah, it's a lot. I think the connection is made now. But again, scientifically, they want to wait another thirty to forty years.

I run a foundation now that helps police officers, and that [connection between illnesses and working on the Pile] is one of the questions. My anger was that you get these professionals that come on and state that there is no way cancer can begin that fast. You have children that get cancer. How does that happen? That was my question, because you can't state that it can't. We've never had anything in history like this. They're the experts, basing their analysis on miners or people that worked in contaminated areas their whole lives. "There's no connection, there's no connection."

There was paperwork flying around for months. Pictures, IDs, everything you'd pick up. I think that's the hardest part right there—seeing the pictures of the people when I was digging, me collecting pictures of families and putting them in my pocket. I took it really hard because I kept on thinking of my children, and I'm not scared to die—far from it. I'm scared to have my children live their lives without a father.

Locator beacons and the photographs of husbands and wives taking their Christmas pictures—knowing that they could possibly be dead. I think that's what hurt me the most.

I don't want to say it was something given to me genetically by my dad. But a lot of the guys that were there were second-generation, third-generation cops. A lot of firemen that died were second-generation, third-generation firemen. We were just put in a machine. You do what you have to do. You're doing it for your country. You're doing it for your city.

In November of that year, I wound up getting really sick, and I was studying to be a sergeant. My lieutenant had me going down there every single night, and he put me in a position where I do perimeter security in a truck, and I was able to study a bit and go out of my vehicle every once in a while and do what I had to do. But I was sitting right there. I didn't know, but that's where my illnesses started. I was deathly sick.

I came to work deathly ill. I was vomiting. I was coughing up blood. My fecal matter was green for weeks. I must have caught something. My wife was begging me not to go to work. "Call in sick, call in sick." How can I call in sick? I just had brothers that I lost. I could deal with this. And you think about the families that lost their fathers, brothers, sisters—no complaint in the world is going to match what they went through. So you just do what you have to do. I don't think I ever thought of it.

MY FAITH WAS TESTED

I went to a lot of funerals after 9/11, probably a few months afterwards. One in particular, which I think had a lot to do with 9/11, was my lieutenant. He was Lieutenant Goodbody, a good man. He started having the signs during the rescue and recovery. We brought him to a hospital a couple times. I begged him to go.

In November of that year I got a phone call from his wife. He'd had a massive heart attack and died eating dinner with his kids at the table. This man was an eight-mile-a-day runner. There was something wrong there.

At that funeral, again, I was deathly ill. I couldn't even stand at his coffin to give my honor in my uniform. I actually sat there in a wheelchair. From coughing so much, I had pulled my back muscles out and, again, I was still going to work.

I think of his children and what he accomplished in his life. He was forty-five years old, he was a professor at St. John's University part-time, and he was a lieutenant for the New York City Police Department, and I had so much respect for him as a man and a father. He was a good friend of mine.

Going to the funerals became hard after December. After the New Year, it became harder. I wouldn't go. I almost lost all my humanity in a way. I was a Christian man from the beginning, and my faith was tested that day. I think I lost my faith in God, but I think it came back to me on the Pile. I lost it for a few months, and I got it back.

I think it was February or March, and I was put back down there again, and I think I was doing an overtime tour. It was morning, and I just got there and I was sitting in my truck looking around again doing perimeter security. A Catholic priest and a young lady from a Christian church out on Long Island came to my truck. They asked me if they could go [into the site]. I happened to be guarding an area that they didn't allow civilians, and they came to me and asked me, "Detective, would you mind if we went downstairs to this parking garage? We need to see something down there."

My curiosity was, What do you need to see down there? They said they couldn't really explain it to me, that I needed to come see it. I called one of my buddies over, another partner of mine. I asked him to take over my spot while I go down there. I'm glad I did. It was in the North Tower, the southwest corner of the Tower. There's a parking garage. I don't know if you remember, the North Tower had an office complex off the side, a small square building.

Underneath that there was a parking garage. They started explaining to me what was down there. They said to me this is going to change your life. I said, how's it going to change my life? So the priest goes to me, "You believe in God, right?" I said, "Absolutely I believe in God, but I still haven't gotten my answer to why this has happened." He said, "I think you're going to get an answer."

I walked down there with him and this lady, and as I turn the corner, I see this beautiful ray of sunshine coming through this wall. And, behind this wall covering the parking garage is where I saw the sunshine coming through. I walk towards it, and I made a left and I look at this hole in a wall. It was like being hit. I couldn't understand it. I fell to my knees and started crying like I'm doing now.

The whole time I was there [working on the site], I didn't know there was a cavern inside the building. They finally uncovered it sometime in February, and this cavern went down probably 150 feet. As I look through the wall, I see three crosses had impaled themselves in the ground in perfect unison.

They were draped in clothes and paper like arms, and I said to myself, this has got to be God's work. My roots are in Christianity and Catholicism, but I was losing faith in Him, my faith was being tested there. To me, it was God telling me these people didn't die in vain. I thought of the Holy Trinity: the Father, the Son, and the Holy Ghost. So I think that changed my life. I became very cynical. But I think my faith in God really came back to me that day, and I always reflect on that.

After a while, I composed myself, and the priest came over to me. He said, "I've been down here many times already, and I never, ever heard anyone compare this to the Holy Trinity." He didn't want the media to know about it, though, because they would want to make this a holy site. I understood that. I understood that completely because it moved me that much.

Maybe these things happen for a reason, and they're too grand for me to understand, but I was there, and it's the way I felt.

Anyway, some of the crosses were taken out, and one of the crosses, I believe, was put on display. I think two others are in storage or will maybe be put on display after the Towers are up. If you look online, you'll see vague references to that site and the crosses.

I think there were a lot of responders who saw it, but I don't think anybody spoke about it. I didn't speak about it. Again, you're a police officer. You're macho. You're not going to show what your beliefs are and why. You're a big tough guy. You can take this—you can take getting shot at, you can do anything. No big deal. I'm not going to bring my sensitivity or my faith in God to somebody who may not believe in God. They'd think you were crazy.

I didn't actually come out with that until I retired. I just kept it to myself for many years. I went down there for the five-year anniversary; I spoke, calling out the names. I got to meet one of the construction workers that had pictures of the site. And he remembers me, and when I saw him, I broke down again and started crying. He goes, "I remember you, detective. You were down there. The Holy Trinity, the Holy Trinity."

"WE NEED YOUR HELP"

After I retired, I think I put my family through hell a little bit. I started becoming sick, I became very cynical, and I couldn't understand why. It wasn't a pity party. It was just—I didn't understand psychologically what was happening to me. The help I received from the Hauppauge crew here and Doctor Luft, when they'd just opened up in 2004, saved my life. If it wasn't for them, I think I'd be dead right now. I was living life cynically, probably mentally abusing my children and my wife, blaming myself for a lot of things, regretting not being there the day it happened and not dying.

There were a lot of survivor issues of that type. I really wasn't aware of the PTSD thing till after I retired. My wife will tell you, she'll say, thank God for this whole monitoring program. She has her old husband back, and even better, she says. I'm so glad that this is available to us and my brothers and sisters and anybody who was down there. It's very important.

There've been something like forty-nine suicides among the responders, and absolutely there's a connection with their 9/11 experiences. In my foundation alone, we've had over five suicide attempts that we were able to stop and get them help through this system here that you have in place. Men that you'd never think would have any problems, men that stayed in their homes for five years after that and never left the house, became hermits. Wives calling our foundation up, crying, "Can you please do something for my husband? He's going to kill himself. We need your help."

So people feel isolated. That was another thing I had. I had nobody to talk to. In our group, we were lucky because we had each other, and we started communicating. We kept on saying, "Can you imagine if this is happening to us, what is happening out there to other guys?" In 2008 I felt I was wasting my time, wasting my life. I thought that I could at least do something with my hands.

I sat down and wrote up a 501(c)(3) charity, and I started the 9/11 Police Aid Foundation. I'm glad I did because we were able to educate cops and their families and help a lot of families out. We're still doing it to this very day. We've saved many lives. It's one thing that a cop won't open up to, let's say, a civilian, but he'll open up to a fellow brother cop that was in the same exact situation. Cops are funny like that. But when it comes to this, to illnesses, these guys who were trained to be heroes and then put out to pasture, it's like emasculating them.

So, absolutely, guys feel abandoned. When they finally started getting calls from our organization, they can't believe it. "There are other guys like me? There are other people like me?" And, generally, what I do is take them for trips with us when we do our fundraising or education, and they can't believe it. They get to tell their stories, and it brings me sometimes to tears. Sometimes I ask, "Why am I doing this?" I have my family I'm putting in jeopardy. They never see me, and they say I'm putting too much time in this. But, when I get that one guy who goes, "Mike, you saved my life," I feel like my life is worth something. It's why I do this.

It's sad. You have things like the Zadroga bill. It provides $4.2 billion for health care and monitoring for responders and Lower Manhattan residents exposed to World Trade Center dust. The statute carries the name of James Zadroga, an NYPD detective who was the first responder whose death was linked to the particulates and toxins at the site, where he spent some 450 hours. We had to fight for it for six years. I think that's unfair.

I go through the United States and try to educate people. You get some congressmen who are very indifferent. They feel like it's a New York problem, that they've given enough money to New York, and that this is an issue that New York has to deal with. This wasn't an attack on New York; it was an attack on the United States of America. Hundreds of people died in that incident in Russia [Chernobyl], but I think it's going to pale in comparison with the deaths that result from 9/11. I think the number is already way over 1,000 people who passed away from illnesses. I think we're up to 890 in the State of New York. I have police officers in almost every state that have died and aren't even memorialized. Their families aren't even getting anything. I think it's just sad.

I go away to the Midwest to speak, and I even speak on the West Coast. No one can believe what is happening. They have no idea what is happening out here. It's a shame. There should be some sort of national educational program, especially with these tragedies, so they don't happen again.

Were something like 9/11 to recur, I think I would respond the same way, but I would be a very outspoken opponent of going in and staying on-site if there was no human life to be saved. If life is already gone, I think we should sit back and look at the situation. No money is worth anybody's life. It's almost like we're second-class citizens in a way. I think I would probably disobey an order after two weeks.

After 9/11, my view of the federal government changed. I have a lot of disdain for the Bush administration. I've been conservative my whole life, and I think he did more damage to us than anybody. He could have really helped us out. He used us as a political pawn. He went on the Pile with the firemen and said, *I'm there for you.* It's sad that, looking back now, it makes me sick. It really makes me sick how politics in the United States works.

I just hope in the future there aren't tragedies like this in the first place. But if there are, I hope they take a look at history and say, *Let's not do that again.*

CHAPTER 25

TO SEE IT WITH YOUR OWN EYES

Rafael, also known as Ralph, was a detective in the NYPD assigned to the Community Affairs Division at Brooklyn North. When the attack occurred, Rafael and his partner were at a car wash on Highland Park, where they witnessed both planes hitting the Towers. Rafael comes across as very self-assured and talkative, with a florid style of expressing himself and a biting sense of humor, making it is easy to see why he was assigned to Community Affairs. By his own admission, he also has a vivid memory, so he provides a remarkably long and detailed account of the day of the attack and the few weeks following. As he relates the events blow by blow, he also offers profound insights about the culture of policing: how they work, how they think, and how they relate to each other. And he manages to insert some humor into his tale, which, he later explains, is part and parcel of the police culture. Through his eyes, we can see and feel the horrendous hardships he and his fellow policemen suffered while taking care of everybody else.

9/11 WAS A TUESDAY, AND IT WAS A PRIMARY DAY in New York. I was actually assigned to work the later tour, the 4 p.m. to 12 a.m. tour on 9/11, and then I was going to service my own vending machines in various stores at the World Trade Center. So I figured I'll do that in the morning and then I'll do my job.

But that night they called and said everybody has been reassigned, so we all had to go do a day tour. That was for the election detailing, so that meant that I had to be in at 7:30 a.m.

When Rafael got in, he found that someone had used his Community Affairs vehicle and left it dirty. They went to the car wash before going to their assignment.

The police van got stuck in the car wash. I don't know why, but it did. So we were just standing by, waiting there for them to get my van out of this car wash, and I turned around, and I saw the first plane strike the first Tower.

Immediately you heard chatter over the radio that the building had been struck, and they didn't know what it was. I turned to my partner and said, "Phil, a big airplane like that flying into the Tower, that can only be one thing, and that's terrorism." It's really odd, because the first time they tried to bomb the World Trade Center, they drove a van into the garage and they detonated. I remember responding to that, and at that time telling the people I was with: If you really want to take these Towers down, all you really have to do is fly a plane into it. You could see the air-traffic patterns. If I could figure that out, you got to figure anybody else could figure it out. We're just the cops, right?

It was very surreal, because it seemed almost like the plane was moving in slow motion; like you could see it coming and you're looking at it and saying, "Is it going to hit the building?" and when you saw the impact, then it became very real. Even as the smoke was billowing out of the first Tower, until you saw the second plane coming it really seemed very surreal. Almost like something you would see in a special-effects movie, because you're watching it, and you're seeing this plane coming in, and it's moving very fast, but it seemed almost like it was in slow motion, coming frame by frame by frame.

As the officers gathered at Brooklyn North SATCOM (Strategic and Tactical Command), they watched the Towers collapse on TV.

One of the officers that worked with us, her brother was a fireman. She knew he had responded to this event. All of a sudden, you could hear the officers who were trapped in the building calling for help on the radio. They were still alive, and they were calling for help. As a matter of fact, the female officer who perished, I've forgotten her name, but you could hear her very clearly that she was calling for help, and that was one of the most helpless moments I've ever experienced in my entire life, because unless I wore a Superman suit, there was no way I was going to take 110 stories worth of debris off of a building.

But at that point, the only thing I could do was turn the radio off because I knew that was having a very negative effect. All the officers in that room were crying. I'm not ashamed to say that, because you would have to be more than heartless not to understand what was going on. We already knew, based on the radio chatter, that people were jumping from the buildings, so at that point I told Sergeant Rodriguez, who was in charge of us, I said, "Sarge, there is no point in us being here."

Police officers and firemen don't get angry until after the event, because that's just the way we are. If we got angry, then who's gonna go in and help? For us it's duty first, and when it's all said and done, then you do two things: One, you use a certain number of expletives to express your anger, and second, after that you start making levity and jokes to help you get past it. There was no time for either one at this particular moment.

We knew what needed to be done. The officers that were in that room needed to be comforted, and they were, but we couldn't stand there in our own grief. That's not what we're called to do. We're the Police Department; we're in the hero business. So it was time for us to go out and be the heroes. That's what we get paid to do.

IT'S WHAT THEY DO

I parked my van all the way down by South Street near Beekman Hospital. I just had this thing washed. So I took it that you have to laugh at these things, right? I left it all the way down by South Street Seaport, and it's a good thing I did, [because] all this smoke and everything was all up in the air [and] we didn't have any protection. I did not want my vehicle to be destroyed and, oddly enough, I have pictures of all the vehicles that parked nice and close, and they all got destroyed.

There was an ambulance that was open, and we borrowed some of the few paper masks that they had, and we also determined that we were going to need water, so as we were walking towards the buildings while everybody else was going this way, we saw a water truck.

So we took some water with us 'cause we're gonna need it to wash our face and our hands and everything else off. I remember Detective Hannah asking me, "Ralph, do you think it's okay for us to be here?" I looked at him and said, "Phil, if you look up, the sky is orange. All of the stuff that's in the air, it's the sunlight going through it." I said, "We can't think about what's gonna happen in the next few minutes or the next few years. We have a job to do. Let's go do it and we'll go home." Well, we did just that.

We also had the foresight to borrow a camera, and we took some pictures as we were going along so we could document. [It's] just like a World Series game—everybody says they were at the World Series, but the stadium only holds 58,000 people. Yet, 100,000 people say they were there. We were determined to say we were there.

I had already had a colorful career where I had a number of situations where I had to keep moving, and it becomes automatic when you do it. It's what you do. It's like a doctor who commits surgery. It's what they do. They walk in, and once they open the person up, it doesn't matter what they see. They know what they have to do. If they saw something that they weren't anticipating, they improvise, they adapt, they overcome it. It's the same with us. We just knew what we had to do. We knew we had to get there. We were there for one purpose and one purpose only, and that was to find people that were hurt or alive and extract them before anything more serious occurred.

ON THE SITE

One of the funniest things was, after a while we got hungry. We were there on that side, where all the restaurants were. We went in, and one of the restaurants that happened to be there, somehow the entire front of the restaurant had gotten blown out. But, anyway, there was no obstruction for us to go in. So we went in, and we got some water, and I remember this guy we were with getting a frozen apple pie. He's standing out in the middle of this, on top of the rubble eating this apple pie, with all of this stuff falling down.

I look at him and say, "Eddie, why you eating that?" He said, "A man's gotta eat, right?" I said, "Yeah, I guess you're right." I'm sorry I didn't take a picture of that, because that would have been really interesting. That's one of those moments you just had to be there to understand the logic of it. Hands were dirty, whatever, but you couldn't think about that at the moment.

Again, it was just get back in there and dig, find somebody, if you could. And that's what we did. We were there for several hours before we finally realized we weren't going to be able to do much. [At] that point, some of the officer[s] who knew how to operate some of the heavy equipment commandeered some equipment, and I later came to find out that all that equipment belonged to Tully Construction, which is really funny because I now know the people from Tully Construction.

With our hands we weren't going to move too much of anything. Some of the guys had taken some of the equipment, borrowed it and helped to excavate, to move. But even that proved to be futile because it was just so much, and it needed to be done in a more organized fashion.

At a certain point, the fire chiefs began telling all the officers and the firemen that they needed to evacuate the area so that they can get a better assessment. We ended up going over to the side of where 7 [7 World Trade Center] was located. That proved not to be a very good idea because eventually 7 collapsed, and we were in the back of that because you could see the flames from the open garage area—you could see the flames burning on the ground floor. We're looking at this building—it was a marble building— and you could see how it was slowly beginning to dip in the middle.

We're just watching this thing [and] saying, "This is really not a great place for us to be. This building is going to collapse." And, eventually, it did. When it collapsed, we started running away from there, going all the way over to the American Express building, which is on the other side of the highway, because we needed to make sure that no civilians were in the area.

They started sending us out to make sure that everyone was out of that entire downtown area. The whole area had to be evacuated because nobody knew what else was going to happen.

You have to understand that there was no real communication, except by telling people word-of-mouth. When you see other guys tell them to start looking and moving everyone out—that's what we ended up doing. We went all the way, as far as where the marina was. Which, by the way, those buildings were also damaged by the debris from the aircraft. A lot of the other buildings surrounding the World Trade Center were ablaze. Then there was the threat of the Millenium Hotel. You could see that it was just off. To the naked eye, you could actually see that it had moved off a little bit, so now they were fearful that that was going to collapse. So, basically, we didn't know where we should be. We just knew we needed to be out of that area.

We had no radios or communication. The only thing that was working was land lines because cell phone service was dead. I couldn't call my family. I couldn't do anything to let them know that I was still alive. Obviously, even my wife knew that I would be there, and, in fact, it wasn't until three days later that I was finally able to get home. When I got home, my youngest son at the time was watching the news and just crying because he couldn't believe what happened, and they hadn't heard from me in three days.

My wife, when I walked through the door, she just broke out crying. To me, it just seemed like I'm safe now. That was the first moment out of the seventy-two hours that I actually felt safe.

The second day, if you recall, they actually had the military. I never thought I would see in my life the military invoking almost quasi–martial law in that whole downtown area. No vehicles were allowed to come into the area. No one was allowed to be there. I remember just standing and watching as the National Guard and military vehicles went up and down securing the locations. I don't really know what they were looking for, but I guess they thought there was still another threat that may come to the area.

That's pretty much what we were doing. Just making sure that there was no additional threat and that there was no other collateral damage or persons that may have been injured, disoriented. People are funny: If a house is burning, instead of running out of the house, people go into the bathroom and lock themselves in. So we were going in and out checking buildings, making sure there weren't people stuck in elevators, because the power had cut off. So there were a number of things that needed to be done. A lot of logistics [were] involved in securing the area. So all that had to be done first before they could even consider starting to let people rest and other things like that.

PRAYING RIGHT WHERE THEY STOOD

I remember we were allowed to use the church, I believe Saint Paul's Church, which became my home away from home. That's where we rested, and that's where we ate, if we chose to eat something. In that church there is a pew, a box actually, and when George Washington had been sworn in as president in Federal Hall, he went directly from there to the church.

In that pew, there's a plaque, and I remember reading that plaque, and I don't recall the exact words, but it had to do with what he was thinking at the time. Here he is now, the president of a country that is devastated. I sat down in that same pew, and I just looked at it, and I understood what he was thinking: that no matter what, we were going to overcome this. That was the morale and the thought of the officers and the people that were there: We were going to overcome this.

I think that people were praying right where they stood. I don't think they needed a church at that particular moment. People can say they don't believe in God, and they can say whatever, but like a good friend of mine said, "As long as they have tests in schools, there will always be prayers in school." That was a great test for the men and women in that area, and I can tell you there were a lot of people who were praying, and a lot of people who were in grief and needed counseling. It was a good place for some people to get support, because some were exhausted.

They really needed a reason to continue, especially since we weren't finding anything. We knew at a certain point we weren't going to find anybody alive. It stopped becoming a rescue mission rather quickly, and became more of a salvage mission. The most important thing was to keep people's spirits alive and moving forward. I remember we got a lot of letters from kids from different schools telling us how they supported us. All of that stuff was very inspirational.

Two weeks directly after 9/11, the crime statistics in New York City were very, very low. You would think the criminals would have had a heyday, but even they had the decency to stop for a moment. Even they realized that something badder than them was occurring, and that they needed to show the respect and restraint.

I was assigned primarily to that area, right there by the church. We were assigned to secure that area to make sure nobody could go in. We did the escorts for the people that were coming in to do cleanup. We eventually ended up doing the escort for family members and people from the pilots' union, who came to see the site where their comrades had perished.

It was a little stressful, because when you're with your own—again, like I said, cops have a certain gift for the macabre—we try to make humor out of tragedy so it doesn't affect us. It's a defense mechanism. Somebody on the outside might say, "Wow, these people are very insensitive." No, that's just the way we deal with it so we don't realize the true trauma of it. When we had to deal now with people who obviously were totally devastated—there is no way to tell a person to stop crying—you either hold them or you cry with them. But you... take all that grief with you. They're unloading it, which means it has to go somewhere.

I had to act as an interpreter for a lot of the people who were Spanish-speaking. There were a number of people who worked at the restaurant who were undocumented, and they were Spanish-speaking, and now we had to take them around through the whole process to make sure they got all the benefits.

FULL OF LIFE

The pier started out as a good thing. They had this long wall which ran the length of the pier, and it was covered by a curtain, but you had to walk through that corridor. Some of the people started taking pictures and posting them on this wall and making little comments, and it started as a good thing. Then they started leaving teddy bears, and that became known as the teddy bear wall. The first few days it wasn't so bad. But, after a while, you would read the stories and you would see these children, eighteen years old, nineteen years old, twenty years old—full of life. The little comments that were left, and all the teddy bears. Hundreds of teddy bears.

After a while you found a different way to get wherever you needed to go because you just couldn't walk that wall anymore, just reliving all the stories. That was the worst part of the entire thing. I could close my eyes right now, and I could see some of the pictures—young women, young men.

I remember there was this little girl. She couldn't have been more than five years old. She had that beautiful platinum blonde hair and the bluest eyes. I could see her from a distance, and I told the guys working with us, "How much trouble do you think I would get in if I walked that little girl right to the edge of the Pit?" They said, "Ralph, you would get into a world of trouble."

I said, "That's right." I walked into the crowd; I looked at the father. I said, "I'm going to take your daughter into the Pit," because you could see she wanted to see. She was just holding onto the fence. I said, "You can come along with me." I said, "Bring your camera; don't worry about it." I walked her all the way to the edge of the Pit, and I stood there and I told her, "Do you know why I brought you here?" She said, "No," with the innocence of a child. I said, "Because when you get to be my age, there's going to be a lot of people who are going to tell you that this never happened.

"[R]ight where you see this hole, there is going to be a beautiful park, and they're going to build big buildings here, and no one is ever going to know. But you're going to know because you saw it with your own eyes." And with that I walked her all the way back, and everybody thought I was crazy, but I knew exactly what I was doing because thirty years from now... The same way the Holocaust never happened, and the same way they make up all these other stories. There's going to be those people who have their own agenda, and they're going to say, "It really wasn't that bad. This really didn't happen; look at this area. How could it be possible?"

WE ONLY HAVE EACH OTHER

Initially I went to as many services as I could, but to be perfectly honest, with each one it took a little bit more, and then finally I couldn't do them anymore, because each and every time we went you saw the same people, and they were grieving and crying. It just took too much.

I think people made more of the "battle of the shields" than it really is, because at any major emergency you'll always find firemen and you'll always find police officers. If you go to any place where they hang out, you'll always find firemen, you'll always find police officers. I think there is a certain camaraderie that goes with the two, simply because of the nature of the work. Both jobs are the type of job where you get up in the morning, you kiss your wife goodbye, make sure the kids had their homework done, and then you're not entirely certain that you're going to come home. We understand each other. Do we argue? Yeah, like two brothers in the same house. Why? Because one wants to be in charge. That's the only thing that ever happened, and they settled it in the football or hockey field. That's all it is, but for anybody to think that cops hate firemen or that firemen ever hated cops—that's foolishness. We're two peas in a pod, and when all hell breaks loose, we only have each other.

Happiest day in my wife's life was the day I retired. As a matter of fact, I never really smiled much, but the day I got home after I retired, my daughter was standing at the top of the stairs, and as soon as I walked in, I said, "I'm home," and I smiled and she took a picture of it. And to this day she still has the picture, and says, "Daddy, that's the first time I ever seen you smile in all the time that I've known you."

I think what has helped me put a lot of this behind me is the fact that, even with my friends, I do more listening than I do talking. I find that I prefer the listening because when I talk, then I have to relive it. One ... good thing that came out of it was that I had a chance to have lunch with my brother. During the cleanup and all that stuff that was going on, since he worked in that area and once they were allowed back in the buildings, we made a point to have lunch, and I think that for the first time my brother came to realize what it is that I do.

CHAPTER 26

IT JUST BUILDS UP

Glen is a veteran of the New York City Police Department, the Emergency Services Unit. As such, even before 9/11 he had already seen the worst that any New York City cop would ever see. His story is a simple, straightforward, and profoundly sad account of his small unit, which lost so many of its members on that day. When a friend called to tell him about the plane that crashed into the Tower, he got into his car and rushed to his precinct in Flushing, Queens. His group was rounded up, and together they went to the site. When they got there, they learned that they had two teams of officers from their unit—fourteen people in all—inside the collapsed buildings. Glen was at Ground Zero from the day of the attacks until the very end of the cleanup.

When Glen retired in 2003 he did not have this support group anymore, and everything started to build up inside him. He went through a rough time with drinking, fights with his family, and aggression. Luckily, with the help of loving family members, he found a way to seek professional help. The problem, as he sees it, was that right after 9/11 he and his friends did not have anybody to take them through their trauma. The culture in the department discourages police officers from seeking help, which, according to Glen, is the cause for the disproportionately high suicide rate among the officers of the NYPD.

I'M NOT ABLE TO WORK BECAUSE OF INJURIES I received at Ground Zero. I put in about 800 hours down at Ground Zero, from the morning that the Towers were attacked till the last beam was removed, which I believe was in early June. I receive Social Security disability.

I jumped in my car and headed to my precinct that I work out of, the 109th in Flushing, Queens. On my way there, I took the Northern State Parkway, which is one of the most direct routes. And as luck would have it, I was doing about 100 miles an hour on the parkway, and I just flew by a state trooper. He came alongside and wanted me to pull over. I held out my shield and he just gave me a wave to follow him.

He turned on his lights and escorted me all the way into Queens. On my way, I called the precinct to see if anyone else was there. There were a few other police officers, and they were just about ready to leave. They were in one of the vehicles, and the garage door was going down, but they heard the phone ring and they figured it might be something important. So they went back in.

I asked the officer, "Do me a favor. Just wait for me. I'll be there in about five minutes. Let's get together and take some of the spare vehicles and throw some equipment in, then we'll head into Manhattan." Everyone in our group worked together the whole day. All of us went back to the precinct together about two the next morning.

We took about fifteen, twenty minutes to load the equipment, but we were monitoring our radios and we heard screaming: "Stand back from the Towers, there's bodies coming out the windows!" That's when we knew it was going to be something really bad.

They formed a caravan and headed downtown.

A civilian ran over to us and said there's a police officer injured down the block. I was the senior man at the time, so I sent two guys down. "Go down the block and see what we've got over there." It happened to be one of the police officers from my unit, ESU.

They brought him back, and his uniform was completely gray because the Towers had collapsed on him. Thank God he wasn't seriously injured, but he was covered with debris and choking from inhaling all that garbage. We put him in my vehicle, which had the air conditioner on, gave him some oxygen, and got an ambulance for him.

We finally got through to a supervisor despite all the radio traffic, found out where we were supposed to meet, and headed in that direction. That's when we learned that we had two teams of guys, fourteen in all, in the Towers, which had already collapsed. My lieutenant didn't think they made it out, but I knew we were the best-trained police officers in the world, and that if anybody knew how to survive something like that, it was our guys. For two weeks, I thought we were going to find them somewhere, like in a little pocket underneath all the debris.

I'd been in the World Trade Center a lot. We trained there. We rappelled in the elevator shafts, and I knew that there were stores in the lower sublevels. I thought it was possible that people could survive in there. There's food, there's water. All they had to do was find a pocket. That didn't happen. Of the twenty-three New York Police Department officers killed on 9/11, fourteen of them were our guys. Most weren't even found. Some of their remains were found on some of them—guns and handcuffs and things like that.

Our mission that day was to go around the outer perimeter of the debris and see if we could recover bodies, whether survivors or victims. There really wasn't much of either. I remember finding a foot that was still in a shoe, but not much more. We continued doing that for hours. It was very, very hot, and flames were still shooting out. You could get close only to certain areas.

A lot of our vehicles were crushed or burned, and our supervisors asked us to go to find our vehicles that were crushed by debris or burned by debris that came down from the Towers. We carry all types of weapons—shotguns, machine guns, sniper rifles—and they were still out there on the street. We didn't want to leave those out there to get into the wrong hands, so we formed teams and went to find vehicles that weren't too badly buried. We recovered some of our weapons and more expensive equipment and kept working till about two Wednesday morning. That's when they told us to head back to the precinct or to head home and take a shower and try to get a couple hours of rest, because we would have to be back again early the next day.

When we got in the car, I'm not sure if the enormity of the incident had even set in at that point. It was very quiet. We were exhausted. It was a pretty warm day. We were sweaty, dirty, tired. Some guys did want to go home and see their families, and I was one of them. I hadn't been able to reach my family to let them know I was okay. As a matter of fact, my girlfriend at the time—she's my wife now—thought I was dead. Some friends of mine who saw me that day thought I was in one of the Towers and told her, "I think Glen was killed." So she was pretty glad to see me when I came home. From what I can remember, though, it was a pretty somber mood. We spoke about our guys who were missing, even though we thought we would find them alive.

We went back the next morning. I don't remember exactly when. Soon we were put on sixteen-hour shifts, seven days a week, straight through till January. We got breaks, of course, at our temporary headquarters at Stuyvesant High School, which is off Chambers Street and West Street. That happened to be one of the areas where the EPA did an air-quality check and found it to be okay. I knew the air quality wasn't good, but I didn't know it was as toxic as it actually was. Anyway, we took off our respirators, and they had a buffet set up for us, so we ate. Not only did we inhale contaminated air, we also ate it.

The first day, we had paper masks. But we already had tear-gas masks in our emergency-service unit. We were a SWAT team and sometimes had to use tear gas. The first day, I put on my gas mask, which I think probably helped me a lot. But gas masks aren't designed to filter particulates, so they quickly clogged up. Not only that, but the gas masks stick out really far, and they're cumbersome and uncomfortable. They're not made to use any longer than it takes a SWAT team to throw a tear gas canister and get the bad guy. Then you take it off. You don't work in it six, seven, eight hours. It was the next day before we got the respirators. They told us we'd used the wrong cartridges—ones that couldn't filter the micron particles—for quite a few days.

So we worked in a hot, dusty environment for 16 hours a day wearing an awkward piece of equipment that's designed to use for fifteen minutes. This went on for a couple of days. Not everyone in my unit had a gas mask. Let me be clear. On 9/11, there wasn't a gas mask for every police officer in New York City. Now quite a few of them do, because they have to be prepared for a terrorist attack. Before 2001, though, my team members had them. We had them that morning because we left a little bit later than everybody else. The first teams thought it was an accident. By the time we headed into Manhattan, we knew it was a terrorist attack, so we took along our tactical equipment—flak jackets, helmets, and gas masks.

MISSING VICTIMS

I think the only thing that kept us going was adrenaline. The best way to explain it is that when it turned into a recovery situation, we wanted to bring home whatever we could, not just our members of the police and fire departments, but also the civilians, the innocent victims, who at that point didn't have anything. It got to the point that finding a bone or a piece of flesh was a big to-do. It comforted us because we knew that DNA testing would give victims' families some closure.

There were so many missing victims. We went down there with the intention of sifting through that debris and finding something every day. After we found all the bodies, when most of [the] major debris was cleared out, we went through those little piles with rakes, and we did find bones and tissue. Didn't look like it. We couldn't tell what it was, but we bagged what we thought might be body parts, and a lot of it turned out to be bone fragments or pieces of skin or internal organs and things like that, covered in dirt. But I guess the Medical Examiner's office did whatever they had to do to clean it up and find out that it was in fact DNA parts from a body.

At the beginning, the first week or two, it was chaotic. It seemed like just about anyone who wanted to do rescue work was there. We had volunteer firefighters from Long Island. And I saw people freelancing, off on their own, and we would tell them, "If you're going to work down here, work with somebody, because if you fall into one of these holes here, you may become a victim yourself." There were voids that went down two, three stories deep. The beams down there were hot from the fires that were still burning.

I'm not sure exactly when they put the fence up and started issuing IDs, but I think it was at least two weeks after the attacks. By that time, the authorities told the volunteers and police officers and firefighters from around the country that they weren't needed anymore.

I'M NOT WHO I USED TO BE

I had two children at home when all this was going on. My son was four, so he was a little young to be aware of what was going on. My daughter was six, and she pretty much knew. They're children, and I wonder whether they really understand what a terrorist attack means. They knew something big was happening, and that daddy wasn't going to be around for a while.

I was separated from my wife at the time. So I picked them up after school almost every day, and that stopped for quite a while. I explained that I was busy doing stuff at work. I didn't really want to go into it any further than that.

The schools did a good job of telling the kids what was going on, and I pretty much left explanations up to them and their mother. It was quite a few months before I saw them on weekends as much as I used to.

I lost a lot of guys I'd worked with every day for many years. These were fourteen of my close friends, and twenty-three police officers in all. Spent more time with most of them than I did with my immediate family. Eight-and-a-half hours a day, sometimes more when there was overtime. I did side jobs with a couple of them when I was off. So to me, it was like wiping out my family. I took it really, really hard. And I still do. Most police officers take it hard when another officer gets shot and killed. Now you're talking about twenty-three in one incident.

I'm not who I used to be at all. I'm suffering from post-traumatic stress. The irony is that, in the Emergency Service Unit, we dealt with death and destruction every day. I mean, we went to every homicide in New York City, every bad car crash where people were trapped in cars. We took bodies and body parts out from under trains, hostage situations, people who jump off the bridges. We were there for every really bad thing that happened in New York City.

We always felt that there's no way anything can bother us. We're hardened to that stuff. And I believed that, even when I retired back in 2003. But our team had something that was pretty special. It's true that we didn't have critical-incident stress teams like the Fire Department does, but we had our own. Our critical-incident stress debriefing was to go back to our command, have a cup of coffee and sit around the table with everybody who just handled that situation, and talk about it. And sometimes even joke about it. That's how we dealt with it. When I retired in 2003, I didn't have that anymore.

Everything started to just build up inside of me. It got to the point that I started drinking really heavily. And I was never a drinker. My family started to see this. I began fighting with my wife and yelling at my kids. I started punching holes through the walls in my house. Then my wife said to me, "You need to go get help." She's a medical professional. She said, "You need to go get help or you're going to be divorced again." I listened to her and sought help. And thank God I did because, otherwise, I don't know where I'd be right now. I may not even be here. I'm still going for help, and I'm not embarrassed to say it. I'm on medication. I see a great psychiatrist. I love the guy. He's great.

I still take the attacks very personally. I still can't stand the fact that Osama bin Laden is out there, and all these innocent people are dead. It's under control, though. I was at the point where I was jumping out of my car. I had road rage, and I was going after people in their cars. It was going to get to the point where either I was going to get killed or kill someone.

I'm not like that anymore. I'm calm. I don't have road rage anymore. I very rarely even argue with my wife. I see the more important things in life now and how easily your life can be taken from you. Anger took over after 9/11, and I didn't have anybody to work through it with. Here's a big problem in the Police Department: There are lots and lots of police officers who need help, who have post-traumatic stress who are still on the job since 9/11. The problem with going for help is that right away the department sees you as a liability. They think you may do something they don't want you to do, and for which they may be liable. So the first thing they want to do is take away your guns. You're labeled as a crazy person, and nobody wants to work with you anymore.

So a lot of cops who may need help don't go for it. That's why the suicide rate is so high in the New York City Police Department, and probably in police departments all over the country. If you go to what's called the Psychological Services Unit and you're not careful about what you say, they'll take your guns and put you on desk duty, or they'll transfer you from a precinct to the Central Repair Shop and let you check in cars for the next ten years. You lose all your overtime. Guys don't want that.

I hope that fifty years from now people aren't going through what we're going through now, waking up every morning worrying about terrorists attacking and blowing up subway trains. I hope the wars are over and our country is more secure, and there's peace in this country and you don't have to go through what we went through here.

What we did down there should never be forgotten. The people who died that day, don't ever forget them. It's a part of history that I know will never be forgotten.

CHAPTER 27

THE UGLY BRANCHES

John was called to Ground Zero on September 12 in order to clear out debris. His specialty was large demolition jobs. "I'm not a cop or a firefighter," he says, "but I knew that with my expertise in construction over the past twenty years, and my having been in the military, I was going to be needed." Even as a civilian, the sense of duty to his country at a time of emergency trumped any commitment to his regular job. He refers to it as patriotism.

John is one of the non-military responders who rushed to Ground Zero to help, and ended up needing help themselves. So he decided to turn his misfortune into a powerful tool. He spearheads groups that lobby and advocate for the needs of his fellow responders. He now runs the FealGood Foundation, a not-for-profit organization that spreads awareness about 9/11-related health problems of first responders while providing them with financial assistance.

I NEVER REALLY STOPPED

IT WAS THE MOST SURREAL THING I'VE EVER SEEN, the most horrific act of violence I've ever witnessed. Getting into Ground Zero, there were tens of thousands of people that were literally clapping and cheering like you were Elvis—like you were going to save the city. I found that a little odd because I was just going there to do my job. I knew I wasn't there to save anybody; I was there to remove debris and remove the pile of devastation so that those trained to find survivors could do their job.

I think everybody inside had some sort of patriotism in them.

But when I got in there and saw the devastation…Listen, I've seen devastation. I was in the military. I've seen a lot of carnage; I've seen some things that I don't choose to speak about. But you're not programmed to wake up in the morning on a daily basis and see what we saw.

When I initially got there, I worked about forty-three hours straight.

I was at Site 7—Building 7. I was in charge of delegating orders. I took orders from the top and I delegated them on the ground. That was my job. Building 7 was one of the most secure buildings in the world. It came down later that afternoon, after the Towers. Everybody was gone. They were all evacuated, but the rubble from 1 and 2 and 7, they crisscross.

We took five- to ten-minute breaks here, twenty minutes there. I ate there on the Pile. It wasn't until September 15th that they started the twelve-hour shifts. Within a couple of days the Red Cross had tents up. The local church, other organizations, United Way—they all had places where you could go and talk to somebody. But my main focus was on work. I never really stopped. A lot of celebrities came, dignitaries, political officials. I never stopped to bother to talk to anybody—not when there's a job to be done. I'm a strong believer in work hard and play hard. I didn't sleep the first forty-three hours and then I went home, slept about three hours, took a shower, and went back. I haven't had a full night's sleep since 9/11.

EIGHT THOUSAND POUNDS OF STEEL

At the time, before 9/11, nothing was physically challenging for me. I was in the best shape of my life. Mentally, I'm a pretty focused person. But since then, my life was physically and mentally altered. Well, there were a lot of grown men taking time out after working and just sitting there by themselves crying, and you see that, and then cops, firefighters, big burly construction workers with tattoos on their necks, and they're sitting there hugging each other and crying.

I really kept to myself. I didn't really know a lot of people there. I knew I had a job to do. I come from a strict family background where my father told me to work hard, get it done. I can't say I'm like the thousands of other 9/11 responders that might have made friends for life, but since my injury was so high profile, people would come up to me and say, "I remember when you got hurt." I wish I could remember them, but I can't because I was in the process of losing a lot of blood.

I was there for five days before I got horribly injured. On September 17th, eight thousand pounds of steel crushed my left foot. The man next to me fainted when blood was shooting out of my foot about six feet in the air. I was a human sprinkler. When he fainted, I made a tourniquet. I took his belt off of him and I put it around my calf. I don't panic. When the Fire Department got there, within three minutes, four minutes, I was 120/80.

I got my boot off and bones were sticking through my sock. I couldn't get my sock off. I was rushed to Bellevue Hospital like I was Elvis. They were waiting for me. I spent ten days in Bellevue and I got gangrene. At the time, I thought gangrene was like from the 1800s like when someone gets shot in the belly and guys are like, he's gonna die of gangrene. I didn't really think you could get gangrene anymore. I told my mother to get me out of the hospital and I went to North Shore University Hospital on Long Island. I put my mother and my sister through family hell. Every day, they were worrying if I was going to be okay. And then when I got hurt, they literally were at the hospital every day. They altered their life for months for me.

I spent ten weeks at North Shore fighting for my life. I eventually lost half of my foot, which at the time I thought I could handle. I went to therapy for a year. If I didn't do that, I probably wouldn't be here today. I can honestly say that. All of these cops, firefighters, construction workers—all these macho, burly men—they're embarrassed to admit that they take medication for their post-traumatic stress or their depression, or they're embarrassed to admit that they went to therapy.

Take 9/11 out of the equation, and three-quarters of America is medicated because of depression or something. I went to therapy and it saved my life and it gave me hope, but while I was in the hospital, when you lay on your back for eleven weeks, your life changes. It's not like staying home from work for three days with a cold. Your life is literally altered, and you learn to appreciate what you have and what you don't have and what you don't need and what you might want in the future. Or there's something that you had in the past that you think is now frivolous because your priorities are more focused. I learned the hard way. Really, the hard way. I had multiple surgeries. Every year from 2001 to 2006, I was always in a cast or on crutches. So even while I was suffering and even before I started the FealGood Foundation, I was advocating for others since 2003, just as an individual.

IF 9/11 IS A TREE

9/11 made me a better person. I'm about solutions and problem solving, and what can we do to make those people who were affected by 9/11 and this country as a whole whole again?

I'm never going to be the same person I was on 9/10/01. But I'm damn close—a lot closer than other people, even with my debilitating injuries—to being that same person, but better. But there are so many people who need that help. They're in there; they're in the shell of the person they used to be. 9/11 has really laid its ugly hand on so many good people.

I don't know if it's a curse or a gift, but I can block 9/11 out. I can block out what I did there for five days. Again, that goes back to going to therapy. I don't have nightmares anymore. I don't think about 9/11 per se unless somebody brings it up. But I live 9/11 every day 'cause I run a foundation. People that come to us for help and we hear their stories. The burden is heavy on me, and my board and my board members are affected by 9/11. They're medicated, too, like the 9/11 responders they help.

What really hits me the hardest is the kids that are affected because their parents are affected. Misery needs company. Daddy used to be the breadwinner in the family and he brings home a paycheck. Now Daddy doesn't do that no more, or now she doesn't feel like the woman she used to be and now the kids are in therapy or the kids are in rehab for drug use and the families are getting divorced. People just think that two buildings fell down and that 2,751 lives were lost that day. Three buildings fell down that day, but it has just affected so many families in so many different areas, that if 9/11 is a tree, it's got hundreds of ugly branches that have just worked their way into mainstream America's households. It's painful.

THE AMERICAN PEOPLE WHO MAKE THIS COUNTRY GREAT

There is nobody more patriotic than me, in my mind. As an American, as an army veteran, as a 9/11 responder, I'd say I'd do it all again in a heartbeat. If this building fell down right now I'd try to save you all and get you out. But as an advocate—as a leading advocate—I would say no way: You can't get me to go there because the government lied to us. We're sick because we were told the air was safe to breathe and the water was safe to drink. Since 9/11, people say I'm the grandfather of the movement, 'cause with all my work, our [struggles have] been publicized. We're sick because the toxins that we swallowed, that we inhaled—that toxic soup—without the proper mask and ventilation. We're sick because of neglect and denial.

9/11 brought this country together. Everybody loved everybody: black, white, different religions—it didn't matter. Everybody was united. It didn't matter where you were from, what you did, how much money you made, what your tax bracket was. You could cut somebody off on the L.I.E., it's okay. Or somebody would hold the door open for you. Everybody hugged each other; everybody said hello.

Now we're back to the same way. Oh, you cut me off; let me throw you the finger or give you the F word. We lost that loving feeling. Poor leadership, bad politics, and the desire not to help men and women who risked their lives without prejudice trickled its way into society. The American people now have a bad taste about our elected officials in D.C. I work with many officials in D.C. It's my home away from home. I've been fighting now for four years for a bill. There are so many good elected officials that get a bad name because of the whole scope of D.C.

I'm an optimistic person. It's the American people that make this country great; it's not our elected officials. I just wish more people would find a cause, even if it's not even 9/11. Find something you believe in. I sit here living on a government check, but I was able to donate $250,000 in the last five years and to donate a kidney. As Americans, we have extra money. We have extra food, and we have extra body parts. Just imagine if everybody just took a couple minutes out of their day.

On September 11th, 2,751 people died, perished because of an act of senseless violence—because evil people wanted to do evil things to the people of New York. But they did that because of ignorance. It's the way they were brought up. They don't know any better. But in the true, classic form where evil meets good, people from all over this country, not just New York, came to Ground Zero. Of the 435 congressional districts in the United States, people from 431 of them came. The good came to fight that evil, and it was the largest ever showing of good. I know good will always prevail over evil.

Since then, all of these people that are sick and dying, evil met them again, but in a different form. But now with the doctors, like the World Trade Center clinics and the Centers of Excellence, good has fought evil again. Even 9/11 heroes need heroes, and the doctors and the lawyers and everybody that has championed our cause—they're our heroes. It's true a hero does need a hero. They just might not say it or show it. Your government might not always be there to step up and do the right thing unless the goodness in the people forces the government to do the right thing, embarrasses them to do the right thing. I love my country. I love my history. I certainly love my future. And I love everybody that I advocate for.

PART FIVE

RENEWAL

In the wake of the ten-year anniversary of 9/11, the horror and pain of the responders' experiences has hardly quelled. In fact, their raw pain has been complicated by a sense of abandonment and, in some cases, isolation. And yet, there are those people who have taken up the 9/11 responders as their cause. They continue to provide them with medical and emotional support and legal assistance. They are in the fight to help the World Trade Center responders move forward with their lives in a meaningful way. Since these interviews with responders began, one fight was won with the passing of the James Zadroga bill, which establishes a national health care program for 9/11 responders and for disaster survivors. Renewal is a long, hard process that some responders may never achieve. They will never be as innocent, as lively, as strong as they were before 9/11 marked them, but with people devoted to their cause, they have a chance at getting there.

▲ **The interior of St. Paul's Chapel,** located across the street from the World Trade Center site, offered responders spiritual support, medical treatment, massages, and hot meals. The chapel's priest, Reverend Harris, recounts his 9/11-related experiences in Chapter 32. *Photo by Steve Spak.*

▲ **A makeshift memorial in tribute** to some of the firefighters, police officers, and emergency medical technicians who lost their lives in the World Trade Center disaster. *Photo by Steve Spak.*

▲ **A "teddy bear wall" where mourners** left hundreds of stuffed animals and other items in memory of the victims of 9/11. *Photo by Roy and Lois Gross.*

▲ **Responders form an honor guard along a huge ramp** extending into the Pit to salute bagpipers from the FDNY, NYPD, and Port Authority Police Department at a ceremony held on May, 30, 2002, to mark the closure of the World Trade Center site following the cleanup. *Photo by Steve Spak.*

CHAPTER 28

THE SMELL OF DEATH

Frank is a psychiatrist who worked directly with 9/11 first responders. He grew up in a family dominated by people in police and military professions, and he naturally gravitated professionally toward helping the responders cope with the stresses inherent in their work after the attack. He himself is identified as a responder, and as such was exposed to the same horrors as his patients and suffered similar medical consequences. His story is a fascinating description of his own struggle as a doctor and psychiatrist to cope with both the vast disaster that would be part of the rest of his life, and the overwhelming vortex of psychological pain that spared no one that day, including himself.

TRAINING VOLUNTEER PEERS

I'M A PSYCHIATRIST, AND MY ROLE POST-9/11 was mostly as a psychiatrist volunteer responder and a medical advisor to POPPA, the Police Organization Providing Peer Assistance, which is a voluntary, peer-based assistance program for New York City police officers. It had been in existence a few years before 9/11, assisting the peers and, at times, being available for clinical emergencies and doing support at the various sites. At Ground Zero, those included the morgue, the landfill, and Ground Zero, mostly Ground Zero.

As a clinician, we sort of automatically do what the emergency responders do, and we go into that work mode. I could barely let myself feel, "Oh my God. How many people are going to die?" And barely start to feel and think about the emotional impact, the psychological impact, the physical injuries and dying, because I have to get through my day; I have to see all these patients on the unit and got to be ready.

Five or six months out, we sort of had an idea that it was around 3,000 that had died, and we knew about the twenty-nine in white [medical professionals], twenty-three members of NYPD, twenty-nine from the Port Authority, and 343 firefighters.

I remember saying to my wife, "That's going to be nothing compared to what we're going to see over the next ten or twenty years." How many are going to die from the traumatic stress? Just wondering when is that going to start happening. What can we do to help all these people? We're learning about all these physiological interactions between stress, depression, PTSD and heart disease and the immune system and other things that shorten lives, but I still wonder how many of these people will end up, unfortunately, dying by their own hand. I'm sure, as much as I'd love to be wrong, more than that have died so far.

Some people think I founded POPPA, but I did not. Bill Genet founded it. He's a retired police officer and the current president of POPPA. It started in the mid-90s after a crisis where the suicides really spiked. There were twenty-six in a two-year period, mid-1993 to 1995, and everyone was up in arms in the city. The police commissioner's office, the mayor's office, the city council, and the press were demanding a solution. And Bill, who had been around for twenty some-odd years by then as a police officer/union leader, had been trained as an EAP [Employee-Assistance Program] professional, was there with a solution.

His idea was: "Let's train volunteer peers to be the liaisons." The liaisons do the same police work, but they get officers with these stress-related issues and link them to professionals who can assist them. But it's got to be an outside agency, because officers are afraid to go to the department for help.

POPPA is now accepted around the department, but there are still obstacles. I think that because POPPA was around since 1996, and now it's fifteen years, most officers have come across POPPA at some time over their career, particularly with all the work that was done post-9/11 at Ground Zero—the morgues and the landfill. There's been a lot of outreach and support work done by the peers and the clinicians who also volunteered, and the work that has gone on since then. So, I think ... officers know who POPPA is, and they get it that stress-related problems, depression, anxiety, post-traumatic stress, alcohol problems, and other problems can happen as a result of this work.

HOW WE RESPOND TO RESPONDERS

It's still a challenge for each individual, though, to recognize in themselves that they're affected by a problem and then have the courage to reach out. The suicide rate in the NYPD is 40 percent lower than it was over the ten-year period before POPPA's existence. Now people reach out through other channels. For example, they reach out through the Trade Center Medical Monitoring program. Some reach out through the Red

Cross, others through word of mouth on their own. Although some of the volunteer peers are very comfortable helping others, it can take a long time for them to say, "Maybe I'm being affected."

I think a big reason for that is most people who choose to become an emergency responder, a police officer, firefighter, EMT, and certainly even us, doctors, are, on average, more able to handle traumatic events than maybe the rest of us. There are screenings as well, there are psychological screenings, physical screenings, and so on, and certainly people are weeded out. The other thing that happens is that, as they do this work, they learn from others how to adapt and how to push these things aside and do the work they've got to do.

In some ways, how we respond to responders is a societal issue. It's okay that we expect them to be professionals and to be able to handle the crisis. But it's not okay that we sometimes lose sight of the fact that they are human and that they are impacted just like you and I are. They may be better able to handle an individual event than the rest of us, but over their careers there are so many events, especially if someone works in a busy firehouse or busy precinct or command or task force, that they could be exposed to hundreds and hundreds of things, that you could almost think of it as a repetitive-stress injury. And we know enough about traumatic stress that it really does affect us physiologically.

I really think of it as a physical, psychological, and spiritual injury that, after a while, it can just be too much like another version of a repetitive-stress injury. But, also, there could be sudden individual events that are so over the top. A job-related shooting, a fire where civilians died, particularly children or an infant. 9/11 was one of those kinds of events, that it's so big in and of itself, and a lot of times, I think the press and the public look at it as though it was one event. It was a terrorist attack.

But it was hundreds of events to any one person who responded. That's what these responders taught me from the get-go. Common sense said to me, well, it was one plane, a second plane, it was fires, it was explosions, it was one collapse, a second, and people forget a third building collapsed later in the day.

As I listened to their individual stories, I realized that this was a crisis intervention, and that while individually people might talk and share some stories or talk as a group about their experiences, I realized that each officer responded to many events, a lot of them concurrently. They went in and out of the buildings, guided civilians, and assisted the wounded and injured. There were fires, there were explosions, there were tons of steel and debris falling. There were jumpers, there were bodies falling.

Somebody who dodged a falling body on their way into the building just went through a life-threatening event, and they barely perceived it, and yet it happened. It's etched in their brains, in their minds, in their memory and their spirit. These people were exposed to dozens and dozens, hundreds, of events. Any one of them is enough to cause post-traumatic stress.

Seriously traumatic events that happen in thirty seconds, or a minute, are enough to cause PTSD: An officer tries to fire a weapon or is fired at, someone gets stabbed, there's an arrest and the perpetrator becomes violent. Responding to a rape or an assault, a child who has been shot in a drive-by—these are really severe traumatic events that unfold for most police officers. Yet, that's enough to cause PTSD, and that's the type of thing that I mean—that over a career, the trauma-related stress ratchets up, and there could be an event or circumstance that could be the final straw that breaks the camel's back.

Now we have this 9/11. If you responded before the Towers came down, was it twenty minutes, was it thirty minutes, was it three hours that your body was in this heightened state, as if the stress of a shooting was happening not just in an instant, but for hours? If you responded afterwards—after the Towers' collapse—and you were doing security on the perimeter, you were in some of these caverns searching for survivors or remains, or you were guarding an area where there were bodies, and you were waiting for people to take care of these bodies and remains. And then a week later you realize that now there's warnings that no one is allowed to go there because this is unsafe, and here you were standing guard for eighty hours over the last week.

This 9/11 is so over the top that it's beyond ridiculous, and that's what hundreds and hundreds of these people were exposed to over those weeks. Here are people for hours and hours, day after day, week after week, month after month, at that heightened stress level. After a while, whether the alarm went off or not, you wondered each time whether you couldn't get out. Some people I worked with, civilians or the emergency responders—because there were civilians, such as electricians running lines, or workers cutting steel—side by side with these officers, exposed to remains, exposed to the same dangers. After a while, sometimes when the alarm went off, they didn't move. That wasn't because they didn't care, but because they realized that if a building is collapsing, they can't get out anyway.

I don't think that the public or the press really appreciate that level of what these people went through. When people say, "Get over it," I know that every one of the responders would, in a heartbeat, love to work with a guy like me and say, "I talked about my stuff, I got a handle on it, so let me just put it on the shelf and be done with it." If it were just that simple.

If only they could get over it. If only the nightmares would stop. If only all the reminders, the jumpiness, all the ways their stress reactions are triggered would stop, and they could just live their lives comfortably. If only they didn't have these physical illnesses that, again, remind them of danger.

They're affected with anxiety attacks that are a big part of traumatic stress. People hyperventilate; they feel short of breath. Two-thirds of the responders have lung disease that's new or worse than it was before. I count myself lucky, by the way, that my asthma, that I've had since childhood, is better now than it was on 9/11. Why? Luck. It's only luck, and also because I don't have the level of exposure of many of them. So luck and less exposure.

But what if you have traumatic-stress symptoms every time you're short of breath and use your inhaler? Every time you're feeling anxious because you've been triggered by a reminder, you feel short of breath, sometimes you don't even know if it's asthma or anxiety or both. This is what people are dealing with every day…

CIVILIAN RESPONDERS

When I was walking around Ground Zero, we would talk with civilians. If somebody looked like they were hurting, we'd reach out and put a hand on their shoulder. "What's up? What's going on? How are you doing?" We didn't care who it was. The public and the press were saying, "These firefighters, EMTs, and cops–they're heroes." People recognized the traumatic stress and were being supportive.

But people were forgetting these civilian responders. I really remember at the time wishing these guys had a POPPA. I wondered what their EAP programs are doing. I could only do so much while I was helping POPPA. I still had my practice, and of course my own family. I remember being grateful that I knew people from the Red Cross and Mt. Sinai's disaster-psychiatry outreach program. Some psychiatrists that I knew volunteered, and they were there for all of the workers, and maybe they focused on the civilians. I've met people who may be more in construction or engineering or electrician work. Whether they worked for the phone company or the MTA or whoever, and here they are, side-by-side with these firefighters and officers. Some of them are just volunteering on the Pile and removing debris and remains. Some are running wires, running cables. Cutting steel and doing these other things exposed them to the same risks, the same elements, the same body parts and remains, all the sights, the sounds, the smells, as the emergency responders.

Civilians are probably more vulnerable to post-traumatic stress for the same event, compared to the average police officer or firefighter. Some of them were okay for a while and had their own way of pushing it aside, just like cops, firefighters, EMTs, and docs do. Some of them were experiencing anxiety attacks, were experiencing nightmares and insomnia, and still felt an obligation: "I've got to go back, and I've got to help out." They knew their role was important and that the official emergency responder needed them to do their work so they had power, they had equipment running, they had phones going, they had lighting, etc.

But they were hurting along the way. In many ways, I think they are forgotten because it's more obvious to recognize, say, the civilian who was in the building, or someone who was injured or grieving the sudden, traumatic loss of a loved one, and to forget about these civilians who responded. They were exposed to the same things.

A POTENTIAL EPIDEMIC

It's funny, but I've learned that sometimes things work out the way they're supposed to. By day three, POPPA had been donated space, and it had established this initial emergency-crisis center on the ground floor of the Federal Reserve Bank when power was out in the area. They had some power generators to keep some basic functioning going in the building, and I had planned on going in, knowing that they were going to start being available that Friday. I was told by the director and clinical director to stay home and stay in my office. I was pissed.

"What do you mean?" I grew up in the family of responders. "I'm coming in." [They said,] "Look, everything is disorganized. We know we have a plan to be involved and to start being available for outreach, and so on and so on." I wanted to come in and they basically said, "No, you're not coming in. You wait till we're sure things are up and running, and we know we can use you in a way you can be helpful."

I was furious. I had canceled my day and arranged for coverage for the weekend because I was going, and I didn't know when I'd be coming back. But I knew that I could be helpful. It turned out that same day—this is the part where things work out the way they're supposed to—an officer brought a friend and colleague to the crisis center who was clearly florid PTSD and really suffering. She needed to be seen in somebody's office, so then I got the call from my friend, Gene [director of POPPA], who I was furious at and was never going to forgive for telling me I couldn't go in with him and be a part of the response. I saw her in my office and just started helping. She was actually so symptomatic and so struggling that I think if I wasn't available, she would have ended up in the hospital.

In some cases, the problems were pre-9/11 traumatic events that they maybe hadn't fully dealt with, or they had dealt with to some degree but they were already changed and were more susceptible to a future event. This person had been involved with two job-related shootings and was having severe sleep deprivation, really looking like a punch-drunk, delirious, sleep-deprived kid. As parents, we've probably all seen that once when our kids couldn't sleep, and this is what it almost looked like. Once this person received a medication that could help them sleep, they realized, as bad as Ground Zero was, and they were there within the first couple of days, that wasn't the problem. What was coming up in the nightmares was actually these shootings that had never been dealt with.

It turned out that, for this officer, 9/11 was easier to deal with once we dealt with the shootings. My worry then was, well, three-quarters of the NYPD had some direct exposure to Ground Zero, the morgues, or the landfill. Whatever the official estimates are, my bet is that some 5,000-plus had some significant response within the first few days to a week, and however many thousands officially or unofficially volunteering, assigned here, quietly going to help out like good officers, firefighters, and EMTs do.

With all that exposure causing PTSD, some would limp along and do the work they feel they've got to do and get worse. What else are they exposed to over their careers? For this person it could be a shooting, and then Ground Zero was just the straw that broke the camel's back. [Or] Ground Zero, the morgue, and the landfill caused traumatic exposure and, then, one, two, five, and ten years later, there's the death in the family or the car accident or the shooting or another so-called normal traumatic event, and that then becomes the straw that breaks the camel's back.

I really believe that PTSD is already so widespread that you could call it an epidemic. I do believe that there are some who have traumatic-stress symptoms, but not PTSD, who are more vulnerable over the rest of their career. I don't know the answer—if there's enough help from POPPA and other agencies, and even the work we're doing with the World Trade Center Medical Monitoring. There are people that we're picking up that may have traumatic stress, depression, and anxiety symptoms that otherwise wouldn't have been recognized. I don't know how much we may be able to decrease that long-term difficulty. Based on the number of people we've already seen, my worry is that there are still many more that we haven't identified.

TEACHING RESILIENCE

Prevention is something that people are looking at. We are all looking at ways to see if we can train people with skills and techniques that may make them more resilient. I think that by their nature, police officers, firefighters, and EMTs are more resilient than the rest of us, but it's really a difficult question. I believe the answer is we can do something to prevent it or to decrease the rates, but I will readily admit that the data is not there.

I do believe a program like POPPA does this, and I do believe that 9/11 has made it easier for people, because now traumatic stress and psychiatric illnesses are more out there in the forefront. That process was happening little by little anyway, but 9/11 and all the news and information about it, I think, has accelerated that. More people are now getting help earlier when we believe these illnesses may be more treatable. We saw over 5,000 people at the crisis center where we did individual and group crisis work. We've kept the help line running. Hundreds of people are getting help through the help line every year. There were others setting up programs to assist, and I knew people would get help. But I still knew, with help from my friends in Oklahoma City who came to help us, that the majority of people who responded in the first few days would really be affected at that so-called clinical level. And I knew the majority of them were not getting clinical help, and I knew no matter how good POPPA is, this is a tough nut to crack to get these guys to come and get the help.

A FEAR OF OPENING UP

Now, years later, we've seen that some officers would report symptoms, and our care managers would recommend they get help, and some would get it, but many would resist. Others would underreport symptoms. But many times the symptoms were there all along, and they were still afraid to admit the symptoms to us at the Trade Center Medical Monitoring Program. It has nothing to do with their fear that it could somehow get back to the department. Sometimes there's that fear that, "God, if I open up that can, I'll never be able to close it."

It's cops, firefighters, EMTs, people who volunteer to serve in our military—sometimes people forget it has been an all-volunteer military for nearly forty years now—they are often people who, in one way or another, grew up and developed, however their personal story unfolded, into people who wanted to be the person who could help protect someone from a bullet. They're putting their own lives at risk for the sake of helping and protecting the rest of us. In many ways I really look at this as transcultural medicine. Just as people are more and more aware of others' different ethnic and religious backgrounds, you have to understand that the emergency responders are a culture. They respond to, and see things, in a different way.

Sometimes an officer is struggling with symptoms all along and they make this Herculean effort to try to keep the symptoms in check and continue to do that work, and it's mostly out of loyalty to their brothers and sisters in that unit. "They've had my back; I'm going to have theirs." That's the similarity between police and the military—that loyalty to the unit, to the life-and-death situations they face. It's magnified even more in the military, especially with the way things are in Afghanistan and Iraq in the last nearly ten years. For some of them, it's there all along, and they just keep muddling through. Then, when they're retired, they're more comfortable getting help.

THE SENSE OF SMELL AND TRAUMATIC EVENTS

The first time I went down to the site was about a week after 9/11. I remember it was a very rainy day, and we were on the 1st floor of the Federal Reserve Bank. It was partly a tour just to get a sense of what was going on, but also what we were doing was, as people were taking a break, asking, "What's up, officer? How are you doing? How is your family?" We let them know of our availability at the crisis center. They could come by for a break, a cup of coffee, a meal, and, if they wanted to talk, we were available. Also just to talk officer-to-officer, peer-to-peer.

We never interrupted someone when they were involved in their mission. You don't want to mess with their rescue-and-recovery effort. That's why they're there, and that's their profession, but when people were taking a break, we would basically reach out. We encouraged them to get their rest and have their breaks and try to do healthy things and make connections with their family and friends in their down time. We watched for signs of when they might be hurting enough that they might really want to get more help.

I remember walking around Ground Zero, and the sights, the sounds, the smells, and even in the rain I remember saying to myself, *I smell death here*. There were a few smells, and I was really trying to figure them out for myself…I have seasonal allergies twelve months of the year, so my sense of smell is generally fairly deadened. But you could certainly smell the smoke of the fire and debris burning. There was also the smell of fuel, probably partly from fuel burning and what was underground and seepage and soil and pockets and puddles, but also from the diesel of the machinery, the generators and so on.

But the biggest thing for me was—and I remember just doing a double take—one of the sites that was photographed so much was a huge piece of the Tower that had collapsed. It was almost like a huge arrow or javelin sticking out of the ground. And, of course, there were 100 floors of dust and rubble underneath it. I could be standing a block away and look at that. But if I turned around and looked the other way, it could look like Lower Manhattan or like a calm still of the city. And then you could turn around and look toward the center of Ground Zero and go, *Oh my God! I'm in the middle of a war zone. Do people really get this?* You couldn't quite get it from all the photos and all the video and so on, and I just couldn't imagine what it would be like.

The smell was a huge thing. It's when we think about a traumatic event, and smells are part of every traumatic event.

They are a sensation that's part of it…Officers will say, "I have a recollection, and I'm smelling it." They're afraid that, because it's a sensation, someone's going to say they're crazy because crazy people hear things, see things. "And now I'm smelling things. I don't even want to admit it." The way I explain it to officers is that smell is not only a very strong sensation, but it can be tightly associated with a memory, a traumatic recollection. The smells often come back because they're a part of the trauma. The olfactory nerve right at the top of our nose is like a cable line that goes less than a centimeter right into our brain. And right in that area, where our brain processes smells, is the hotbed of our emotions, the limbic system, and our memory. It's all right there.

I remember waking up one Thursday morning, which was a day that I would always go into the crisis center, and the alarm goes off. My feet hit the floor, and without thinking, I let it out and said, "Oh shit. I smell death." I couldn't figure out what it was, but I know I smell death, but I wasn't smelling death and the way it provoked visual reels of Ground Zero. I couldn't put it together. It wasn't a full-blown flashback. I'm walking around the house trying to figure whether there is some dead mouse somewhere that smells. And it had rained heavily, and where I was living in Oakdale at the time, it could puddle. So I'm looking to see whether some dead animal is in a puddle or something.

I can't find anything, but I can smell it. And I remember at some point from then to the time I took the Long Island Rail Road and then the subway down to Lower Manhattan, it was gone, and I couldn't figure it out. I remember mentioning it to a few of the POPPA peers, because I know about traumatic stress, and we're all affected by it…And they basically said to me, "Don't worry about it. You'll figure it out. You always figure it out."

I said to myself, "None of them is saying, 'Gee, you look like you're rough around the edges, you look like you're hurt,'" so I figure I must be okay, but I gotta keep an eye on this. That weekend, this throwaway newspaper, the *South Bay*—it's like a *Pennysaver* of car ads, and some political articles by the owner of the paper—had an article. There was a fish kill in the Great South Bay. A bunch of bunker fish had died. They had washed up to the mouth of the Connetquot River, and my house is about a half mile due south or a half mile due west. I really was smelling death, but that triggered all the recollections.

Imagine if you were there before the Towers collapsed and [gone] through dozens or hundreds of life-threatening events yourself that happened so fast you can barely remember them. The alarm goes off, there's an explosion, or some of these officers or firefighters are repelling down and going into caverns and looking for survivors and so on, or bringing out remains, and all the while this smell is there. Think how that gets seared into responders' experience of the event.

Every time I give a talk, I teach, or speak at some public situation and we talk about traumatic stress, I always make sure we talk about smells, because I know there will be somebody in the audience who is dealing with it. They may even be in treatment, but have been afraid to talk about those symptoms. Often, knowing what triggers the smells, or what the smells trigger, can reveal some of your key exposures. But it's healing to know, *I'm not going crazy. I'm not that abnormal.* There's thousands of other people experiencing it. Even now, when I mention scent-association to these POPPA volunteer peers or the trainings I do every year, inevitably, if there are 100 of them there, one or two of them will come up and say, "Dr. D., thanks for mentioning smells. You shared your story. This is what happened with me. Now can you help me make sense of it?"

FEELING NOTHING IS SAFER

Ground Zero responders often say they felt like robots while they were working such long hours. I think what happens with a traumatic event— and most are fairly short in duration—responders put their emotional selves aside, usually without thinking about it. It happens naturally, and they do what they have to do. The event happens, and then afterwards, some of them may experience it, or they're moving on to the next thing.

We all dissociate. That's what this is: In some ways taking what's going on and pushing it out of our awareness. It's a normal thing to dissociate. One of the best examples I can give is if you're driving to and from work, or to and from the same place, over and over. Initially you're paying attention to every stop light and every turn, and every this and every that. You're actively aware. But after a while, you know where you're going and you could be thinking, listening to something on the radio, having a conversation, and you wake up, so to speak, and you're there, and yet you weren't unconscious, you didn't crash. You obviously were paying attention, so there is a natural way we all do that.

Though we dissociate, we take something out of our active awareness and put it aside. In many ways that's a healthy thing, but what happened at Ground Zero is that this exposure was so intense, so severe, and [lasted] so long that some people will say they just don't remember huge gaps. They still don't remember what happened on 9/11 or the ensuing days. It's not just because they were there for hundreds of hours. How could you remember every detail? This is what their mind, their brain, did to protect them. One might just not remember. One might say, "I felt almost distant emotionally, or flat."

This is how the brain helps avoid PTSD. Feeling nothing is safer than feeling all this god-awful stuff that's too difficult for words. Sometimes when people dissociate, they can emotionally feel a distance, like they're outside and watching themselves do things. That's when they can feel like they're a robot and just going through things. I had advised some people who may have said some things like that. I told them, "You might be okay, but that could be a warning sign that you were on overload for so long that you were like a robot going through things."

Your mind can protect you by inserting gaps in your memory, and that may be a warning sign that you have post-traumatic stress, or you're more at risk for it. Really look out for it, and come back if you're worse. Some officers can do that so well that they're not aware of the symptoms, and they might not technically meet criteria for PTSD when asked about nightmares, vivid recollections, or flashbacks, because they're so good at pushing it aside and not feeling much of anything. This emotional detachment might feel more like numbness than sadness. They may deny that they feel depressed. So it's missed by us because it's missed by them.

CHAPTER 29

PROVIDING PEER ASSISTANCE

Bill is the founder and director of POPPA, the Police Organization Providing Peer Assistance. The peer counseling and crisis intervention group was still in its infancy when the 9/11 attack occurred. Police officers are caretakers. They have an innate need to "fix" whatever problem is at hand, and they often forget to care for themselves in the process. Bill discusses the challenge of convincing officers to seek mental health care and the importance of an emotionally well emergency response force.

POLICE CULTURE—LIKE OTHER EMERGENCY responder cultures—is one of caretaking. Police officers are the helpers. To change their mindset about asking for help, to pierce that curtain of resistance to getting assistance for personal problems, was very difficult culturally. We collected something like 180 peers prior to 2001. We intensely trained them in the word-of-mouth of peer to peer, saying, "There is help available. You don't have to wait till you reach a crisis point."

When 2001 came we had impacted approximately 10 percent of the Police Department, which was 35,000 at the time. We were an outside-the-department agency. We had confidentiality agreements with the New York City Police Department, which they agreed to. That could assure the officers that if they came forward on their own with personal problems, it would not be entered into their records in any form.

We were 10 percent into the population by 2001, by September 11th. Since then we [have] impacted almost 90 percent of the population, meaning that they have a full understanding that they have a safe place, and that it's a good idea to get help before you're really in crisis. That was a result, a positive result of September 11th.

A year before September 11th, we got all the people to take the crisis training. And thank God we did, because without it we wouldn't have been able to respond to 9/11 the way we did. So when 9/11 came, we had a core of well-trained peers. Nobody knew we were ready for 9/11. It was that we were preparing for 9/11 all along.

Oklahoma City actually became a guide for our response. There was a fire chaplain who was extraordinarily active in this area of crisis intervention and crisis response to disaster—manmade disaster. We contacted him to see if we could assist when Oklahoma City took place. We didn't actually physically go out there, but we began a correspondence. He did come in, and he gave us a lot of points. And then when 9/11 happened, he did come in and assist us. The highlight of that was, "Make sure that you take care of yourself."

Because we were overlooking that—including myself and my peers. My peers and the mental health—we had mental health volunteers that were working with us also—and the self-care part of it was totally overlooked. And they learned in Oklahoma City that was a disaster for them. A lot of the helpers had serious problems—two, three, four, five years later—because they didn't do any self-care; they didn't pay attention to that factor. So we learned a lot of lessons from them.

The police departments have a mission to protect the citizenry. Recognizing the needs of their personnel is done in a very quasi-military approach: "Fess up and deal with it." At least, that's the message individuals get. That's not necessarily in the training, but the training does not perhaps go in-depth to the importance of self-care, particularly in the emotional, psychological areas. It wasn't even thought about.

So you're at a disadvantage, because they have no training, or very limited education and training, in these areas through the years. So that's why we focus very strongly on intensive psycho-education and outreach. We knew we had to educate them first for them to accept the help that we were going to be offering. They had to really buy into it.

SEPTEMBER 11TH

I got there rapidly because POPPA's office was located on Fulton Street, which was only about five, six blocks from the World Trade Center. I didn't have a clue of what we could or would do, but I knew I had to start moving and start planning right away. We got down to the office, and our building was incapacitated; everything was down, everything was shut. The dust was all over the place.

Our offices were within the office of the Patrolmen's Benevolent Association, and they had about 100 some-odd employees that were impacted severely. We were stressed not knowing what moves to make. What the heck do we do here?

It turns out, it was right before us: The office people had to be addressed.

They were in panic mode. Their supervisors came to us: "Can you speak to our people?" And we did. We started to group them into small groups and fill them in with whatever information we had. We comforted them that we're going to be okay.

I saw the droves of people walking up Water Street, covered in the gray dust. It wasn't so much walking as trudging. It was… it was like one of those horror movies, like these people were not real; the whole event was surreal.

So we started setting up a communication system to all our peers. I knew I was going to go to the site as soon as I could get over there and find out what's going on. We worked that day, right through the day. Obviously we got all the office people to get out of there and go home.

THEY'RE COMING IN

[Once] we did get over to the site, we saw how the officers were doing, and rather than assigned officers there were more nonassigned, meaning off-duty people—police, fire—that were coming by the throngs. Everybody's going out, and they're coming in. They're not being ordered in, they're coming in—which is not something unusual to me. Of course they would be, because that's just the makeup of an emergency responder, … to fix the break.

In some diluted form we took the blame for [the attacks]. "How did we let this happen? We gotta fix this." It was the epitome of evil. And as a sworn police officer, sworn law enforcement officer, that's our job—protect people from letting evil happen. And this evil was so huge. It was immense. How did this happen? Of course, I know intellectually what actually took place, but that's not what was felt.

Between the anger and the *What can I do?*, I do what I'm trained to do—I start helping people. I start rebuilding. I start doing whatever I can do, as fast as I can and as effective as I can. That's what a good law enforcement officer does. Let's fix this situation.

The offices that we had were: one, incapacitated at least for a week; and two, way too small to handle the numbers we were going to be dealing with. My focus was on "How are we going to do this?" and the process of getting a feel for the officers that were there—both on-or off-duty—on the scene. My wheels were pretty much going that night, so there wasn't much sleep involved. I had a couple hours' sleep. Whatever it was, it didn't matter. I was racing because there was a lot to be done.

I got up the next morning early, and I went down early. I was so grateful that I did go down early because we didn't have a home, we had no place to go, and I was walking around the site and I saw about 200 officers mustering, and I happened to know the chief that was there in charge, from my police career. I just went over, chatted with him. Whether it's a handshake or a hug or whatever it is—we're going to take care of each other. So I went over to the chief for that very reason, and we did this back and forth. And as we're talking, two gentlemen in civilian clothes come by, and they go to the chief and they told him, "We have a facility two blocks from the Trade Center, ... and we'd like to make it available to your people." I had just finished telling the chief my needs. I said, "I'm looking for a place. We have to start setting up a crisis center."

So these two guys were the director and assistant director of the Federal Reserve Bank. They were offering the space—not only a space, but a space that had hot and cold running water, electricity, and food. The chief turned around and said, "I don't have a use for something like that, but Bill does."

CRISIS CENTER

We went right into the Federal Reserve Bank, I think it was that day. We literally had orange crates and boxes as tables. I had my key people come down because we had already communicated with that many. The police officers, the volunteers, were hard to get because they were out there working as police officers, so we couldn't move them too well.

So we set up a mini–crisis center right off the second day. We were in business the second day. It was an adventure and exciting in its own way, including the boxes and orange crates that we used as tables and chairs in the lobby of the Federal Reserve—because they weren't up in the building yet; they hadn't gone up in the building.

From that pretty much for four days I worked around the clock. Foolishly, I didn't go home and didn't get rest. 'Cause there was a lot to be done.

One of our peers, he went from being a police officer to being a firefighter—because his wife thought being a police officer was too dangerous—and out of the Fire Academy was assigned to the firehouse across from the World Trade Center. And he got caught under the rubble, but he dug himself out, minimal physical injury. But he walked into our crisis center, and he had the 20-mile stare. He was damaged goods. There was no question about it. He only came to the crisis center to find out how he could help, and we immediately took him into a session with one of the mental health [professionals] and one of the other peers. And we worked very much with him, and thank God, to this day he became a poster boy for a national depression campaign, and he did very well.

But it was a clear indicator of what was to come. We also had two persons who were killed in the Trade Center that were very significant to us. One was a Sergeant John Coughlin, an emergency service sergeant, and a peer support officer also. The reason for his significance there was that he brought an individual to us as a sergeant, maybe about two years before, that had some problems. And they were addressed, and that person got his life back. We give an annual Peer of the Year award—it's called the John Coughlin Peer of the Year award. His wife insisted that she would only take part—because we wanted her to present the award to the people—if we get away from the grieving part of it. Because John was a strong believer that life was more important; [to] live life. Grieve what you have to grieve, but don't mourn and don't go on and staying in the death.

The second fellow was one of our clients who had a substance abuse problem, and he had two years out of his problem. He had gotten back with his family, with his wife. He had a full life, loved being a cop again … and the obvious significance of that, because it was conveyed to us by family members, was that he got his life back before he lost his life.

THE START OF SELF-CARE

The news stations were by this time looking for coverage, and I literally—when they put the mic in front of me and went to talk—just about had a total meltdown. I didn't realize I was having a really rough time with all that was going on. My personnel, my staff people, got me right away, forced me out. And I said, "I'll be back in the morning." And they wouldn't let me in the morning. I was forced to take at least a day. That was the beginning of us understanding—our medical advisor particularly was involved with us also—that our understanding of self-care was going to play a key role. Remember Oklahoma now, what Oklahoma told us.

As we set up the crisis center with more structure, we built in self-care. Every peer was required once a week to have a self-care session with two mental health [professionals], and the mental health [professionals] themselves would do the self-care. We kept pretty good records, because they would do everything they can to escape it. They didn't want to do it. They don't need it. They're fine, they said. There are people out there that need it more than they do, and that seemed to dominate. Once it set in, they were okay with it.

We had over 100 crisis-intervention teams coming from around the country. A team would be two peers and a mental health professional. We have them from Alaska, from Canada. Many of them would leave and return a month later. We had a constant rotation of about maybe ten teams here at a time. They did a lot of work. Every day we would send groups of teams out to the Pile, out to the site, and just walk around. We had donated immediately, overnight, POPPA T-shirts—dark blue shirts with big letters, POPPA, on it. And no one ever heard or knew what POPPA was, so it was a great attention-getter because it didn't look militaristic or institutional.

When I went over in my shirt, I had a firefighter say, "What the heck is POPPA?" Then we would explain it to them. We dealt with all personnel on site, not just police officers. We would tell them that it's really important to take care of yourself. We're not telling you that anything bad is going to happen, but we'd like you to come over and visit us at the Federal Reserve. We got something that we think will benefit you. And even better yet— because we know what helpers are about—the best way to get through to a helper is not telling them they have to help themselves, but more importantly you might be able to help your partner or your buddy. And they say, "Okay. I can do it for that." That was the segue to get them to realize that it's for them, but maybe not necessarily. So nobody has the stigma if they come over to POPPA:

"What are you doing over there? You need help?"

"No, they're helping us to learn how to take care of each other."

"Good."

We were able to generate that. So it was becoming accepted in the sense that they were coming over. They did come over to our center.

By this time we had a huge office space, plenty of phones. The Federal Reserve did an incredible job providing for us. They fed us, which was incredible. We used a little trickery, so to speak, to get people over there. "And by the way, they have a full cafeteria and it's free, and you can go there after you go to us." They would come over to get the meal, and then come to see us thinking they had to, which wasn't part of the deal—they could have gone anyway.

We had them, and it started to become a little bit of a trend that they were doing it. Not in great numbers, but in good numbers. Mainly because of our onsite outreach. One of the pins we had was, "We care." We're volunteers because we care. Remember, the energy of 9/11 is there. It was incredible how many people wanted to help from around the world. It was just there. It became okay.

The best example I had was one of my teams went to the Emergency Service Unit people. They're the elite, the SWATs. They had a trailer, and they walked in, [but the ESUs] … were trying to chase them out: "We're too busy." My people would explain, we're with POPPA. Then they would get it through, and they'd say, "Just take this flyer." We had mini-flyers that gave a brief identification of what PTSD is, and that we'd love to talk, and we're all police officers, etc. And what they observed, they'd go back each day, they were persistent because they were of that nature. They knew their people. The next day they go back, the same people who were throwing them out still had the flyers in their pockets. They weren't just tossed. And we started noticing that throughout the site. People were keeping them, because on it was our phone number too. They could get a hold of us, so it was catching. It was very much catching.

The problem came in when they returned the officers from the site—which was about two months after the attack—back to their precincts and their commands. As much as we may have been embraced by the population, they're not making trips down to come and see us. The Police Department is very supportive of POPPA's activity, and they worked out kind of a mandated kind of thing that everybody had to report down at least once. What they also gave us—and they do to this day—[was] training time. The department, especially today, the manpower resources are really stripped down. It didn't matter. They would make time for anything that they felt was going to benefit people and help their people get a little bit better, so they would allow it.

We knew we were, at the most, doing good Band-Aid work. We know we actually contributed to mitigating the PTSD in many officers. Within weeks, sometimes even months, we addressed trauma, where they were given the opportunity in a safe environment to really process through what the experience was for them. The impact we had was on the over 5,000 officers that we saw in a ten-month period. They were affected by the work we did. There was no question in my mind about it, because they would come back. Many of them later on we would speak with. There was a lot of damaged people that we continue to see till this day. We still get residue PTSD from 9/11.

WE WANT THEM IN GOOD SHAPE

Do we all have to wait for another 9/11 to understand that we have to have our people in good shape? Our primary goal today is to say, no. We don't want to wait till it happens anymore. We want them in good shape before they go in there. Because the people who had the most problems, in our estimations, were the people that had a lot of accumulated stress ... unaddressed stress.

We created an entire resiliency program around that premise, which we learned mostly from 9/11. Don't you think we want our emergency responders at their peak performance? Isn't it time that we recognize the psychological and emotional toll that their day-to-day work takes? And that we should have a regular checkup on them? We push very strongly for them. I believe we will see it one day, that at least twice a year each police officer should have a mental, emotional "oil check," I call it—a checkup. It's the process we have.

That's our resiliency program process. Just come in once every six months, get rid of that personal life trauma. Perhaps you were divorced, perhaps you lost a child, whatever it might be… so that when the 9/11 is faced again, you still aren't carrying that—that you're less vulnerable.

LIFE OVER DEATH

John Coughlin was the closest [person I lost]. I had an admiration for him, at a professional level somewhat, and on personal attributes in the individual. He was a former lawyer. He was just [a] guy, and he ran over on his own. He worked in headquarters, ran over to help, and got caught in the Towers, and lost his life as a result of it.

I'm working on letting it go. Let it go. And John Coughlin was the inspiration, because his wife says—she's adamant about it—he's a giver of life. That's where we pride ourselves. We are givers of life. We talk about life. Death is a reality we have to deal with, and we have to do what we have to do with it, but let's get life back here.

The tenth anniversary is coming up so… we're trying to get all the people that helped back from outside the city and take part in the event we have built around it. We thought it would be sort of a reunion to recognize that we've come through. However, I get a sense that we're not going to get many numbers for the very reason we're talking about. People want to move on from it. They don't want to memorialize it.

I'm hoping we can turn it into [a renewal]. Come out of the closet, and let's make it a life-giving thing. I was actually told directly by someone, "You're going to offend the people that lost someone." I don't think so. Some people you would perhaps, but I think if done with love and understanding, it's not something that's done to offend; I honor somebody's death by living better.

GOOD AND EVIL

I had a lot of anger that I thought people just shut it out, [who say] oh, it never happened, and move on. I don't want to get political, but that's how we got in trouble in the first place: [Assuming] this would never happen in New York, and it happened. It impacted me in the sense, though, that, as an American, I'm as vulnerable as anybody else, anyplace else in the world.

I show my vulnerabilities without hesitation, my imperfections. I believe that we are all equal, in the sense of our imperfections. None of us got it right, but jointly, the core thing of being a decent human being to another human being isn't really that hard. And I think police officers in particular are extraordinarily, understandably, highly sensitive. And they project the image of just the opposite for professional reasons—because if you saw me shaking and baking and scared, you would not think I was doing my job in protecting you. I could act out and choose to do things on that anger, but I thank God I haven't. I choose to do the opposite.

To this day, my wife also, we kind of shy away from going over there. I am like many 9/11 responders—we have many of our officers that can't even come near this area. They can't. Outside of that, they're fine. They function quite well. Come down here? No, not going to happen. When I discuss it, the memories come back. It's those wounded emotional cords. I thought I dealt with that and I did, but it's still there. It's not necessarily a bad thing. It's there.

CHAPTER 30

LEARNING LESSONS
THE HARD WAY

Micki is the Health and Safety Director for the Communications Workers of America (CWA), a union that represents workers in a variety of industries. Micki was on a bus in Queens when the Towers were hit. It was her job to keep people protected from hazards, and, if possible, to eliminate those hazards. Now, ten years later, Micki is still fighting for her workers. In conjunction with local unions and various agencies, she has been trying to ensure proper health care for those affected by the disaster. She continues to fight with government agencies about the extent of contamination and the lack of testing that took place.

MY JOB IS TO WORK WITH OUR LOCAL UNIONS to make sure people's rights are protected at work. So when they're faced with various hazards of all types, I work with the local union, and often with the company or agencies, to help keep people protected and eliminate hazards.

I returned to Lower Manhattan less than a week [after 9/11]. When I got out of the subway, the streets were white and there was hardly anybody walking around. When I got into my office, the windows face Ground Zero, so I always looked particularly at the South Tower. It was directly in my view. When I walked in on that day, that's when I first just broke down…because there was no Tower.

We had members who were working on site at Ground Zero. As a matter of fact, our Verizon workers were responsible for getting the Stock Exchange up and running. The reason that went down was because of the loss of the communication network, and it was because those workers immediately rushed in that they were there on that first day. And that's why the Stock Exchange was open. Within the unions, you first figured out where different people were, what was going on with companies where we represent members, and what was happening with folks on site.

There were endless conference calls to make sure people had protections they needed, but as you can imagine within the first couple of weeks, it was just a lot of chaos. The communication wasn't great. There were people who were sent down there at the beginning and, to a certain extent, afterwards, and they had no protection. They went down there not just because they were being told or asked to go down there, but I believe it was voluntary at the beginning because everybody really wanted to help. There was a real pulling together at that time, and part of that cost people their health in the time that followed.

QUESTIONS RAISED

There were certainly questions raised immediately. A lot was known at the beginning about what was potentially in the dust and in the combustion, the materials that were released in Ground Zero. That body of knowledge wasn't secret, about what was potentially there, things like asbestos. I think there were less health concerns in the area at the beginning because it was a horrible tragedy. The beginning was just focused on finding people or searching for people.

It started to change very rapidly with regards to concerns about health. It was also very early on, within a couple of days, that government agencies started saying that everything was okay, that the air was safe: New York City, the EPA, OSHA. It was safe for everybody to return. My role, because of the different groups of members we had that were affected, was really to try and keep track of the monitoring data that was coming out and figuring out what it actually meant: Was it really safe? What wasn't being done? It was hard to know from what was being released if it was safe or it wasn't safe. As time went on, and as we learned, there was data that was polled that was hidden. I don't even think we use the right monitors in terms of how we monitor and make decisions about people's safety.

Because of how the response was handled by the government agencies, one of the problems was that it also allowed companies to not be as protected as they should have been. For example, since there were no occupational health standards supposedly being violated, because the EPA supposedly said okay and gave the all clear, our telecommunications workers were given the opportunity to wear a type of respirator, but it was voluntary, and when you have a voluntary respiratory program, it means that you don't have to give all the training that is needed. You don't have to do fit testing, which is a test to make sure it is actually sealing properly on the face, so that contaminants don't get in. They don't have to be cleaned. There are all sorts of standards that don't have to be followed, and that's what happened. So some people used respirators sometimes, some never used respirators. We're seeing the results of that, unfortunately.

NO WAY TO PREPARE

There was no way to prepare for what was there. I ended up not going to the site of Ground Zero until the very beginning of October. So that was a couple of weeks after the event, mostly because there was miscommunication about what credentials you needed to get onto the site. I remember the first time I was meeting with the Verizon Health and Safety Director to talk about what was going on for the Verizon workers and within the Verizon building, which was the building on the north end of Ground Zero, the Pit. Heavily damaged, it was the building that 7 World Trade Center fell against.

Our CWA members who were at Ground Zero and who were affected by those events were not only Verizon, but other telecommunication companies, Lucent, AT&T. We also represent traffic enforcement agents and supervisors and various sanitation titles for the City of New York. So they were all part of the response. We represent nurses at New York Downtown Hospital, which was Beekman at the time, so that was the closest hospital, just a few blocks from Ground Zero. Our members who were working that day were the first to actually treat victims of the collapse before people started to be sent to St. Vincent's and other hospitals.

There were a lot of different groups that were there, as well as volunteers, by the way. We had some CWA members who were volunteer firefighters, or those who just came down to help. So several thousand at Ground Zero doing work. We also represent workers in the area, which would include city workers for all agencies in New York City. We represent our guild workers, reporters for the *Wall Street Journal* and other publications. The *Wall Street Journal* reporters were at One World Financial; that building was not destroyed but it was greatly affected, and they needed to evacuate that area.

We also had workers who had to evacuate the Towers. We represented Port Authority workers, who worked in the Towers, and other Verizon workers, who were in the Towers and buildings close by. And one other group: our broadcast and engineer technicians, who were the news cameras and camera people who were down there.

HEAVILY CONTAMINATED

Questions would come up. I was mostly in touch with the local union leadership, and they were, to varying degrees, on site as well. So much of the communication happened with the local unions. There were constant questions, actually, about safety issues, both on the outside, because we had workers who also worked at Ground Zero in the neighborhood, as well as the Verizon building itself.

Initially, with the Verizon building, it was breached, so there were many windows that were blown out, and a piece of the fuselage from one of the planes went into the building and sort of blew a big hole into it. And 7 World Trade Center collapsed on it at the end of the day on 9/11.

The Fire Department was stationed in that building several floors above to pour water down below. There was diesel fuel within the building in the subbasement levels. The cable vault, which is also below ground level, had a giant hole torn into the sidewalk. So it was heavily contaminated, and very dangerous, so for the first few weeks, particularly with the work that was going on in the cable vault, there were questions about the integrity of the building and whether or not it was safe to go in there. It was a really large area with racks and racks of cables coming in and serving the telephone system in Lower Manhattan.

There may be nobody working in the cable vault on a normal workday, or very few people working in there, but we had upwards of ninety people from all different locals trying to make repairs that needed to be made. The whole back, the east side, was the area of concern: whether or not it was stable enough, whether or not there would be a collapse of the Verizon building because of the collapse [of 7 World Trade Center] and the fires that were in there. There were a lot of safety concerns that we had at the beginning, and those concerns changed to those about health and contamination, and what should be done about contamination.

Those answers were not always clear, and certainly there was a lot of conflicting information. With that company in particular, it's not something that they really were prepared to respond to. Their whole safety organization was actually away at a conference on 9/11. It took two weeks before that group came back. So you have the operational managers making decisions about things, just to get the work done, but without any safety guidance from the company.

PARTING WAYS

The growing concerns about health effects really started in October, with the World Trade Center Cough reports, even from our members, and I think at that point when we started to press for additional protections, precautions, we started to really part ways in terms of what we thought needed to be done at the site.

We certainly didn't know the extent of the health effects that we do now, but there were definite concerns. I know they were having arguments with local managers, who just wanted the work done, and [were] not providing respiratory protection. They were told, "Go get it from the Red Cross." It took a while, even for what was provided in some systematic way. I think people had concerns early on, and I think those concerns grew.

At that time, there were other 9/11-related issues going on as well, besides the work at Ground Zero, besides people returning to their offices with literally no guidance or clearance from any agency whatsoever. By the way, that's why I was also getting calls from locals who were returning to the buildings: "Was it safe?" And there was no answer, because nobody was saying that there had to be certain testing to figure out what kind of indoor contamination existed. It did in most places. Besides that, very soon afterwards, there were anthrax scares, if you remember that.

So that also affected our locations where we had members in office buildings that were targets, or where there were scares. Remember, this is the Bush administration era. Very soon afterwards, the administration decided that smallpox vaccinations were going to be required for health care providers and emergency response personnel, ... even without the facts, without a threat of smallpox, even though it is a vaccination that can have serious effects, life-threatening side effects. So with other unions, we had to launch a whole campaign to fight that from actually happening, because it was without purpose and provided no protection to the people who were getting vaccinations. It was a constant barrage of health- and safety-related issues that were all about fighting terrorism. So it was constant, and it's remained that way to the present time.

MEDICAL MONITORING PROGRAMS

I never imagined that there would be one safety issue that would take over, and certainly the World Trade Center work has been, and will continue to be, a defining issue for me in my life. It's been something I've been involved with continuously, with very few exceptions, on a daily basis. Issues having to do with contamination and issues around health ... and also trying to get health care provided. None of the medical monitoring programs existed. We had to fight for that. We were involved early on, trying to figure out how we get our members screened somehow.

Nothing was available. For a short time we were working with the New York State Department of Health and that fell through, and we began working with Mt. Sinai and others on the proposal for the first screening program. I have been involved in that as a committee member ever since. In July 2002 was the first screening. As a matter of fact, our local unions gave out to as many members as they could what we call an Exposure Assessment Questionnaire. Because of concerns about health, we wanted to collect information. We wanted to know who was there and have some information—contact information, and also information about what people were doing down there—even though at the time we weren't really sure how it was going to be used. Maybe for Workers' Compensation. So we had collected these forms, just these one-page forms from our memberships, and the locals would send them to me.

It was because we had this pile of information for our members who were working at Ground Zero that when screening programs first started, we were able to take that—essentially it was a list—and work with Sinai and the other medical centers, so that they could start making phone calls. One of the largest groups for the initial screenings were CWA members. Because there was no registry of people who were down there. There was no list, no official sign-up anywhere. Even the companies and the agencies did not have the best records. To this day we've had trouble getting information. It's not complete what we have, but it's actually helped us in many ways as another record of what people did and what happened to them, at least for the Verizon group if not for all of the groups. Looking back, we would certainly do that in the future.

ONGOING CONTAMINATION

There were things I wish we could have done. I wish we could have done our own monitoring and sampling, for example, at Ground Zero. I wish we could have provided other kinds of things to our members, but we just don't have those resources. I also spent a great deal of time fighting around issues of contamination. I don't know if most people realize that to this day there has never been an assessment of contamination in Lower Manhattan—never of workplaces, and very little of residences—and yet those same agencies feel perfectly at ease saying everything is fine.

My personal feelings about the contamination issues and the health effects—it was never addressed. I believe there are places that still have ongoing issues of contamination. Obviously not like it was on 9/11, and not in most office spaces, but there are buildings we know weren't cleaned, and a lot of these contaminants don't go away unless there are sufficient kinds of remediation. That was never done, and there was a refusal to do that, particularly of workplaces.

Not all of it was a surprise, but I think the extent to which it was blatantly ignored, and the way in which the science was twisted to validate the viewpoint that everything was fine, and the ways in which it has come back to haunt us over and over again to the present day, have been quite amazing to me. In 2002, the residential community was obviously very concerned about health and contamination, and they had pushed the EPA to do something. So the EPA was starting this residential test and clean program. At that time, the New York Committee for Occupational Safety and Health organized labor unions to meet with the EPA, and one of the questions we asked was, "What is the scientific rationale for not including workplaces in any kind of assessment or cleanup?" I'll never forget that meeting. We met with Kathy Callahan; she just looked at us. There was silence, absolute silence. It was probably no more than a couple of seconds, but it was astounding. She said, "I'll get back to you."

CALL OSHA IF YOU NEED TO

We had to push... and after a few months we were finally able to get another meeting, and at that point she [Kathy Callahan] brought in OSHA and basically said they didn't have the resources. That began a very proactive battle with the EPA. Senator Clinton was able to come to an agreement with the White House Council on Environmental Quality to get the EPA to set up the World Trade Center Expert Technical Review panel. It was a panel that was going to be made up of representative government officials and experts to discuss health needs in the affected areas. This was public. These were going to be public meetings. They were supposed to happen every single month for approximately a two-year period. There was a community liaison representative on the initial panel; there were no worker representatives.

I eventually became the labor liaison on that EPA panel. They really did nothing. It was a year and a half. They shut it down prematurely, announced at the end of 2006 that it was going to be the last panel meeting. They came up with a scam of a test and clean program and said thank you very much and that was the end of that. Even agreements that had been reached along that process, the very difficult process to include workplaces, to extend the geographic boundaries of what was going to be part of that program, they rescinded on all of it. Workplaces were out. Basically they said, "Call OSHA if you need to," and they were done.

I think that's part of what has been not just so frustrating, but keeps me angry all the time. At a certain point, there was overwhelming evidence of ill health. People are getting sicker; there are more diseases. But even faced with that overwhelming evidence—that the initial proclamations that were directed by the Bush administration to Christie Whitman and the EPA that the air was safe, and by the Giuliani administration that it's okay to return to work and go shopping, which he actually said—that they stuck with that.

And because of issues of liability and really financial decisions, they have stuck with that line and that approach, despite proof to the contrary in terms of health. We'll never know the full extent of exposures. There was a lot of information that was purposely not collected, or that was not coordinated. Obviously, we know that people were exposed, but to what extent, particularly in indoor spaces… nothing. We know there was heavy contamination. The reason we know that… in particular [was] there were several buildings around Ground Zero [that] were publicly owned—the Deutsche Bank Building is a good example, and Fiterman Hall of the Borough of Manhattan Community College—those results, the results of sampling, were publicly available. So all those documents were available and you can see the extent of what was there. Those weren't unique. So any of the buildings that were breached—again, even other buildings brought it in through air conditioning, and so on—the potential for contamination existed and, again, unless a private company was hired, there's no public knowledge of what happened in those locations. There are a lot of reasons why that will never happen. Property values, again, financial interests.

WE DON'T TAKE A PROACTIVE APPROACH

The events are in the past, but the impact is still not understood, and it's still not addressed in the way that it should be. Certainly not in terms of health. We have continuing and growing concerns about people's health. The medical and monitoring treatment programs, even though it was a great victory after so many years, that was another part of what's gone on over the past ten years, constant battling to get funding. It's a five-year funding. That's not a long-term program.

We don't take a proactive approach. When I say we, I mean society or the government is not proactive, in the sense that we want to protect people as much as possible, and then let's figure out how bad the health effects are. I think that the extent to which the labor community, the residential community, other advocates, the occupational health community, came together to fight around these issues has been very positive. Whether or not the government has learned any lessons, I can't speak to that, but I think that we learned a lot. I think that we would do things very differently in the future.

I think it changed me in a lot of ways, certainly in how I view information from the government, and the politics that were involved. I'm much more cynical. If you're not directly involved and affected by this, I think there's a view out there that it's done. It was done nine years ago. Other than seeing occasional news stories about health, or occasional news stories about the Zadroga bill and possibly activities going on around that, I think that many people have moved on and assume that the community that has been affected has also moved on, or should move on. There is definitely not a sense out there about all the work that has gone into trying to do right, trying to address health issues to this point.

As a society, we think of emergencies as short-term events: The emergency happens, you have all kinds of relief organizations pouring in— just like the horrible events that are going on in Japan—and after a short period of time, because the news stops reporting on it, it should be done. But the people that were affected continue to be affected. I think that's another thing we need to change in terms of responding to emergencies.

Look at them as having the acute immediate phase and what's needed [for that], but also what's needed in the long term, because there are always long-term needs. People will continue to need social services and mental health support. Any person who's been affected by the events of 9/11, that hasn't ended ever, or will ever end. So that kind of continuing support is also needed.

CHAPTER 31

A BEACON OF GOODNESS

Father Mike has been a priest for thirty-two years, more than ten of which have been spent at Our Lady of Lourdes Church in West Islip, Long Island. On 9/11, he didn't hear the news from his parishioners, the fire department, or the police; he found out while walking on a treadmill and watching television at the local gym. He quickly headed back to the rectory, but as he pulled in, his phone rang. Some old friends from his previous church were worried about their son, a volunteer firefighter who was near the Towers when the planes hit. They needed comfort, and Father Mike drove straight to their house to provide it. This was just the first of many similar calls and many similar visits. Father Mike chose not to go to Ground Zero, deciding that his place was with his community; it was there that he felt he could do the most good. That night, he held an impromptu Mass at Our Lady of Lourdes, lighting candles in hope and in prayer. The church was overflowing.

AS I WAS GETTING BACK TO THE RECTORY, I got the first phone call of many. It was from friends of mine from my old parish in Melville. They were home watching TV, as well, and their son worked in the Tower. They just presumed that he was gone. They were hysterical, saying that he was a volunteer fireman and that he was that kind of person. They said if anybody had run to the center of it, he would have done that. I just talked to them for a couple of minutes on the phone, then I got in the car and drove to their house.

It took maybe about twenty minutes to get there and, of course, along the way, I'm not watching TV, but I'm listening to the radio, and they're talking about how the Towers are collapsing, that the first Tower collapsed, I guess, at the time I was listening. I was in complete disbelief. I was thinking, "Maybe something fell off it or something." I couldn't get my head around the idea that the whole building could have collapsed, and what that would have meant.

When I got to my friends' home, they filled me in. Their son had actually escaped. He had called and he was outside on the street when all this started to happen, and took a look because he was a volunteer fireman, because he knew something about it. He realized, though, that it was just an enormously dangerous place to be, so instead of running back into the building, what he started to do was to help the people on the street understand that they should start to move out of the area, that they should try to find a way to escape. He ended up helping them in that way, and that was obviously key to his survival.

A VERY CONFUSING DAY

The next thing I remember happening was a phone call from our school. We were in session that day, so we had three hundred kids in our Catholic school, and families of firefighters who were there, families who were just beginning to hear what might have happened. There were people coming down to take children home, to come get them. I ended up wanting to go right back there to see what was happening.

People suddenly felt very vulnerable. Everybody had the sense that if this had happened in the city, maybe it could happen in our community, maybe it could happen to our school. So parents were coming to get their children just completely afraid that something very out of control was going on.

WE BROUGHT PEOPLE TOGETHER

People started to call the church asking what we were going to do to respond to this. We told everyone was that we were going to have Mass that night. Anybody who wanted to pray for people, for what was going on, for people that had lost their lives, for people who just didn't hear or just didn't know what was happening, we would get together in church.

That night there were more people there than probably on a Sunday morning, and that was just from word of mouth. It was absolutely jammed to the doors, and people had just told each other about it, just reached out to each other and got together. We ran out of candles in about ten minutes. We had this big entrance way to the church, and there were probably two to three hundred candles in there, all lit. We were just putting out boxes of candles and people were lighting them. It was just, I think, everybody was looking for some sense of being able to pray, of being able to reach out to God in order to relate to this in some way.

There was a whole gamut of emotions. I'd say by late afternoon, early evening, we knew that there were several firemen and police officers from the parish that were among the missing. We knew some of those people that were there that day and nobody knew where they were. There were some business people, workers in the Towers, and families that had also not heard from loved ones. Then there were people who had friends and family who escaped and had the harrowing tale of what they had seen and what had happened that day, and how some were still in various different places trying to make their way back to Long Island.

People were anxious about what was happening; they felt out of control. Was this going to keep happening? Had it happened and was over? Was it just the beginning of something? They didn't know. They really didn't know what to expect and I think they just, in that insecurity, wanted to turn to something that was very centered and grounded and familiar. And so we brought people together.

A STACK OF ADDRESSES

The very next day people began to call in directly for help. The calls came from friends and family, who told us names of different people. Everybody at that point was among the missing. We really didn't know who had died and who had escaped and who had been injured. We just knew that a lot of people didn't come home the night before.

I just had a stack of addresses, a lot of people I never met before. Some names I knew, some people I knew casually, some people I had never met before. I had a map where all these homes were and went from place to place, spending a little time with everyone. It was a tremendous sense of anxiety. People were missing. People didn't really want to talk much because they were waiting. That was actually one of the reasons why there was so much of actually going to people's homes, besides the fact that we would want to do that anyway, want to go there, but people would call and say, "I'm getting off the phone right away because I'm tying the line up. What if that call comes in while I'm on the phone?" So there was a lot of silence on the phones that day because people just wanted to be available.

There was one family where they actually found someone. He was a man who worked in the Towers. They found him, his body, pretty quickly—I think within three or four days. They had a funeral Mass after that. It was a very concrete, familiar type of experience to find that he had died; they had his body and they had the rites of burial. But there were other situations where the question began to be: When do you have a funeral? If you think the person has died and you don't know when or if they'll find his or her body, when do you actually start to move ahead with that?

Many people thought that perhaps the person is injured and somewhere, but that they can't identify themselves. Maybe they have a head injury, maybe they were knocked out, maybe they have amnesia, maybe they're just unconscious and they're somewhere in Manhattan, in a hospital, a nameless person. We were beginning to understand that that really wasn't true, but nevertheless, there was also the feeling that well, maybe any minute, or maybe there are people trapped. There were rumors about how there may be hundreds of people underground. It was a roller coaster for people's hopes. They just went up and down.

THE HUMAN JOURNEY

This is one of the things that is part of the human journey, of how people approach things. Some people that just needed to hold out their hope. Some of the rescue workers were telling me, after probably not too many days, that they're not going to be finding people alive. That wasn't the message to go back to those families with. They needed to hope and they wanted to hope. I think that what I know about people, spiritually, is that they deal with that in their own way, that it's part of the journey. They hold out that hope until they come to some place in themselves where they can say, "Well, that's not going to happen, so now I have to deal with this a different way."

Some folks had services pretty quickly. Others, it was as much as a year later that they finally decided to do that. The services themselves, the funerals, were sort of unprecedented, because they were without the bodies of the people who died.

That was a very difficult thing. When someone has died, I think people really need to see that, to know it and let it sink in, to let the reality of it be there. Thinking that someone has died, but you just can't see their body, is a real deprivation. Without seeing, there is always an unreality about it. Like, I believe they're gone, I believe they died, but I just wish that I could be sure.

So even in the funerals within the Catholic faith, we turn to things, to the actual body of the person or sometimes, with cremated remains, their ashes. And these become central to the rites themselves. We bless them, we care for them, we bring them into church, we bring them for burial. It provides closure. It provides a way for people to heal in their grief, so we began to think about what to do when we couldn't do those things. It was the first time in my experience that I ever confronted, certainly to that scale, having these rituals, having these funerals, without the bodies of the people.

In the Catholic faith, there was an interesting connection because we believe in the resurrection of Jesus. The experience on the day of Jesus's resurrection was that his body was gone and the disciples went to the tomb and they failed to find his body. They began to conclude over time that the reason was because the resurrection was true, that he had actually been raised from death. Things like that became helpful to people, too. That's something that priests and ministers do; they try to make the connection between things in our faith and the experience that people are going through to try to help them with that.

EMBODY THEIR LIVES

Then there were things that people brought to it. I always thought that in the absence of people's bodies, we should try to embody their lives, so something that became very important was the possession of symbols. I remember one family where they never found the man's body, but what they put in the casket were all of the things that belonged to him. They put in his uniform, his tools, and some of his personal things, and in that way, formed a remembrance that they could hold on to and treat in that same way that we ordinarily would have treated the body: we let go of it, we put it in the earth, or in its own grave, and are able to say that's where we resolve things. Stories became immensely important, too. At our funerals, we had many people who would come up and talk about the person's life. I think in its own way, it really filled in for the absence, giving people something else to focus on.

The funerals themselves were enormous; they were public. Once in a while in the life of a parish, there will be a person who passes away who was a very public figure and their life has touched more than just the people they were intimate with, but those are usually people who lived their whole lives. To have ordinary folks, day-to-day people, suddenly become the center of so much publicity was both consoling and difficult for the families. To have the mayor of New York in your parish church—or the representative of the mayor or the fire chief, or any of the other public figures that would come to these funerals—was, on one hand, a really great gift to the families, that their loved ones' lives meant so much that these people of importance and stature in the community would come to their ceremony of burial, their remembrance. On the other hand, it made it difficult because it made it a big, public event. Ordinarily, people would plan a funeral around a table talking to their priest, their pastor, one of our deacons, one of our ministers, and just plan things out. Now we were involved with police departments and fire departments and public relations and the press and schedules…It became a much bigger thing.

TRANSFORMING HOPE

It brought people together. That was one of the things that was amazing about this time. It just seemed to thrust everybody out of their ordinary preoccupations. All of the little things that we worry about every day seemed completely out the window. There were big things to think about. There were important things to pay attention to.

There were some families that held out for a year. First it's the hope that the phone's going to ring and the person's going to be alive, then that's not going to happen. Then the phone's going to ring and somebody's going to say, at least we found his or her body. Then it was, at least we found part of their body. It just gets to the point where people just wish they'd find something. Even a boot, a shirt, clothing, or a tool. Just something to say with some assurance, "he was there," or "she was there."

I spent most of the time at that point with the families. They really appreciated what was being done. In my own parish, people got together and they brought food down for the rescuers, they brought clothes down, they brought socks, they brought shoes, they brought whatever they could, even bags of dog food for the animals down there that were doing the search and rescue. Anything to try to connect with what people were doing. To feel a part of it, to feel they were contributing to it.

The children did some of those things, gathering clothing and food and supplies and things, bottles of water. They took part in that. We had some grieving children in the school, and whenever that happens we just really pay a lot of extra attention to them, and realize that sometimes the school day has to stop to take care of somebody. The teachers, people who work there, were great with that, but it was something that went on for a long time. Life has to stop for a minute, so people can feel deep things.

There was also an interesting sense of wanting to return to something that was familiar. There was one family in the parish that lost a fireman working at the site. They had several children, one of which was a kind, nicely outspoken young man who got the attention of the mayor, Mayor Giuliani. At one of the meetings, the mayor went up to him and asked him what he wanted to be when he grew up, and he said, "the Pope." At that time, that September, the Yankees were playing the Arizona Diamondbacks, and the mayor called him up and said, "Since you want to be the Pope, why don't we fly you out to Arizona and see the last day of the World Series?"

And his mom said, "No, he has school the next day." So he didn't get to go, but I tell that because there was that sense that we have to get back to normal. It was almost like, "Too much already."

OF TWO MINDS

We can be of two minds at the same time. We can put closure on something and move on, and at the same time there's a little part of you that thinks, "Maybe, just maybe, a miracle will happen." You see that sometimes with people who have a family member with a very serious illness. There's a part of them that knows that their loved one is dying. Then there's another part of them somewhere that's saying, "But there might be a miracle. You never know." I think it's interesting that just that little window of hope there gives people so much ability to cope and deal with things. It's just amazing how that works.

I was talking a good bit with another priest that was spending a lot of time there, and he extended the invitation, asking, "Why don't you come in?" I said, "No. I got a lot of things to do here and I think I'll stay on this side of it. I can talk to you, though." So there was this sense of supporting each other and also, too, I think there was an enormous cost for those people. I was very aware of that. One of the things you know when you work with people for a long time is that this is really going to be a big wound for a long time. People are really going to be hurting about this. The responders, the rescuers, the families, the ministers. This was going to be with us for quite a while. I found myself doing, working with families that have these losses, and being with them, sharing that pain, and not saying anything at all about it, but just sitting there and being miserable with people.

I think that these events are very dangerous. I would say that if I look at individuals and I look at my community and I look at the way people responded to each other and helped each other, it unquestionably brings the best out of us. At the same time, though, it can bring the worst out of us. You can see people who really are irreparably damaged by it. I know there are people who have been changed by this forever, and not in a good way; their own resources to deal with it and their own ability to put things in perspective is just not there. I would never talk about that in a way of judging people like that. I've learned that it could happen to any one of us—we could experience something so terrible that it would really harm us that deeply.

I look at the workers who went down there and worked on that Pile day after day, and I understand what they were doing. They had to. The only way to make sense out of that was to pour every ounce of effort into being there and just doing whatever they could do, whether it was searching for people or picking up buckets of stuff. It didn't matter what it was. It mattered that they were there, it mattered that they were caring about it, it mattered that they wouldn't let go of it, it mattered that they would keep being faithful to it.

Those are the kinds of things that we are talking about when we discuss spirituality. Spirituality is about people's inner lives. Spirituality is about who you are and what makes you the person that you are. It's really about what makes you a human being. I guess most days we can get away without bringing that into clear focus because we can sort of live our lives on autopilot and sort of just do things, but then something happens to us and all of sudden it brings everything into focus. People go through life and it's hard to think about what's really important and then a loved one becomes sick and they just want to be there. We did that as a society, with the sudden outrush of patriotism, which was so important: to feel proud of who we are, to feel proud of what we had, to feel a sense of connection. We turn to religion and the things that comfort us and are there for us, and it is so important for people to turn to each other, to turn to God. That's what comes out when you're searching that way for spirituality.

I believe all those things. I think that people found a tremendous amount of religious connection. There were many Christian people who saw crosses down there in those broken beams and made a connection. It's a way of saying that we really believe God is with us in this moment. We really believe God is here. It's a tough act of faith, because the first thing people feel when something bad happens is that we've been abandoned by God. How could God let this happen? How could God allow this? How could God permit it in any way?

So there are also people whose spirituality is actually more shown in their anger. It's the same, just two different sides of it: One person would express that the rising smoke is the souls of good people going to God, and another person would find that the whole thing is just so enraging that how could there even be a God? And so we're grappling with the big issues at the center of it all. We're never that far from it.

MAKING CONNECTIONS

I think that people preached about and talked about what it meant for a long time in churches. We kept making those connections, the bigger connections. Like how do we think about the world that we live in? How do we think about the people that might have been responsible for this? How do we think about the other cultures, the other places? What anger might have motivated this? Can we be peacemakers? Can we do something other than retaliate? Is that the only thing we can do? Is there really a way that this can teach us something that we can use in a different way in the future to be better, to make these sorts of things not a part of the world? These are the things religious people think about, big-picture things about God's world.

For a long time, the pain was very acute, very raw. I think that what has happened over time is what happens very frequently over time: It's not that it becomes not painful, it's not that it doesn't bother anybody, but it becomes a tender memory, a memory with a lot of love in it. Some people are in a whole different place in their lives. There are people who have lost loved ones and remarried, as people do, and found some hope in another path and are moving to a new place. But they still look back with a lot of warmth and affection and care for what happened that day.

It seems to be like a singular beacon of care for each other. I think of this one town that I drive through, where they have a whole bunch of candles in the center of the town all the time. It's the thing that you drive by and you look at that, and you think about it all for a minute. It's just really part of us now, which is an interesting thing, because in the world these days there are so few things that people share together, so few things that we can all relate to. But the memory of September 11th is one of those few. It's part of everyone; everyone was touched by it.

CHAPTER 32

A COMMUNITY OF FAITH

*The Reverend Harris was working as a priest at Saint Paul's Chapel when
the Towers were struck. After leading a group of seventy preschoolers to
safety, Harris returned to the site, hoping to help, but expecting to find
the Chapel in ruins. Finding it miraculously spared, he opened its doors
to the rescue workers, providing food, counseling, and general support.
He not only offered a refuge for the responders, but also gave volunteers
a place to work in the Chapel.*

I STARTED MY JOB AS PRIEST IN CHARGE of Saint Paul's
Chapel in April of 2001. I was brought in to create a new congregation
there. It's the oldest church in the city, dating back to 1766. George
Washington frequented Saint Paul's Chapel often. My job at the time
of 9/11 was to develop a jazz Mass for Saint Paul's Chapel, as a way
to renew worship in the congregation and reach out to the community.
Whenever anybody asked me how many people I had in my congregation,
I would say sixty thousand, because that's how many people worked in the
World Trade Center site.

CHILLING CLARITY

Thinking this happened with the Trade Center, this is my parish. I made my
way in that direction with John Allen, our Director of Communications.
He and I went together, and we thought we were going to help in some
form with some triage, possibly as humanitarian first responders. We got
to the corner of Liberty and Church, right there where the Burger King is,
when the second plane hit the South Tower.

I was not looking up, was not expecting anything else to happen, but
the terrible sound and the smell and the impact of the second plane on the
South Tower directly across the street...The fireball that we could see in
our peripheral vision was overwhelming, and debris began falling. So we
literally had to run for our lives, and we ran into the first building whose

door was open, which was the American Stock Exchange. We went into there and had a moment of, I guess, chilling clarity—it was pretty obvious that it was more than an accident.

We eventually made our way back to our office building, which was another two blocks south, and we were all standing there together, not having any idea about what was going on, but just an ominous feeling about what was unfolding. I was frightened, petrified, and scared.

EVACUATE THE CHILDREN

I got back to the Trinity Building. We had a preschool at Trinity. It was decided we should evacuate the children from the 3rd floor preschool to the basement, standard safety procedure, thinking that would be best. So we brought all the children downstairs, between sixty and seventy children, I guess, and we were all corralled in the basement, trying to get any word on whatever news there might be about what was going on.

They [the children] of course didn't have any idea what was going on. So they were just being children, but they could sense an air of urgency and worry. We were in the basement, just waiting, wondering what was going on. I would go upstairs frequently and look out to see if I could see something, anything. I remember, specifically, the windows in the building next to us shattered at one point while I was standing there, which was really scary. The teachers were very courageous. They were following their safety procedures, of course afraid, but nevertheless doing their job. No one was losing control or freaking out. We were all very subdued, but wondering, "What's next?"

So we were corralled in the basement for a few minutes, and then the first Tower came down. The ground literally shook as the floors pancaked, one on top of the other. The sound was horrible. It was like a sonic boom. As the ground rumbled and the noise frightened us, the smoke began coming into our basement through the air conditioning system, just pulling it right in. We were filled with this dark, thick cloud of smoke. We couldn't see, we certainly couldn't breathe. It was burning our eyes. We inhaled all that stuff. So what happened at that point, we started wetting paper towels to place over the mouths of the children.

I remember going into the bathroom and there's this paper towel dispenser and I couldn't get the thing to function and the adrenaline rushed and I just punched it, knocked it off the wall. That's not my usual behavior, but that was a crisis. Then we got the big roll of paper towels and tore them off, wetting them down, handing them out to each of the children and the adults, and then we each grabbed a child and went out the back of our building and made a run for it. We ran south, away from the Towers, thinking we would go towards the Staten Island Ferry terminal, which would be, maybe, the safest place.

The children were still very subdued. They knew something was going on, but they were quiet. They felt safe. I remember running away from the office building towards the Staten Island Ferry terminal, when the second Tower collapsed and this massive wave of dust just descended upon us. You could see it coming upon you. I was carrying a little girl named Jasmine and didn't quite know what to do when I saw that cloud of dust coming, so I just kept running and ducked around the side of a building, hoping that whatever was in it would not hit us.

Of course, it was just dust and there was no real hard debris in it reaching that far south. We were covered head to toe like zombies, but eventually we made our way to the Staten Island Ferry terminal. Everyone had split and spread. Some of our guys were brought into a construction camper trailer, and that's one of the delicious ironies: One of the construction workers brought in a bunch of the spiritual leaders that we convened for that day, including the future Archbishop of Canterbury, and said, "I'd like to say a prayer for us," not knowing the people who were with him, which is really wonderful in a way.

I was not a part of that group. I ducked around the side of a building, but I remember running and women were losing their shoes, especially if they had heels on, and I'm thinking, "They're going to get their feet cut or damaged." Then this cloud of ashes descended upon us, and of course I wear a lot of black, and my black suit that day was charcoal.

I thought I had a mission. I think Jasmine probably was a real blessing to me at that time because my focus was not on panicking, but on making sure she was safe. It was looking beyond myself. I never saw her again after that day, but that was a bonding moment that we had. So we got to the Staten Island Ferry terminal and the teachers were all there, corralled together, and they had all the children together. It was decided that many of them would go on a train to Brooklyn, I think it was. Fortunately, the head of the school had enough of her wits about her to call in and change the message on the machine of the school, so it was able to tell parents where our rendezvous point in Brooklyn would be. Every child was reunited with their parents that night, which itself is astounding. While we were caring for these children, I was thinking, "How many of these children won't have parents at the end of the day?" Most parents worked in the Trade Center, and it was a drop-off point for their children. One of the attractions is it's a really good school, and close.

The teachers said they would be fine, and took the children to Brooklyn. I got on a bus that took me up to 34th on the East Side and got out there and just started walking home from 34th Street. I lived on 8th and Broadway, so I'm walking along and people are looking at me and others with me as if we were some alien intruders, we looked so horrible. They embraced us, I think, of course, but we were all so shocked. We didn't know what to say or do.

THE SPIRE OF SAINT PAUL'S

I think the primary motivation for me at that point was to see what I could do to help. I grew up in the Boy Scouts and all of that, so I was formed with that idea of helping others. I knew there was a crisis; I just didn't know how to help. I was reunited with my wife and daughter. Knowing that I would have been right there and she didn't hear from me for hours, it was pretty traumatic; traumatic for my daughter as well. When we reunited, we just wept and held each other. Even though the phones didn't work, email still worked. I was zipping off emails right and left, wondering how some of my friends, some of my congregation members, were doing. I was obsessed to find out if they were okay, and I was also obsessed to see what shape Saint Paul's was in. I assumed it had been demolished. How could it be standing right across the street? I never got any word, and there was never anything on the news. I never saw any footage that showed Saint Paul's still standing. So I assumed it was demolished.

I had got out of bed and decided to go and see what I could do to help early the next morning. It was harrowing because there were the National Guardsmen, Marines, and other people in the Army who had cordoned off the area. There were so many checkpoints. The only way I was able to get through was my clergy collar and my Trinity Saint Paul's ID. I was able to get through the checkpoint at Canal Street because I was already lower than 14th. Going down, seeing all these bombed-out cars and computer monitors and all this debris everywhere was really pretty scary.

I had two goals that day. I wanted to go help and I wanted to see if I could rescue the painting that was in Saint Paul's Chapel, one of the very first oil renditions of the nation with the national bird, which was Benjamin Franklin's idea. The national bird, a turkey before the eagle. A very important painting, but I also wanted to see how we could mobilize the community to help.

I got to just about where City Hall is, and there I could see the tower, the spire of Saint Paul's, still standing, and it totally blew me away and I burst into tears. I couldn't believe it. Saint Paul's was spared. Maybe that meant we had a big job to do. So I went in, opened the doors of the church, and walked through, eerily, and surveyed the inside of Saint Paul's. It didn't even have a broken window, but one of the windows was open, so we had a film of dust, maybe a quarter-inch thick, on everything. It just took my breath away. I was really surprised, and then grateful, because I knew then that we could fulfill a mission of helping in a way that we could not have otherwise. But I didn't know if the building was safe, so I didn't let anyone in really until a structural engineer checked it out a couple days later. But right there at the site, it was pretty clear that we could be mobilized in a way that could make a huge difference. So I started thinking about that.

A SYMBOL OF HOPE

I hesitate here, because to say that Saint Paul's was spared and others weren't implies that we're holier than anyone who died, but that's not the case. If there was divine intervention, maybe it was for us to have a space to do the important work that unfolded over the next few months. It had everything to do with a symbol of hope. In fact, that's how I like to talk about the story now, and have done for quite a while. 9/11 happened and it was covered by every media outlet in the world, but the equally important story is the day of 9/12, when we got out of bed and responded to those acts of violence with hearts of courage and compassion.

Tragedies happen. You can't roll back the hands on a clock. Even though they can't be fixed, tragedies can be healed, and there was important work of healing to be done at that time, in rescuing as many survivors as we could. So that became the complete motivation of everything we did: every person available to rescue one survivor. Whatever it took. We set up a whole service industry at Saint Paul's Chapel to empower the people doing the digging to do their job in the best possible way. I also spent time in the site doing some of the digging as well.

I am very proud that in a time of crisis, 9/11, that our church showed up and we stood there; we stood there with courage and we stayed at the site until it was finished, until the last square inch of dirt was removed. We were there every day, 24/7, for eight and a half months. We served over half a million meals; we had over five thousand volunteers; we had so many different services offered: music, massage therapy, chiropractic care, food ... the food was exceptional. We wanted to do every little thing we could to encourage and empower people in the site, doing that work, to do it their optimum best, and to support them in this emotionally traumatic time. It was very difficult.

I walked through the site almost every day, and many days I would do blessings and last rites on body bags, and it meant the world to the workers to have the clergy in the site with them, sometimes even helping with the digging. There was a symbol, a connection, a solidarity of goodness even in the midst of devastation that I think is a lesson that we can delve into and learn from today. We don't have control over a lot of the tragedies that happen to us, but we can respond in a way that's life-giving and compassionate and helpful. That's what we wanted to do. That's where we're going to find our healing, moving forward as a country.

Mr. Rogers was asked at the time, "How do we talk to the children about 9/11?" He said, "Tell them to keep their eyes on the helpers," and that's who we were serving, the helpers. It was our privilege to do that. I never had a policeman as a friend in my life, but, automatically, I have a little police force as my friend: the firefighters and the sanitation workers and the Verizon guys. It was really an amazing experience that changed my life.

You couldn't have more of a stark contrast than life and death, working in a militarized zone. We were in a battlefield, literally. So how do we live out the sort of core values we have as people of faith, as leaders of a faith community, regardless of what faith tradition? How do we embrace and embody compassion and mercy and kindness and courage and hope, and how do we share that with people in such a way that it helps them heal and makes us all better? It was really the laboratory to try it out, to explore. It really was life-changing for me.

A NEW CONGREGATION

As I mentioned, I was brought there to start a new congregation, but I didn't know it would be this one. One of the journalists wrote that Saint Paul's Chapel had a new congregation: They wore respirators instead of neckties and Kevlar vests instead of Brooks Brothers suits. So this was a community that was brought together out of love, through love and compassion and service. I like to describe it as a season of love, and I'm using that song from *Rent*. I love that. When people try to outdo one another in showing kindness and courage and compassion. And it was bottom up, not so much top down; outside in, not inside out. A very different way of understanding church ministry. In other words, we had federal judges thrilled to serve sandwiches and coffee to sanitation workers. Stockbrokers so excited about mopping the floor. It really was amazing.

So we found healing together, as a community working for a greater good, but for many of the workers at Ground Zero, myself included, we put a lot of personal stuff on the shelf that would come back to haunt us later. The adrenaline of doing that work and focusing on the critical needs of every given day became the sort of organizing principle of our lives, more so than paying attention to our own grief and our own post-traumatic stress and other things. There was a comeuppance that would happen to many of us after June 2nd, 2002.

I FOUGHT THE HEALTH DEPARTMENT

It was all very organic. I didn't go in with a set idea of knowing how to organize anything. We started one thing and it led to another. Or we started something and decided it wouldn't work, so we didn't do it. There are checks and balances all along the way, sometimes even comical, if you can imagine that, in the midst of this disaster zone.

For example, we started a food service that weekend, on the Saturday after the attacks, and the first grill to be fired up was the grill from the men's shelter that we had at Saint Paul's Chapel. But since I didn't know if the building was safe, we did it out on the sidewalk, out on Broadway, right there on the corner of Broadway and Fulton. We have pictures of this; it's really quite stunning to see them. Out there grilling burgers, and those of us who were serving felt so rewarded to be able to do any little thing we could to help out.

So before long, I had eight grills going at the same time and we had a volunteer pool of people coming in to flip burgers and people coming to get food and cold drinks. The Health Department shows up, and they start shutting us down. They would shut us down twice a day. So after they would leave, I'd start it back up again. They had good reason: There was all this stuff in the air; we didn't know the source of the food. It was crazy, but we were driven and we were hell-bent on serving food to the hungry people doing the work in the site, regardless.

Ultimately, after being shut down so many times, we got the police captain to come over and help us out. He said, "Let me know when they're back." So they came back and the police captain shows up with about eight or ten of his biggest, burliest guys, circled the Health Department group, and marched them off the premises. One of the guys jokingly said the next day, "Last time I checked, the Health Department doesn't carry guns and we do." It was a very dramatic time, when everything seemed to be up for grabs, but we were trying to do our best. Ultimately, though, we were shut down. So then we moved the food service inside. I hired a food service professional to oversee the preparation and serving of the food. The Health Department was happy, and we were happy, and were able to find a win-win to make sure the food was reliable and prepared safely and all that.

It grew. It grew from a few hamburgers to the Waldorf showing up to provide dinners. It really became known as a four-star accommodation at Ground Zero, as we had really great food. I felt that nothing we could do was good enough to show these men and women how grateful we were for what they were doing, and the funds were coming in to be able to provide this. The restaurants preparing the meals gave us a great discount at break-even costs or less than cost, so we had a lot of partners helping make that happen.

IT'S ALL THE SAME STUFF

The Red Cross organized a whole team of caregivers for what we called the T-Morgue—the temporary mortuary. Gosh, I don't know how many hundreds of people were involved in that. They would come to Ground Zero and do a shift at the temporary mortuary, so that when bodies were found and bagged, they would go out and say a prayer, give a word of consolation.

We were finding body parts. I saw them myself. Some of my own flashbacks are some of the images of body parts that I saw. It's just … in a regular situation, you don't even deal with the bodies. You just go to the mortuary and they bring the coffin and do a very dignified service. We did dignified prayers at the site, but it was just a memorial service in a military zone, really. A war zone.

We had chaplains from all faith traditions participating. I think we all wanted to be as inclusive as possible, so the prayers were really offered in sort of an open-ended way, so that the rescuers who were bagging the bodies and those around them would feel comforted as well. I didn't learn any of this in seminary; I learned by doing.

I think we did a great job. I think that moving forward, I have some concerns about how we as leaders in our civic society and how we as leaders of faith communities have helped people cope with this public tragedy. I think we can do better there, but in the immediate aftermath, I think it was very powerfully done.

Our motivation and our decision was to offer a service on humanitarian grounds. In other words, for those who wanted to pray, we had a daily prayer service, but it wasn't required or even expected. It was just one of the offerings. We just wanted to be a place, an oasis, of healing and hope and encouragement, and often times a big, strapping firefighter would walk in and just burst into tears because of something he had just seen. Or a police captain would walk in, would burst into tears, and she would tell us what they had just finished doing. It was a place where people could come to process some of their grief. An oasis of support. Certainly we offered food and massage therapy and chiropractic care, which helped. Podiatrists were working around the clock, too. It was the longest-burning fire in our country's history. The boots were literally melting off their feet. We just tried to reach out and meet the needs of the full human person, not just spiritually, but emotionally and physically. It's all the same stuff. It's all the same.

Death is death and that's horrible, but a death and dismemberment, or incineration, or vaporization, or whatever happened to different individuals, is just so gruesome and so overwhelming that it's hard for us to cope with the suffering that loved ones went through at that time. It's really difficult for families, I think, to process that and to release that grief.

It really wasn't the case that if we had worked harder, of course, maybe there could have been more things or different things done. We can second-guess that, but I think people really responded with their best efforts. We didn't cause the tragedy; we were just responding. But a lot of people maybe feel that they didn't do enough. I would hope whoever feels that could find a way to forgive themselves and to realize that everyone really did their best in the face of this enormous tragedy.

A lot of people felt, I think, that they didn't have as much in common with people at home as they did at the site. There were people sleeping there, about a hundred every night. I guess, not that I'm an expert in any way on any of this, but I would imagine it's the same for anyone who has served in war, Afghanistan or Iraq or any other place.

MAKING SENSE OF THINGS

I think that's one of our biggest challenges right now: making sense of things in the wake of this tragedy. So many questions were asked. How can God let this happen? Or, why would God turn his back on us? I was asked the question many times, as a priest working down there: "Where was God when this happened?" I know a lot of people had this loss of faith experience, or a deepening of faith.

I think my faith remained steady, and my sense is that God was right there, and that the first heart to break on 9/11 was the heart of God, because people with free will chose to do evil things, and that's the price we pay for the world that we have, in which we're equally endowed with the capacity to make decisions. We can make good decisions or bad decisions. Unfortunately, that day, some people chose to make awful decisions that caused much grief and suffering, but really I saw the presence of God throughout the Pile and the Pit. And the embrace and the love of the people who were working, and the honor shown for the deceased when they were found—I saw it as a testimony, really, to a resilience as a community.

The season of love came to an end, and we've been floundering. I think we've lost our way. We've engaged in two wars, the economy has melted down, not entirely unrelated to that, I think. So much seems to be unraveling in the world, but even though I think we lost our way, it doesn't mean we can't reclaim it. That's my mission.

I started the Gardens of Forgiveness after 9/11 based on the Garden of Forgiveness in Beirut, Lebanon. That doesn't mean that we let bad people off the hook for doing evil things. It means that we take the tragic element of our life and make peace with it somehow, so that we can release the bondage and the burden of the past and create a new possibility for the future, and that's what keeps me awake at night now. What keeps me driven is to think about ways to help our communities heal in the aftermath of this tragedy.

The tenth anniversary is coming up. How could this anniversary be different than the others? Will we have the children read the names this year? Or the parents reading the names? And will that be all that we do? Or will we strike a note of resilience and transformation and hope?

I'm writing a book for faith community leaders on how to help congregations and communities deal with losses like 9/11, and then work through the grief and look at new beginnings that can come after them. We never want anything like this to happen, but it's naïve to think that things won't happen. Why do bad things happen to good people? Because they happen to all people; it's just the tragic nature of life.

Why not have Wynton Marsalis write a jazz Mass for a new city? New beginnings to pull through the grief and the suffering and the loss, but then to come out on the other side, maybe not triumphantly, but transformed and to say, in honor of those who were lost and those who were killed, ruthlessly murdered on that day, the best thing we can do for them is to live life to the fullest because that's what they want from us. They long for us to be released from the cynicism and the burden and the bitterness of how we deal with this past event. I'm not making light of it, but we have to process the grief.

The co-chair of the Gardens of Forgiveness campaign with me, Fred Luskin, a professor at Stanford, was doing an interview in October 2001. His book *Forgive for Good* had just come out, and it might have even been *Time* magazine, but someone was doing an interview with him and they said, "Well, Doctor Luskin, is it time for us to forgive the terrorists?" He said, "I can hardly forgive you for asking such a stupid question."

You got to go through the cycles and the process of the emotional response—the anger, the grief, the loss—but we have to move through it and beyond it. To stay there is not honoring those who died. I think on one hand we've stagnated and, on the other hand, we have become apathetic and cynical. I think there are many great projects going on to lead us through this, and I have confidence that we will, hopefully with the tenth anniversary. I see this as a call for a new beginning, and I'm excited about the possibilities for us as a nation. I'm hopeful. And that's different from optimism.

As a person of faith, I'll use a biblical category here. Go to the Book of

Genesis and the story of Joseph, whose brothers sold him into slavery. But as it turns out, he wound up in Egypt as the Pharaoh's right-hand man and had enormous power and wealth. When there was a famine in Israel, the brothers came to Egypt to ask, to beg for food, basically, not having any idea that their brother Joseph was the one in charge of the empire. Joseph greets his brothers, forgives them, embraces them, and he says to them, "You intended it for evil, but God has used it for good."

I think 9/11 was intended as evil, but I think through the mercy of God and through the courage of human beings and communities and leaders, we can make something out of it. It's always the way life is. It unfolds and things happen, but how we respond is really what's important.

I know for a fact that at Saint Paul's Chapel, we posted letters from children that we got from all over the country, all over the world, and that was maybe one of the most meaningful things that we did for any of the rescue workers, because they would read these notes. Just simply a little guy saying thanks for helping all the people, P-E-P-L. That was one of our favorite letters.

Then there was a letter from a little girl in Scarsdale, and she had written this elaborate piece addressed to the firefighters: "Dear firefighters, there are many deaths that I can die: heart attack, I could get stung by too many bees, I could get run over by a car, I could have cancer." She named like twenty-five different things, and then she says, "but I know, however, that I will never die in a fire, because brave people like you would go into a fire to save an ordinary person like me. And that's what makes you so special, amazing, courageous"—another twenty-five attributes—"special people."

That means so much to people. It meant so much to the men and women. That encouragement. So who was helping who? It was all, of course, a partnership, as it always is.

JOURNEY TO HEALING

I had my own basket of issues to deal with, and it was very difficult for me. Moving on from Saint Paul's was a very difficult thing for me. Finding out that I had a lot of stuff in my lungs, losing my job, losing a home, losing a marriage… It was all very difficult and I was bitter. That's when forgiveness became so important for me because I finally heard the Mandela quote, "Not to forgive is like drinking a glass of poison and waiting for your enemies to die." I drank a lot of that poison and I was justified in drinking it, too, but it was still a poison and it was still killing me.

I think there is a lot of bitterness out there, a lot of cynicism, a lot of pain. I think we can help people with that, and if we had the courage and the vision to do it, we could help people become better leaders, better communities, better individuals, a better nation.

I think one of our dangers and our seductions as a country is to sort of fetishize the grief around 9/11 and not look to 9/12. I think it will be a failure for us in ten years' time if 9/11 is a federal holiday in which you can buy another washing machine for a good price or another car, because I really think we should hold ourselves to higher standards than that. We should help our communities grieve, but then move beyond the grief to a resolution of healing and new beginnings, resilience, and new possibilities.

A PRIVILEGE OF A LIFETIME

There are such powerful stories I'll never forget. Way back in September of '01, just a couple weeks after the attacks happened, an elderly African-American woman in the Bronx heard that someone working in Ground Zero had hurt his leg. So she got on the subway and came all the way down to Lower Manhattan, got out, talked her way through the police lines, which was no small feat, came to Saint Paul's Chapel, talked her way into Saint Paul's Chapel, which was an equally enormous accomplishment because we had people at the gate to protect the sanctity of the space for the rescue workers. She came in and gave us her own cane and hobbled off. Unbelievable. I still have that cane, too. It cost her fourteen bucks at Kmart, I think, but to me, it's a priceless testimony to her courage, her generosity, and how we can be better than we are. How we can be more than we are.

I remember the truckload of boots that showed up from Asheboro, North Carolina. A woman in Asheboro went on the evening news and said, "These guys need boots. Let's bring them together." So they rented a U-Haul truck and they loaded it up with boots of all sizes and came to Ground Zero. We were helping them at Saint Paul's and opened up the back and the guys came off the Pile, got a new pair of boots, saluted the guys handing out the boots, and went back in. It was incredible.

The podiatrists that worked around the clock, day after day, after night after night. The rescue medics that were there, not in Saint Paul's, but working in the site. The rescue dogs, oh my gosh. They would come into Saint Paul's Chapel to cool their bellies on the hot days because Saint Paul's Chapel has marble floors. I'll never forget those experiences. I'll never forget on 9/12, making my way to the chapel, and right after discovering that it was still standing, even before I went in, a firefighter came over to me and he pointed to the boots on the fence across the street and he said, "Do you see those boots, Father?"

I said, "Yes."

He said, "Those were the boots of the first responders. They won't be coming back for their boots." And he was weeping. I'll never, ever in my life forget that. I'll never forget the people who came, selflessly, to serve and to bring food. I'll never forget the woman from Dallas, who worked for Starbucks, who said, after she worked one of our food shifts, "Father Harris, you need a cappuccino maker here." To which I could only respond, "Yes, we do." And before long we had a cappuccino maker, and people were lining up for lattes and all that.

The generosity of the people was absolutely amazing. I'll never forget Christmas Eve at Ground Zero. We had a special midnight Mass and brought back my band that had been working with me at Saint Paul's before 9/11. It was very powerful, these acts of compassion. I remember Sister Grace, one of our volunteers who worked with me every day. As we were getting close to Easter, she took me out to the cemetery at Saint Paul's Chapel to see a tree that had been covered in debris, but pointing out to me that birds had begun to nest in the debris of the tree as a sign of new hope, new life, new beginnings.

I'll never forget the tree that was uprooted on the corner of Saint Paul's Chapel in the cemetery. A big sycamore tree took the full brunt of the impact and was uprooted. I always wanted to take the trunk of that tree and make a baptismal font out of it. The juxtaposition between tragedy and new beginnings is so important.

So many memories, so many experiences. I was truly blessed to be able to do that work, and how in the world it happened, I don't know. I grew up in a small town in South Carolina. I'd never even been to New York City until I was in my early twenties, and somehow I wind up here and have the privilege of serving at Saint Paul's, and then to be there during 9/11 to work with those amazing, courageous people. It's a privilege of a lifetime.

A WIDOW'S LOVE

Greta and Rob grew up in Nassau County, Long Island, just east of New York City. They married in their late 20s, only about three years before 9/11. Rob, a Navy veteran, became an NYPD officer after the couple married and, according to Greta, he loved what he did. By 2003, when the couple's second child was born, Rob began feeling poorly. Initially, despite extensive testing, doctors couldn't identify the problem. His weight declined dramatically, and physicians finally discovered stage 4 cancer. He died in 2007.

In her recollections of the past decade, Greta says that while she wishes some things had been done differently to protect workers at Ground Zero, she's not bitter and is proud of her husband's contribution, especially his work with victims' families. She recalls her husband's dedication and sincerity, his enthusiasm for helping people, and the promising life they'd only just begun together when it ended so unexpectedly and in so much pain.

WE WERE ON VACATION IN CANADA visiting my sister for the first time as a couple, and I'd slept in because I was a little sick from being pregnant with my son. Rob came upstairs and woke me up, and he said, "You're not going to believe what's happening." And I went downstairs and we all sat in front of the TV, and we couldn't believe it.

Rob turned to me and said, "I have to cut this vacation short. I have to go home. I have to go home and help." This was the kind of man he was.

We'd just gotten there the day before. The next day, the two of us turned around and drove the ten hours straight through back home, and he went to work the next day. He was worried about getting back over the border, so we took a different crossing where we thought we'd have a better chance of getting through.

Even in Canada, everything shut down. And everybody was just in disbelief. I know you've heard it many times, but it was just—I'll never forget it. All the way back, we listened to the news to get updates on what was happening, for our safety and to find out what was going on. It was pretty much a silent drive. But people were calling us to see if Rob was okay because they didn't know we were away.

Rob had to go into work right away, and they assigned him to perimeter security. From then until March, when Garrett was born, I feel like I didn't see him. That whole time was a blur. He came home, and he told me stories about what he saw. In the beginning, he was very quiet about it. One day, I asked him how he thought the disaster had changed him. I could see that he was okay talking about certain things, but other things he really did not want to talk about. He said, "I see a big change in the way people respect us and what we do." He said that, before 9/11, a lot of people took their security for granted, but now they feel differently about the Police Department, and what a great job they did and continue to do.

I know there were a lot of things he couldn't talk about. But he did talk about all the people who were in there helping. He was so proud to help the people that were still there. He just had this way with people that would comfort them. When he looked at you, you knew he really cared about what you were saying to him, that he would help you and take an interest.

One of the officers who worked with him said, "Rob wasn't one of those guys who just passed you in the hall and said, 'How you doing?' He would stop and really want to hear how you're doing." That was him.

He worked at the family center, he worked at the morgue, and he did the perimeter security. But he especially worked at the family center. He explained how a lot of these people were just so lost. Rob and the others tried to make it a positive place for families to come and collect information. They had the therapy dogs, they had stuffed animals, they had all kinds of things. Those things helped, but did it make it better? People still knew their friends or family were gone.

Right after 9/11, Rob had so much energy, and he loved going in and helping. But, then, afterwards, he started to change in a physical way. He wasn't himself anymore. He started losing weight and was always tired. He went to the doctor, but they couldn't find anything wrong. We'd go on vacation—we went up to Maine to visit my mom—and he got a lot of sleep, sometimes like twelve hours. But he was still tired. That's when I started to see the real change in my husband. He was just never quite right after that.

I knew it wasn't from the mental effects of 9/11. You could see the rings under his eyes, and he just did not feel good. That's when I really started pushing for him to get tests. But the doctors still couldn't find anything wrong other than being anemic.

It's really a blur to me. I have a lot of energy. I was always going, going, going. After Garrett was born, Rob was still working a lot of hours, so that was a little tough. I depended on help from neighbors and friends. I'm one of six, and I was always independent, so having to accept help was hard. We knew Rob was lucky to have a job, and I had a great job at the time. We were preparing for a beautiful thing, our first child.

Two years later, Amelia was born, and that was a little bit rougher. It's an adjustment going from one child to two. Plus Rob wasn't feeling good, and the doctors didn't know what was wrong. So again I depended on help from neighbors and friends. My dad was a deacon at Sacred Heart in North Merrick, right on Long Island. And many of the people there knew of my husband and me and the kids, and a lot of them helped out. Also I have very, very good friends. My dad's best friend Andy and his wife were really true supporters.

Before there was a diagnosis and no one knew and there were so many tests that my husband went through—colonoscopies, endoscopies—and they didn't find anything. It was very, very frustrating. Finally, the doctors identified it as a rare cancer. When people found out, everybody wanted to pitch in and help: the police department, friends, neighbors, family, everyone. They knew I needed the help, and I finally admitted I couldn't do everything on my own.

Rob and I both had to educate ourselves about cancer. Neither one of us knew anything about it when he was diagnosed. My sister is a nurse, and she was very, very helpful to answer my questions, including ones about the best treatment plans for Rob. We'd talk to the doctors, then get her opinion. Once the cancer was staged as being so advanced, the doctors explained that treatment would keep him alive a little longer, but it wouldn't cure him.

I remember leaving the doctor's office. It was the first time I ever saw my husband cry like that. I turned to him and said, "It's just not fair because we never had a chance." I mean, we just got married, then 9/11 happens. Our children were born, we were just starting out our lives together. We got our house out in Suffolk right before 9/11. He's so young.

Even so, he never regretted working all those hours at the site, and neither did I. The problem is, why weren't they given the proper protection? I go through stages when I'm a little angry. Then I'm fine. I accept what's happened. I know he's in a better place, because you can't sugarcoat the fact that my husband was very sick. He went from 180 pounds down to under a hundred when he died. I remember standing in the driveway one day and looking at him. He was so thin because of what the cancer did to his body.

My only regret is that the cancer hadn't been caught earlier, because there would've been a better chance of surviving. I could be mad at the terrorists, I could be mad because the workers didn't have protection. But you can't change what happened. So it's tough. I'm mostly accepting because I still have his memory. Rob gave me two beautiful children. I want what he did and what happened to him and so many others to make a difference. In the future, I want the responders to have masks and whatever else they need to protect themselves.

I thought I was doing a really good job until Amelia, who is now six—and she was only three when Rob died—we were cleaning her room about two weeks ago and she turned to me and she goes, "Mommy, I'm really upset. I can't remember Daddy anymore." I told her that it's okay, that I don't remember anything from when I was three. As far as preserving his memory, I show them photos, I tell them stories. Amelia's favorite story is how she used to put her head on Rob's lap. She couldn't sit in his lap because he had two major surgeries to take out big sections of his colon and do radiation on his liver to prolong his life. So the only thing she could really do was sit down next to him and put her head in his lap. So I talk about that a lot.

Besides the videos, Garrett's favorite thing is to listen to the music my husband loved, so I'll put it on and I'll play some of his favorite songs. Then they get out the air guitars and start playing. So we have a lot of great memories together. They talk about him every single day and ask questions. Garrett, who's eight, had a very rough time in the beginning of this year, because I think as he is maturing, the real sense of the fact that Daddy is really gone has really hit home. And a little trouble in school.

My son is on the spectrum for autism. So, besides the troubles that typical children have, he has additional trouble processing things. An amazing child. Sees the world in a whole different way. He's very gifted. But emotionally, he is still growing. A little behind other children his age. And I'm just trying to give them the gift of support and love and do the best I can for them, to keep them emotionally stable and make them feel that Daddy is still around them. Although he's really not here anymore, he'll always be their dad. So.

Right after my husband died, I took them both for hospice counseling. Garrett is part of a program at school where they meet once a week. It's families who are different, that have had something happen to them. We have an amazing support system through all of the widows that I know and their children. Being around them, Garrett and Amelia realize that they're not alone, that there are also other people that are like them—their fathers died of cancer from 9/11, or of other causes.

More recently, in January [2011], I met John Feal from the FealGood

Foundation. He and all his workers are just amazing people. They have helped me because, really, through it all, you hear about other people's stories, but until you meet other people who are going through the same thing that you're going through, it's a lonely life. When you lose your husband and then put the 9/11 thing on top of it.

Not everybody out there really understands how many people have gotten sick after 9/11. A lot of people would look at me and be like, "Oh, your husband died after 9/11? What do you mean?" So I tell them the story and they say, "Oh, my gosh." They can't believe.

Getting together with other families has made a difference for Garrett, Amelia, and me. The gatherings give us something to look forward to and people to share experiences with. There's something very special about other families that have been through this. You don't have to sit and tell your whole story. They already understand how you feel.

There is one woman who I'm very close to and lives near me in Hauppauge. Rob died in August and her husband in November. I saw her at a police event, and I turned to her and said, "This is so nice, being here. All I want to do is spend time with my children." She said she felt the same way. Because both of us were taking care of our husbands literally all the time. I spent time with the children while my husband was ill, but not enough.

But at the time, my husband was more important. Toward the end, when Rob was in hospice, I didn't bring them in to see him as much because I wanted them to remember Rob when he was healthy and loving his job and full of energy and full of all those great gifts that he had. So she understood and said the same thing, that she just wanted to spend time with her children again.

We had lists of medications, emergency room visits, and long hospital stays. To this day, I can't stand hospitals and doctors. It's tough, because it brings it all back, all the times that he was in the hospital. When I had to leave, he was looking at me and saying, "I'm lonely. Don't leave me." And I couldn't stay. I had to go home and take care of the children. Rob was in the hospital seven weeks at one time.

I tell the kids that their daddy was a hero because I think, to the kids, it's a little uplifting. To me, I know my husband loved his job. And up until the end, he said, "Greta, I just want to get better so I can go back to work." That was what kept him going. He loved his job. Like, to me, that's not being a hero. You know? People said to me, "Oh, you took such great care of him." I think "What?" Like, why would I do any different? I feel like it's almost like the same thing.

Some people have been supportive. But I've had people come up to

me and be like, "Oh, you lost your husband three years ago, and why is
Garrett still talking about him? Why is he still upset?" Like, get over it.
I've had someone say that to me. I said, "How could you sit there [and say
that]?" Some people just don't get that this is something that has changed
our lives forever. It's changed Garrett's and Amelia's lives forever. It's
changed the lives of so many people I know forever.

I think some people get it, other people don't. They just want to put
it behind them and forget about it. They say, "Hey, listen. It's almost ten
years. Let's put it behind us. They're not going to get us again. We're
protected." I don't know. They don't understand that it wasn't just my
husband. That's why I like to tell his story, to make them realize that it's
beyond my husband. He's a part of something else, greater, that happened
to these men and women.

Two weeks ago, we were at the NYPD Police Museum, and they inducted
twenty-nine of the shields of the police officers who died after 9/11, that
got sick, my husband being one of them. Those people that were there, you
could just feel the emotion in the room. Like, the deep passion for the fact
that they're just so proud of what their spouses or sons or daughters did. But
also you feel the pain in the room, of all the people that were there, because
they're still in so much pain. Then you walk out on the street and no one
knows really who you are or maybe why you look so sad that day.

Most of the time, though, you look happy and you have to go on with
life, which is what we do. But I think people are forgetting about it. And
really don't understand it. Actually, I recently did join up with John Feal
in a project to create a memorial in Nesconset for the over 900 responders
who have died since 9/11. I started out helping in the project, and now I'm
vice president of the committee.

I'm doing this not only for my husband's memory, but for the many
people who died after 9/11. It's important to create a special place to
have all of their names together, whether or not they were FDNY, NYPD,
handing out water to volunteers, Port Authority, whatever walk of life they
came from. I think it's very important that their names be in one spot and
be commemorated together. So I've joined up with that project. I've also
had the wonderful experience of going down to Washington to tell my
husband's story to help pass the 9/11 health bill. Because even with great
medical coverage, my husband and I really struggled financially.

The finances were difficult, besides all the other stuff that we were going
through trying to save his life. It was a real struggle. And these men and women
deserve good health care, really good health care. They didn't know that they
were in danger. And here they are all sick. It's tough. I hope that my voice can

help them, as far as the health bill, and also keep their memories alive.

You just want to shout out to them and say, "What's wrong with you? Why, why, why do I have to be here to pass something like a health bill?" My husband is dead. This bill should've been passed way back when. So part of me asked why I had to be here. Even responders who have a hard time breathing are down there in Washington because they have so much passion to help pass the bill. Very inspirational people.

And most recently, the scanners at the airport. When I see people going out there and complaining about being scanned, I say, "How could you?" I don't see myself as an individual; I always feel like I'm a part of something greater than myself. How could they worry about themselves? Like, this is for the protection of them and our country and to prevent people getting not only hurt but dying, being killed. So I'm glad they put the protection systems in the airport. I feel safer since then.

I feel better being able to tell his story and help people. That's what drives me. Then the children see that and they go, "Mom, we're so proud of you. We saw you." And it's amazing to see how uplifted they are.

But it's hard, because, at the end of the day, my husband is gone. And I wish he was back. I miss him. Miss him a lot.

I'm not the type that prays every day. But I know that God is always there. He's always surrounding myself and my children. I know he's with Rob. Listen, I lost my dad the same year that I lost my husband. I don't know if I mentioned that before, but my father died suddenly a few months before Rob did. So that was a double whammy. If I, and not only me, but if my whole family can go through that, it just makes you a little bit stronger. And I keep saying that now I have no excuses. I have my health, I have my beautiful children, and I have an amazing family, although they don't live around me. My dad was amazing. He was a real charismatic individual that helped many, many people. I'm told I'm a little bit like him. That's what drove my husband, too. He loved helping people.

Everybody should give back. It really is a healing thing. And in my husband's case, it's also keeping his memory alive and what happened at 9/11. The lesson learned is that now we know how to protect ourselves much better. I think that in the future, God forbid that something happens like this again, that first and foremost, the workers who go in, the volunteers who go in, should be protected better. Many lives would've been saved if they had been protected. And I remember someone asking me one day, "What do you think would have been worse, your husband dying that day or going through…a long, really, really painful death?" And I said that I don't know if one or the other would be worse or different. I think they're both just different and they're both just terrible. It's a life that's being lost.

Are people more patriotic? I think they are. I just hope that people outside of New York and throughout the country realize that there are so many special people, so many special stories, and that they hear their stories. And if they don't know about those responders' stories, maybe they'll change. Maybe they'll care a little more. Maybe they'll do something to help.

I think people should never forget how precious life is. For me, personally, I will never forget the people that died that day. I'll never forget all the people who have died since. I know many of them personally. I know their stories, I know their children, I know their parents, I know their spouses. They were very, very special people. These are people that really cared. Smart men, smart women. What they did was not just because it was their job. It really wasn't. They did it because they loved this country, they loved us. Amazing, amazing people.

And one of those amazing people was my husband.

So don't forget them.

ABOUT THE AUTHOR

BENJAMIN J. LUFT, M.D., is the Edmund D. Pellegrino Professor of Medicine at the State University of New York at Stony Brook and an internationally recognized expert in the treatment of Lyme disease and AIDS-related conditions. He has been at the forefront of the care of patients with toxoplasmosis, AIDS, and Lyme disease, developing new diagnostic tests and therapeutics based on a fundamental understanding of the patient and the disease process. His approach toward understanding these disease processes has often led to the development of multidisciplinary teams of physicians, molecular biologists, chemists, evolutionists, and physicists, and has also brought about many discoveries, including a new bioengineered vaccine for Lyme disease that is now undergoing clinical trials in Europe. His work has also contributed to the development of many of the modalities that are used in the treatment of both toxoplasmosis and Lyme disease.

Perhaps Ben's crowning achievement in this realm has been his establishment of the Long Island World Trade Center Medical Monitoring and Treatment Center at SUNY Stony Brook, which follows approximately 6,000 responders to the 9/11 disaster. Through his leadership, vision, and creativity, the Center has been an incubator of inventive programs that have benefited not only its patients but also medical students, the local community, and, most recently, society at large.

Ben's approach to caring for this unique population at the Center is a perfect example of incorporating an empathetic understanding into a health care delivery system. He developed a collaborative care approach that aims to tackle the difficult task of treating both the medical and psychiatric problems of this patient population, which, due to its makeup, is particularly resistant to psychiatric intervention. By training the internists in psychiatry, as well as providing special sensitivity training for the entire staff, all of whom are considered part of the "team" in caring for the responders, Ben has effectuated a highly successful model of care.

Since 2008, Ben has offered an effective and well-received seminar based at the Center for medical students called "9/11: The Anatomy of a Health Care Disaster." He gathered together experts from a variety of disciplines, including lawyers, ministers, philosophers, social workers, psychiatrists, economists, industrial hygienists, and others who present to and mentor the medical students in a kaleidoscope of viewpoints on the disaster. The student reviews have been exuberant, noting the particular profundity of the seminar. This year the reach of this course will be greatly extended through its dissemination as a webinar as well.

This past year, Ben added an entirely new dimension to the Center through his oral history project, "Remembering 9/11 Responders." This archive of recorded interviews of the responders telling their stories and experiences has generated a whole spectrum of activities that will affect both the local community and society as a whole. These archives are being utilized as a basis for a curriculum being developed for public schools and libraries; in addition, graduate students have already inquired about utilizing the archives for their doctoral dissertation research. In addition, Ben has developed a website, www.911respondersremember.org, where people can view excerpts from the interviews and learn more about the project. The Library of Congress will be the repository for the archives upon their completion in September 2012. These oral histories are the basis for a documentary created in collaboration with public television stations WLIW21 and WNET13, and for an independent documentary film, *9/11: An American Requiem,* which debuted at the 2011 Stony Brook Film Festival.

PHOTO INDEX
By Book Section & Page Number